T0132448

DETERRENCE

AN ENDURING STRATEGY

CHRIS ADAMS

IUNIVERSE, INC.
NEW YORK   BLOOMINGTON

DETERRENCE
An Enduring Strategy

iUniverse books may be ordered through booksellers or by contacting:

iUniverse
1663 Liberty Drive
Bloomington, IN 47403
www.iuniverse.com
1-800-Authors (1-800-288-4677)

Because of the dynamic nature of the Internet, any Web addresses or links contained in this book may have changed since publication and may no longer be valid.

ISBN: 978-1-4401-6978-6 (sc)
ISBN: 978-1-4401-6976-2 (dj)
ISBN: 978-1-4401-6977-9 (ebk)

Printed in the United States of America

iUniverse rev. date: 9/14/2009

With

Grateful Praise

To

The Leaders,

The Commanders

And

The Men and Women

Who

Provided The Deterrence

ALSO BY CHRIS ADAMS

Non-fiction

Inside The Cold War: A Cold Warrior's Reflections, 1999

Ideologies In Conflict: A Cold War Docu-Story, 2001

Fiction

Red Eagle: A Cold War Espionage Story, 2000

Profiles In Betrayal: The Enemy Within, 2002

The Betrayal Mosaic: A Cold War Spy Story, 2004

Out of Darkness: The Last Russian Revolution, 2006

AUTHOR'S NOTE

"Capability x Will = Deterrence"

General Russell E. Dougherty
Commander-in-Chief,
Strategic Air Command

I could think of no better citation from which to draw the title of this project and to begin the narrative than that coined by one of the truly great modern day military commanders, General Russell E. Dougherty, Commander-in-Chief, Strategic Air Command, who we unfortunately recently lost. In his Cold War equation, he characterized "Capability" as the U.S. military strategic nuclear forces and "Will" as the strength of character of the American people and its leaders. If either of the multiplication factors was zero, he explained, then the product would be "zero."

During the protracted Cold War era, U.S. military strategic deterrence was constituted in the "TRIAD," a term which characterizes the three critical elements of U.S. national military deterrent competence. The Strategic Air Command operated two legs of the TRIAD; the airborne force consisting of bombers, aerial tankers and reconnaissance aircraft on the one hand and the land-based intercontinental ballistic missile (ICBM) force on the other. The Navy operated the third leg, the nuclear submarine (SSBN) force. Someone along the way said that if the United States' planning processes had set out to develop a deterrent military force they in all likelihood, would not have devised the TRIAD as such. The evolution of this jointly coordinated "triple threat" became the palpable result of "politics, budgetary realities and new theories." But, importantly, it worked!

Embodied within the TRIAD were the men and women of Strategic Air Command, the nuclear Navy and the weapon systems which combined to

ix

compose the undeniably awesome capability factor in the deterrence equation. The nation's leaders took comfort in these well-developed capabilities and the support of the American people. Western Allies maintained confidence in America as the defender of freedom and oppression. The Soviet perception of U.S. capabilities and the will to use them kept them in check.

With two previous Cold War nonfiction publications and a few spy novels on the subject, I had all but depleted any further thoughts I might express on the Cold War period. But it seems that the sometimes conveniently tucked away 45-year political/military impasse rears its head from one corner or the other.

We need only to fast forward to 2009 and the newly elected President of the United States travels to Russia for an introductory visit only to find himself subjected to a lengthy lecture on the Cold War by the former Russian President and current Prime Minister. Prime Minister Paten's harsh monologue was directly focused on U.S. faults and Soviet triumphs during the tenuous period—'political correction' at its best or worst? My five years traveling within the former Soviet States in the early 1990s immediately following the conclusion of the Cold War conflict made an indelible impression with regard to the historical culture of Russian denial. We need only to look back at their trail of submissions and tragic defeats; dominated for over 300 years by the Mongols, next the czars including a trouncing in the Russo-Japanese War, the Germans in World War I and again in World War II before being rescued by the West. Yet, their faux courage, arrogance, bravado or pride, whatever, always seems to shield their wounds within, if not without, to fight another day.

A cursory investigation into the plethora of notes and collection of heroic "war stories" tucked away in my data base revealed considerable which might be of continuing interest to those who wish to remember, and later generations who have a quest for the important history of our great nation, so I proceeded herewith. The purpose of the work is not to resurrect the Cold War, chastise a frequently passive America, a persistently proud Russia or to critique the successes and failures of the conflict years later—nor is it to further punish the vanquished. Neither is it intended as a textbook or reference source, but rather a compilation of this author's living experiences, those of others, cogent observations and considerable research. To set the stage for the title story, I believed it necessary to provide a brief historical review of the Cold War era for background and reflection relative to the world we live in today.

Special gratitude goes to the men and women who served within our strategic nuclear forces; the "Cold Warriors," my term, whose extraordinary feats of bravery and heroism were, embodied the heart of U.S. deterrence. Many of their exceptional experiences are chronicled herein. I also wish to recognize and commend the extraordinary service, commitment and feats of wisdom, courage and heroism of our national leaders and the military commanders during the period. This is also their story.

I take special pleasure in acknowledging a few very special people who graciously assisted in the many ways it takes to develop a credible story: Ms. Paulette Chapman, editor extraordinaire; Lt. General Edgar S. Harris, USAF (Ret); Maj. General Pat Halloran, USAF (Ret); CMSAF Jim McCoy, USAF (Ret); Colonel Dick Purdum, USAF (Ret) and Ms. Dorene Sherman. My appreciation is also extended to all the others who have marched before me in telling the Cold War story in print and speech, which assisted me greatly in getting the facts straight. Any faults or personal biases otherwise detected herein are strictly my own.

Chris Adams

CONTENTS

Also By Chris Adams. vii

Author's Note ix

Prologue xvii

PART ONE   HISTORICAL PERSPECTIVE 1

Chapter One	The Cold War.	3
Chapter Two	The Forces of Deterrence	15
Chapter Three	Weapons of Deterrence.	25

The Bombers 26
       B-29 SuperFortress 26
       B-50A Advanced SuperFortress 27
       B-36 Peacemaker. 28
       B-47 Stratojet 35
       B-52 StratoFortress 39
       B-58 Hustler 45
       FB-111A Aardvark. 46
       B-1 Lancer. 48
The Aerial Tankers 49
       KC-97 Stratotanker. 49
       KC-135 Stratotanker. 49
       KC-10 Extender 50
Strategic Reconnaissance 50
       U-2 Dragon Lady 51
       SR-71 Blackbird 53
The Intercontinental Ballistic Missile (ICBM) 53
       SM-65 Atlas 54
       LGM-25 Titan I and Titan II 54
       LGM-30, Minuteman I, II, and III 55
       LGM-118A Peacekeeper 55
       The Cruise Missile. 55
       UGM-27 Polaris A1 and A3 58
       UGM-73 Poseidon C3 58
       UGM-93 Trident I C4/Trident II D5 58

Lafayette Class. 59
Ohio Class. 59

PART TWO   HUMAN EVENTS 61

Chapter Four   The Cold War Leaders 63
Harry Truman 65
"Ike" 70
"JFK" 76
"LBJ" 82
Richard Nixon 84
Gerald Ford 90
Jimmy Carter 91
Ronald Reagan 96
George H.W. Bush. 109

Chapter Five   The Commanders. 115
General George C. Kenney, Commanding General, Strategic Air
    Command, 1946-1948 117
General Curtis E. LeMay, Commanding General, SAC, 1948-
    1953, Commander, SAC, 1953-1955, Commander in Chief,
    SAC, 1955-1957 120
Admiral Hyman G. Rickover 128
General Thomas Power, CINCSAC, 1957-1964 134
General John D. Ryan, CINCSAC, 1964-1967 138
General Joseph J. Nazzaro, CINCSAC, 1967-1968 141
General Bruce K. Holloway, CINCSAC, 1968-1972 143
General John C. Meyer, CINCSAC, 1972-1974 145
General Russell E. Dougherty, CINCSAC, 1974-1977 148
General Richard H. Ellis, CINCSAC, 1977-1981 156
General Bennie L. Davis, CINCSAC, 1981-1985 159
General Larry D. Welch, CINCSAC, 1985-1986. 161
General John T. Chain, CINCSAC, 1986-1991. 163
General George L. Butler, CINCSAC, 1991-1992. 166

PART THREE HEROES 169

Chapter Six   The Cold Warriors 171
The Aviators. 173
    Notable Mishap. 173
    Operation "Big Stick" 174
    Sneaky Attack 176
    A Dodged Bullet 177

Siberian Overflight 178
Ensuing Tragedy 180
Migs Over Murmansk 181
Extraordinary Airmanship 183
Gary Powers 185
Incident Over The Barents. 187
BMEWS "Hiccup" 192
Cuban Missile Crisis 193
Ancillary Cuban Crisis Events 195
Curious Trespasser 195
"Routine" Launch 195
Unintended Consequences 196
Operation Arc Light 205
Operation Linebacker 206
Assault on Hanoi. 208
Endurance. 210
The Hustler 212
The Blackbird 212
Assertion 219
The Missileers 219
The Women Warriors. 222

Chapter Seven   The Shadow Warriors 225
    Paul W. Airey, Chief Master Sergeant of the Air Force,
        1967-1969. 227
    Donald L. Harlow, Chief Master Sergeant of the Air Force,
        1969-1971. 227
    Thomas N. Barnes, Chief Master Sergeant of the Air Force,
        1973-1977. 228
    Robert D. Gaylor, Chief Master Sergeant of the Air Force,
        1977-1979. 229
    James M. McCoy, Chief Master Sergeant of the Air Force,
        1979-1981. 229
    Sam E Parish, Chief Master Sergeant of the Air Force,
        1983-1986. 231
    James C. Binnicker, Chief Master Sergeant of the Air Force,
        1986-1990. 232
    Gary R Pfingston, Chief Master Sergeant of the Air Force,
        1990-1994. 232
    David J. Campanale, Chief Master Sergeant of the Air Force,
        1994-1996. 233

Chapter Eight   The Civil Warriors 237

Chapter Nine   They Also Served 241

Chapter Ten   The Last Full Measure. 245

Closing Perspective 247

Sources 251

About the Author 261

Index. 263

PROLOGUE

"From Stettin in the Baltic to Trieste in
the Adriatic, an Iron Curtain has descended
across the Continent. "

Sir Winston Churchill
Westminster College
Fulton, Missouri
March 5, 1946

Few Americans recognized or paid close attention to the outset of the Cold
War and thereafter to its enduring years; first because it came so subtly on the
victorious heels of World War II and second, because it persisted for so long
with but few alarming situations intruded their daily lives. Only noteworthy
events such as Sputnik, the shooting down of Gary Powers' U-2 spy plane and
the Cuban Crisis brought the potential threatening circumstances home, and
then only briefly until the situation calmed and other news items took their
place. Neither did many relate to the excursions in Korea and Vietnam directly
to the Cold War. If anything, those distressing conflicts deflected attention
away from the specter of the underlying Soviet global threat. Nevertheless,
during the last half of the Twentieth Century, the United States found its
national security challenged over the longest continuous period in history.

The Cold War, as it became known, evolved promptly after World
War II into a protracted geopolitical impasse and extraordinary arms race
of unprecedented proportions creating a massive dark umbrella casting
an ominous shadow over the country, world events and lives for forty-five
years. During those tenuous years life within the United States and the Free
World for the most part, continued at a virtually unhampered pace seemingly
unaware of the potential for an Armageddon at most any moment in time.

In the fast moving 'microwave mentality' culture we have come to live within, history seldom has time to be properly baked and savored before we urge ourselves to move on. Accordingly, many noteworthy events, the character of the leaders and commanders and the heroics of many brave men and women who played a vital role in the long drawn-out and tense Cold War era have faded into irrelevant episodes or have been forgotten. Americans love and revere their heroes and it is all too frequent that we fail to grasp the true significance of periods of the past and to recognize those involved. Herein, I want to narrowly focus on some of the prominent figures and true life exploits of many others who were overlooked as they honorably served while performing incredible feats of heroism during the remarkable period.

America has never fallen short of heroes when called upon for the common defense of the nation. When our leaders have sounded the clarion call, young men and women never failed to step forward. Throughout the history of our great nation their stories and their heroics are legend.

The Cold War period of uncertainty called upon America's best and brightest at all levels to respond. As in previous conflicts, America did not send its military directly into combat and engage an enemy. The Cold War was politically unique; it called for recognition, perception, patience and intelligent assessment. As the impasse with the Soviet Union evolved, U.S. leaders, military commanders and an elite force of war-fighters began training with the most sophisticated weapons systems that technology could provide to create and sustain an unprecedented deterrent force.

The much of this journal is dedicated to the men and women of strategic nuclear forces, their extraordinary feats and contributions to deterrence and the decisive end of the Cold War. It was the formidable and enduring collective strength of the men and women of Strategic Air Command and those of the United States Navy nuclear submarine sea-launched ballistic missile force that made up the TRIAD of deterrence that protected the nation's people and interests during the period.

CSA

HISTORICAL PERSPECTIVE

"If we want to know where the country is going;
we need to know where we have been."

President John Adams

ONE

THE COLD WAR

"America was not built on fear. America was built on courage, on imagination and an unbeatable determination to do the job at hand."

Harry S. Truman

President Truman, with fearless determination and courage, had led the country through the last days of World War II. He had made the bold decision to drop the atomic bomb on Japan in response to their persistent acts of defiance to surrender.

Troubled by the questionable outcomes of the strategy meetings between Roosevelt, Churchill and Stalin during the conflict—he had only been involved in the last of the Big Three conferences at Potsdam—he was, nevertheless, buoyed by traditional American optimism that the war to end all wars was over and world peace had been restored.

It was 1946; only six months had elapsed since the final acts of surrender by Germany and Japan. The earlier optimism quickly wilted when Josef Stalin, emboldened by his personal premise that the Soviet Union had been the virtual conqueror in the war in Europe, coupled with the extraordinary concessions by the United States and its Allies, announced to the Russian people on February 9th that, "Communism and capitalism are incompatible and confrontation will likely come in the 1950s when America is in the depths of post-war depression."

It was obvious that communism and capitalism were manifestly incompatible; there was little doubt that conflict between the West and the

3

New Soviet Union would be inevitable. Less than a month later, on March 5th, Sir Winston Churchill, invited by President Truman to bolster confidence in the future, made a 'friendship' speech at Westminster College in Fulton, Missouri. Instead of savoring the end of the war and the defeats of Germany and Japan as Stalin had the month before, he surprised the President and the world with a cautiously perceptive and frankly worded speech, declaring,"From Stettin in the Baltic to Trieste in the Adriatic, an Iron Curtain has descended across the Continent."

With World War II still clearly visible in the rear view mirror, Churchill unmistakably interpreted Stalin's intentions. Victorious in their 'Great Patriotic War', Stalin had ordered a new "5-year Plan" for Russia: Triple production of all war related materials, delay manufacture of all consumer goods until rearmament was completed and for the Soviet people to prepare for a war with a new enemy, the capitalist West. He predicted that war would likely come soon when the United States fell into the grip of a depression resulting from their postwar doldrums. Many government leaders in Washington were shocked at Stalin's bold statements. Some called his provocative speech a declaration of war. Others in the government and the media discounted the Soviets as a serious threat and condemned Churchill's remarks as enticing confrontation with the Russians. Some shrugged as the United States and Britain successfully carried the World War II effort on two major fronts and supported the major efforts, particularly Russia's, toward securing the victories.

Churchill's words enunciated the stark reality that although one war was over, the dark clouds of another had already begun to gather. Seven years earlier during the period that Stalin and Adolph Hitler were engaged in their ill-fated non-aggression pact, Churchill had characterized his frustration with the Soviets to the British people in a 1939 radio broadcast: "I cannot forecast to you the action of Russia. It is a riddle wrapped in a mystery inside an enigma."

World War II had come to an end, but the protracted Cold War period had already begun with its headwaters springing from the three major wartime meetings between the World War II western allied leaders and Josef Stalin. The result of these monumental conferences held at Tehran, Yalta and Potsdam began a convoluted, complex and ultimate failure of an orderly post-war recovery for Eastern Europe. In contrast to the aims of the Allies, the outcomes of the conferences in large part promoted the rapid rise of the Soviet Empire. As the empire quickly expanded, awkward and often flaccid responses by the West served little notice to Stalin.

From the first joint meeting of the Big Three in Tehran in late November and early December 1941, it was obvious from the outset and finally in the end that the negotiations between the U.S. and the UK and Stalin warranted a more astute and tougher stance with the Soviets. In contrast, the following from a joint statement issued by Roosevelt, Churchill and Stalin on December 1, 1941 in Tehran: "Emerging from these cordial conferences we look with confidence to the day when all peoples of the world may live free lives, untouched by tyranny and according to their varying desires and their own consciences."

At the Tehran Conference, Roosevelt had set out to establish a warm and cordial relationship with Stalin such as he had with Churchill. Outside Churchill's confidence, Roosevelt 'played-up' heavily to Stalin. He teased and chided Churchill publicly, embarrassing him, much to Stalin's pleasure. During the Conference, Roosevelt accepted Stalin's invitation to stay at the Russian Embassy. Churchill became disturbed by the conduct of his trusted friend and warned him about being under the surveillance of the NKVD. According to Roosevelt's close confidant, Harry Hopkins, it was the President's notion that even if he couldn't convert Stalin to become a Democrat, at least they could develop a working relationship. Following the conference and according to Lord Moran, Churchill's personal physician, Roosevelt's conduct and illusions about Stalin had left the Prime Minister in a state of "black depression."

It appeared that Roosevelt's tactics worked for a while; Stalin agreed to every term put forth by himself and Churchill—The U.S. and Britain would invade France from across the English Channel; General Eisenhower would be named the Supreme Allied Commander in Europe to conduct the invasion operation; Russia would enter the war with Japan as soon as Germany was defeated; China would reclaim Manchuria, the Pescadores and Formosa; Korea would become free and independent and the borders of European countries would be restored to their post-war positions.

Stalin held out on two issues with regard to Poland. He did not want to recognize the Polish government-in-exile in London, and he wanted to retain that portion of Poland deeded to Russia during its earlier collaboration with Hitler. The Western leaders finally gave n to the Polish government-in-exile issue and formally agreed only to the Polish boundary terms. As one observer described: "This miscalculation led the United States into a tragic triumph—a 'victory without peace'. " It began the first of many political and geographic moves the Soviets would make toward the domination of the European continent.

The three Allies met again at Yalta in the Crimea during February 4th through the 11th, 1945. The war in Europe was winding down and victory within a few months was in sight. The focus at the Tehran Conference had essentially been on wartime strategy and the Yalta agenda called for final decisions on putting the post-war world in order. Roosevelt arrived at Yalta with a principle tactical issue. He wanted the Soviets to enter the war against Japan. While he had been kept aware of the progress of the development of the atomic bomb, he had been given no absolute assurances that it would be successful. Some of his advisors told him that he could not depend on the bomb being ready...or even working. His persistence with Stalin on Japan, as it turned out, would have been better left alone. Stalin requested that in return for Russia entering the war with Japan, the Soviets would be given the southern half of Sakhalin Island and the Kurile Islands which Japan had won from Russia in the 1904 War. Russia would also be granted a lease on Port Arthur for a naval base and "pre-eminent interests" in Manchuria, whatever that meant. Roosevelt agreed and urged Chiang Kai-shek to recognize these concessions.

Churchill was also not exempt from miscalculating Stalin and the Soviets in spite of his perceptive observations and tough rhetoric. Prior to the Yalta Conference, he went to Moscow in October 1944 to further negotiate the post-war "division of spheres" in Eastern Europe with Stalin. The two agreed that the British would control Greece, the Russians would get Romania, and they would jointly control Yugoslavia and Hungary.

Roosevelt and the U.S. State Department were furious with the unilateral concessions. As the war in Europe came to an end, Stalin ordered the hard-line communists in the jointly managed governments to move in. Further, as the three Allied leaders began gathering for the Yalta Conference, the Soviets had already overrun the previously agreed to war-fighting demarcation lines in Central Europe.

Churchill was so badly disillusioned with the unfolding events before departing for Yalta that he sent a cable to Roosevelt stating: "This may well be a fateful Conference, coming at a moment when the Great Allies are so divided and the shadow of the war lengthens out before us. At the present time I think the end of this war may well prove to be more disappointing than was the last."

Stalin had become a master at manipulation. Roosevelt and Churchill agreed to most every condition presented to them, only to have Stalin ignore or deny them later. Stalin chided Anthony Eden, British Foreign Secretary, at one of the conference gatherings: "A 'declaration', I regard as algebra, but an 'agreement' as practical arithmetic."

Stalin's 'practical arithmetic' amounted to a bunker mentality resulting in the clever exploitation of the natural geographical arrangement of the six Eastern European sovereign nations—Bulgaria, Czechoslovakia, East Germany, Hungary, Poland, and Romania—as a buffer zone. Churchill had shrewdly characterized the situation—"From Stettin in the Baltic to Trieste in the Adriatic." Mother Russia would be shielded from the rest of Europe by the Soviet controlled Warsaw Pact nations.

Once an ally who had depended greatly on the United States and the West for support, arms and equipment to defeat the Germans, Soviet leadership with a great sense of empowerment, abruptly signaled to the world that they would now stand alone, control Eastern Europe and exert their ideology across the world as they pleased. They walked out of the Marshall Plan talks, rejected the notion and the agreements that Berlin would be jointly managed while Germany recovered and similarly denounced the Truman Doctrine intended to unify the post-war Europe. The Soviets then tossed down the gauntlet by blockading Western traffic and supplies into Berlin.

Thus what became known as the Cold War began and evolved into a protracted and often perilous journey into history. There had never been such an intense conflict between two highly developed governments which lasted over such an extended period—almost fifty years—without erupting into all-out warfare.

The United States embraced a containment strategy in response to Josef Stalin's declaration to make Soviet communist expansionism his plan for world order. Many prominent American liberals at the time advocated isolationism as a feasible alternative to a containment policy. Some rationalized that the Soviet people had little taste for war after their bloody experiences during World War II and surely would not follow Stalin's lead into another war. As time would tell, there is little doubt that this would have eventually led to a losing strategy given the demonstrated aggressive nature of the post-war Soviet leadership.

The adoption of containment as a declared policy simply implied that the U.S. would thwart any attempts by the Soviet Union to expand their influence beyond those countries deeded to them at the end of the war. It also meant that in order to meet a potential Soviet threat of aggression, the U.S. and the West would have to rearm themselves well beyond the remnants left over from the war. The introduction of the atomic bomb into the war heightened the concern for the technology eventually getting into Soviet hands.

President Roosevelt had kept his vice-president completely in the dark regarding many major issues. Truman had not even been aware of the atomic bomb development project until he was briefed after the former president's death. He learned that Major General Leslie Groves had been placed in charge of the Manhattan Project and had at his side many of the world's foremost physicists to develop an atomic fission weapon. The project had initially begun at the University of Chicago and later moved to the remote area of Los Alamos, New Mexico, in 1943. Dr. Robert Oppenheimer of the University of California became the chief scientist. Two and one half years later, on July 16,

1945, the scientific team successfully detonated the first atomic device near White Sands, New Mexico.

Truman promptly notified Winston Churchill of the successful test, his confidence in the new technology bomb and his intentions to proceed to use the weapon against Japan if surrender could not be negotiated. Churchill was cheered by the news of the new weapon development and in full agreement. The Soviets had steered clear of the war in the Pacific and had not declared war on Japan.

Los Alamos had built two operational bomb devices in addition to the successful test device. The bombs were ready to be handed over to a specially trained B-29 bomber unit of the Twentieth Air Force commanded by a young Major General Curtis E. LeMay on Tinian Island in the Marianas. The President ordered General Carl Spaatz, Commander of the Army Air Corps forces in the Pacific, to plan missions to drop the two bombs on selected targets of his choice on the Japanese mainland if they did not accept an issued surrender order by August 3, 1945. The Japanese responded to the invitation to surrender by stating that it was unworthy of notice and they would battle to the end.

On the morning of August 6, 1945, the first bomb was dropped on Hiroshima, Japan, from a B-29, the Enola Gay, named after the mother of the pilot, Colonel Paul Tibbets. Thereafter and following two days of leaflet drops over major Japanese cities, repeated broadcasts pleaded for the government to surrender. There was no response to the plea and the second bomb was dropped on the city of Nagasaki on August 9th three days after the first.

[Author's Note: Varous sources have cited President Truman as responding, "No, none at all" to questions regarding any feelings of guilt about ordering the use of atomic weapons against Japan to end the war. During my days at Los Alamos I enjoyed a unique experience with the late actor, Charlton Heston, who worked with us doing 'voice overs' for a number of our technical documentary films. At dinner one evening the conversation moved to the bombs dropped on Hiroshima and Nagasaki; Heston quickly offered his personal experience of the period when he was serving as an Army Air Corps B-25 tailgunner staged on Attu Island as a part of a final aerial assault on Japan. "Had we not dropped those bombs," he lamented, "I would in all likelihood be here this evening, much less the father of my sons. I have no regrets; neither should any one." In 2000 while doing research for a previous book, I urged up the courage to place a phone call to now deceased, retired Brigadier General Paul Tibbets, to verify some information. I caught him on a golf course in Florida where he graciously temporarily halted his game and shared with me several personal insights. Living history!]

The Soviets, caught by surprise but determined not to be left out of U.S. actions in the Pacific, declared war on Japan a few hours before the second bomb was dropped on Nagasaki. The first bomb had completely destroyed the Japanese Second Army Headquarters and a four square mile area around it. An estimated 60,000 people were killed, roughly three times the casualties predicted by Robert Oppenheimer and his Los Alamos scientists. The Nagasaki bomb achieved approximately the same damage, killing 36,000. Within six months, residual deaths from burns and radiation accounted for several thousand more.

Truman had previously chosen the August 3rd surrender notice carefully; he wanted to be aboard the USS Augusta and away from the Potsdam Conference he would be attending with Stalin and Churchill when the first bomb was dropped.

George Kennen, a highly regarded political science intellectual and credible charge d'affaires in the U.S. Embassy in Moscow during the war, had previously written a lengthy 8,000-word message to the State Department describing his estimate of the Soviet regime and warning of their intentions toward world communist domination. In his assessment of what he described as historical Russian tendencies toward insecurity and paranoia, he predicted continued neurotic behavior by the Soviets after the war. Any hope of peaceful coexistence between them and the United States would be virtually hopeless, further stating, "The Soviets would stand before history as only the last of a long session of cruel and wasteful Russian rulers who have relentlessly forced their country on to ever new heights of military power in order to guarantee external security for their internally weak regimes."

He concluded that, in his view, "Soviet power was highly sensitive to the logic of force, and for that reason they usually backed down when faced with strength."

The long telegram, as Kennen's message had become referred to, had been received in the State Department in February 1946 before either Stalin's or Churchill's speeches and had been widely circulated even to the President. It was speculated that Truman read it but did not pay much attention to it since he had heard the same warnings from several others, including Averell Harriman, who warned of a Soviet "barbarian invasion of Europe." Harriman had been sent to Moscow by President Roosevelt as ambassador along with General John R. Deane to head the American Mission. They carried with them the President's strategy that offered "providing the Soviets with unconditional aid which would win Stalin over."

After their first year, Kennen and Deane jointly concluded that the Russians were not going to produce any reciprocal displays of trust or cooperation in spite of offered aid. General Deane found that although—"We were fighting the same war," the Soviet military leaders consistently refused to share any information or facilities for joint use. President Truman, one year in office, was caught in the middle in his pursuits to return to normalcy. On the one hand, he had the staunch hold-overs from Roosevelt, including Harriman, Dean Acheson, George Kennen and his chief of staff, Admiral William Leahy. Each had given their own assessments of perceived Soviet intentions.

On the other side in his cabinet was the liberal gadfly, Henry Wallace, Secretary of Commerce and previous vice president under Roosevelt. On the outside was Wendell Wilkie, the 1940 Republican presidential candidate, each of whom made their affinity toward Stalin and the Soviets well-known. In his book, One World, Wilkie glorified the Soviet regime.

The President's characterized middle-of-the-road stance was joined in by his Secretary of State, James F. Byrnes, who consistently sought ways to appease Stalin and the Russians. The appeasement went back to the Potsdam Conference, where Truman had met Stalin for the first time. Byrnes had also worked diligently to influence the President toward the Soviet's desires at the conference. Truman came away from Potsdam fresh from the success of the atomic bombing of Japan and with victory in the Pacific assured, and he felt good about the future of the world. He enthused around the White House, "I like Uncle Joe." We have "...discussed raising corn and pigs in our respective countries." He wasn't alone in his belief that U.S. and Soviet Union coexistence was possible. Roosevelt conceitedly felt that he had charmed Stalin in their meetings and stated that when the time came to seriously work out their differences, Stalin would cooperate.

George Kennen was considered to be the brilliant architect of Truman's post-war anti-communist containment strategy. He had spent several years in Moscow during the war studying Soviet communist ideology and philosophy, but a few years after the war his influence began to fade. Returning from Moscow, he became Director of the National Security Council and began to steadily lose favor with the President's post-Roosevelt cabinet. Truman's senior advisors had begun to question Kennen's evolving assumptions about the Soviets. He had postulated amongst other hypothesis that: "The danger of war with the Soviets was remote; asymmetry with the Soviet Union could be tolerated indefinitely; negotiations with the Soviets, if mutually beneficial, could be productive and diplomacy on the part of the United States must be flexible."

President Truman and his Administration were uncomfortable with the corollary that the United States could safely shift from military dominated containment strategy to one of economic pressure. Frustrated that his thesis was not accepted, Kennen resigned in December 1949. He was replaced by Paul Nitze, also an astute political scientist and historian. Kennen's critics felt strongly that his logic was more 'wishful' intuition than verifiable judgment. Under Nitze, as policy director, the thesis for U.S. Cold War strategy became 'verifiable measurements' of Soviet capabilities and intentions.

The Soviets also served to move Truman away from Kennen's conciliatory approach. They tested their own atomic bomb in late August 1949. The detonation was detected by a WB-29 reconnaissance plane on September 3rd off Kamchatka peninsula. The U.S. monopoly of atomic weapon technology was at an end. It had been the hold card to keep the Soviets in check. The United States, not in untypical historical fashion, had massively demobilized the military after the war from over 12 million at its peak to 660,000 in mid-1949. Equipment, mainly aircraft and ships, had been moth-balled or dismantled. The U.S. defense budget in 1945 was in excess of $85 billion. In 1949, it stood at a little over $13 billion. The Soviets, as noted earlier under Stalin's decree, maintained the largest and best equipped military force in the world. Because of the 'asymmetry' that George Kennen had bet on, the U.S. atomic weapon advantage had been lost.

With the bomb at his disposal, Stalin was now able to counter U.S. containment initiatives and nuclear deterrence became the point-counterpoint strategy of the opposing powers. The result was the greatest arms race and military force build-up in the history of mankind. The strategy was as potentially deadly as its uncompromising nuclear characterization. But most U.S. policy makers felt that nuclear deterrence based on more sophisticated technology and military capability could sustain the containment theorem.

Yale historian, Bernard Brodie, had offered a postulation of the meaning of stand-off deterrence: "The side that prepared most rationally for the ultimate conflict must be the side that was prepared to actually fight a nuclear war and would be the most likely to survive, possibly even to prevail."

With the exception of "preparing most rationally," Brodie was essentially proven correct as the evolving Cold War escalated. During the turbulent period of roller coaster diplomacy between the giant super powers, numerous changes vacillated in political persuasion within both governments. Political partisan solutions to the protracted conflict in the United States seesawed back and forth with the public generally supporting what appeared to be the most compelling arguments: maintain a strong military deterrence while seeking solutions to peace and maintaining a viable economic-driven society during each election cycle. The Soviet manifesto for world dominance remained persistent. The protracted period of conflict witnessed numerous deadly sub-wars fought indirectly between the two major adversaries under the 'umbrella' of the Cold War.

Both the United States and the Soviet Union developed capabilities to support the nuclear deterrence strategy and even learned to skillfully maneuver around under the fragile umbrella. The Berlin Blockade, Korea, Sputnik, Gary Powers' U-2 incident, Hungarian Revolt, Cuban Crisis, Vietnam, Czechoslovakian uprising and the Soviet invasion of Afghanistan—each conflict challenged the West, but without tripping into Armageddon. Each of the crises served to place new and challenging twists on the overriding international state of affairs, the world leaders and ever-increasing demands on the respective military fighting forces.

The Korean and Vietnam Conflicts were the most predominant of these 'sub-war' crises. As we will review later, SAC participated greatly in both military clashes while consistently maintaining a nuclear deterrence against the Soviet threat.

The protracted conflict of the Cold War was singularly unique in the history of military-political conflicts. It was the longest standoff between major nations in modern history. The period saw the largest arms build-up of the most sophisticated and deadliest weapons ever by the opposing governments. None of the vast inventory of those weapons of mass destruction was ever used against the other.

The Soviet Union used virtually every ruse it could muster to promote the communist cause. Their leaders became skilled at probing the West's potential vulnerabilities. After placing a yoke around the necks of Eastern Europe, Stalin's next move was to provoke his former Western Allies by blockading Berlin. The communist empowered government of North Vietnam, encouraged by the Soviet Union and China, moved on its own people in the South. Khrushchev made an ill-fated calculation by attempting to position offensive nuclear forces in Cuba. Each of these, both direct and proxy-supported engagements was designed to distract the United States and the West's focus, and to deplete their economy, military strength and their will. The assaults in Korea and Vietnam inflicted great casualties on the U.S. and its Allies, as well as the invaders. The victimized people caught up in these forays on both sides suffered the most. None of the provocations worked successfully for the world-wide communist movement. The Vietnam conflict came as close as any to disrupting U.S. policy by creating a moral struggle with the conscience of Americans. Many began to lose faith in their government's strategy and military solutions to confront communism.

Many perceived the Soviet Union literally held a loaded gun to the heads of the United States and the West from 1946 until 1991. Their opinions concluded that the gun was secured with a firm grip, by men ten feet tall and made of steel with a finger on the trigger and an equal inclination that it might be pulled at any time.

Finally, after decades of experimenting and toying with strategies to bring the Cold War to an end, President Ronald Reagan introduced a straightforward and simple dictum of defense strategy: "Prevent war by maintaining the military capabilities sufficient to win a potential war and demonstrate the unyielding determination to use whatever it takes to do so, thereby persuading any adversary that the costs of an attack on their part would exceed any benefits which they might hope to gain."

By the mid-1980's, Reagan, confident that he understood the Soviets and their situation, began to implement his own strategy. He began by tightening the screws on all fronts: psychologically, politically, militarily and economically. The war with the 'Evil Empire', as he stridently labeled the Soviet Union, had entered its fifth decade. Deterrence, essentially shaped and led by the United States against Soviet expansionism and the pursuit of world dominance, had taken numerous forms over the years. With a sustained economy, technology base and accessible natural resources far in excess of the rest of the world, the Reagan strategy moved to create a checkmate.

Strategic Defense Initiative (SDI), developed by the Reagan Defense Department, assisted greatly in doing both. Already faced with the prospect of having their territorial defenses saturated with newly developed air launched cruise missiles (ALCMs) and the ground launched cruise missiles (GLCMs) deployed to NATO, fear of the U.S. putting up a shield to defend against incoming missile warheads was more than Soviet technology and economics could manage. These real and perceived U.S. initiatives, coupled with the strong will of a committed president, converged with growing economic and ideological discord within the Soviet Union. The fortuitous surprise advent of Mikhail Gorbachev, the first moderate leader in Soviet history, began the erosion of the Soviet Union and the Cold War.

On August 19, 1991, a quickly organized assemblage of distraught senior Soviet Military and a few KGB officers, along with old guard communist bureaucrats, declared that they had seized power of the Soviet Union. Their intent was to oust Gorbachev and restore the communist central authority. The poorly organized coup failed when Russian people, for the first time in modern history, took to the streets in defiance of an attempted takeover. The USSR collapsed with the failed coup. The declaration of independence by the majority of the former Soviet Republics and an economy in shambles; the forty-five year Cold War standoff was at an end.

TWO

THE FORCES OF DETERRENCE

"It was created out of necessity; maintained by policy and sacrifice of sweat, blood and treasure."

Richard G. Hubler
SAC: Strategic Air Command
1958

"It was quite a day. The sky was full of B-29s, but I am sure they had a better view of it all from down below than we did. There were two things that struck me at the time. One, of course, was the tremendous, historic event that was taking place beneath us in Tokyo Bay. The other was the amazement at being able to fly around over downtown Tokyo at 1,000 feet altitude and not have anyone shooting at us." These were the thoughts later expressed by the late Lt. General James V. Edmundson, USAF (Retired), on September 2, 1945, then a colonel and commander of the 468th Bomb Group, as he led five hundred B-29s in a flyover of the Japanese surrender ceremonies aboard the USS Missouri. A few weeks later, the 468th and the other groups of the 58th Bomb Wing returned from the Pacific Theater to Sacramento, California, where they were told they would be separated from the Army Air Corps immediately:

"Just sign these papers and you are free to go home. The war is over!" the Pacific air warriors were instructed by the personnel mustering-out specialists.

15

The air crews were also told that their airplanes would eventually be dismantled and scrapped by contractors who were eagerly waiting to claim the aircraft. As we know, saner judgments soon prevailed and the initial chaos of rushing away from the war and the demobilizing and dismantling of the military services did not commence with the haste that the bureaucrats and "bean counters" may have desired. Fortunately so, as the dark clouds of another war had already begun to gather.

Only six months after the 468th Bomb Group flyover and their heroic return from the war, Army Air Corps Chief of Staff, General Carl Spaatz, directed the establishment of three new commands: a strategic war-fighting command to address the growing realization that Stalin's postwar goals went beyond Russia and Eastern Europe, a tactical air support command for and a continental air defense structure. The prompt move to respond to the alarming potential Soviet threat created the Strategic Air Command in March 1946 along with Tactical Air Command and Air Defense Command.

The new Strategic Air Command would soon become known simply as SAC. The mandate for SAC was to build an organization for long-range offensive operations to reach any part of the world. Established at Bolling Air Force Base on the Potomac River near downtown Washington DC, SAC was manned and armed with left over scattered remnants of the deactivated Continental Air Command and World War II operational units. General George C. Kenny was appointed SAC's first commander and struggled to develop its directed mission and identify the types of weapons systems necessary to address the perceived growing threat.

The Command began with mostly volunteers, officers and airmen who wanted to remain on active duty in the Air Corps after the war along with 1,300 various types of aircraft.

The conglomerate of aircraft consisted of B-29 bombers, P-51 and P-80 fighters, F-2 and F-13 reconnaissance planes and a few C-54 transports. The hastily begun postwar demobilization process couldn't be promptly stemmed, and SAC's initial manpower amounted to a little over 37,000. The officers and men who remained after the war were the committed and the dedicated; they became the Genesis of the new and exciting command. A program to recover airplanes from the war zones continued, and the B-29 bomber fleet eventually grew to several hundred durable aircraft.

The Air Force still lacked mission coherency with the new Strategic Air Command and its inherited aircraft inventory. In addition to the B-29 bombers, there was an odd mixture of 230 P-51's and 120 P-80's designated for bomber escort duty along with an array of others for perceived reconnaissance missions. Most of the fighter aircraft would eventually find their way to the newly created Tactical Air Command, although SAC retained a few fighters to fly escort duty for a period of time. The modestly configured reconnaissance aircraft were to become a blessing in disguise, setting the stage for SAC to become the long-term single manager of air-breathing reconnaissance platforms. They were directly related to the command's evolving strategic mission planning and later to the comprehensive intelligence requirements of the future Joint Strategic Target Planning Staff (JSTPS).

By 1948, SAC had begun to kick into high gear, creating a dramatic evolution in strategic warfare capability. Lt. General Curtis E. LeMay, who had successfully directed the massive fire bombings of Japan, the atomic bomb attacks on Nagasaki and Hiroshima and the Berlin Airlift operations succeeded General Kenney as commander of SAC. In short order, he outlined the strategic goals of the Command and its people. His task was by no means easy. Saddled with war-worn bombers that lacked "global reach" he envisioned would be required to carry out his charge, he led a torturous political battle to get the B-36 long-range heavy bomber built. SAC evolved to constitute two legs of the United States' Cold War defense structure: the TRIAD, providing the strategic bomber-tanker force and the intercontinental ballistic missile (ICBM) force. The Navy provided the critical third leg of the TRIAD—the nuclear sea launched ballistic missile (SLBM) force. The balance of combined capabilities, power and interoperability were unsurpassed by any other measure in history or the present. In this essay, we will concern ourselves principally with the Strategic Air Command and the Navy nuclear forces, their mission capabilities and the heroic exploits of many.

President Truman, fresh from his close re-election and continuing to work toward recovering the country out of World War II, had called for massive cuts in defense spending. In spite of the saber-rattling by the Soviets, he felt the danger of another war to be minimal. The Soviets were having their own post-war economic problems and distractions with trying to feed and pacify its acquired satellite countries. Following the President's direction, Secretary of Defense Louis Johnson tore into the defense budget, setting an arbitrary goal of $13.5 billion for FY 1950. This would mean a reduction of 45,000 military personnel; he further forecast a budget of $10.5 billion the following year. His first act was to cancel the construction of the super-carrier, United States, the Navy's competing hope against the Air Force's and LeMay's B-36 bomber program. The budget battle with the Secretary among the Services erupted into the legendary "revolt of the admirals." The revolt, in fact, was not initiated by admirals, but by Navy Captain John Crommelin, who was assigned to the Office of the Joint Chiefs of Staff in the Pentagon. Allegedly acting on his own, he released a blistering statement to the press criticizing the administration's budget policies and its impact on national defense and the morale of the Services, the Navy in particular.

17

The Chief of Naval Operations, Admiral Louis Denfeld, was so pleased with Crommelin's bravado that he quietly appointed him to be Deputy Chief, Naval Personnel, positioning him for promotion to flag officer rank. The action was short-lived, however, and Secretary of the Navy, Francis Matthews, promptly rescinded the assignment. Crommelin, not deterred, then released to the media copies of confidential letters signed by three senior admirals supporting his earlier statement. The three admirals included Admirals Denfeld, Arthur Radford, CINCPACFLT and Gerald Bogan, Commander, First Task Fleet, Pacific. Angered by the growing inter-service squabbling and bad publicity, Congress intervened and called for hearings and testimony by the admirals. During the hearings, Admiral Denfeld publicly accused the Administration of "illogical, damaging and dangerous favoritism toward the Air Force" and "relegating the Navy to a convoy or anti-submarine service."

The Chairman of the Joint Chiefs of Staff, Omar Bradley, was called to testify and chastised the Navy for their undisciplined tactics by going public with their complaints and attacking the other services. Truman moved to clear the air, asking Admiral Denfeld to retire, replacing him with a more moderate officer, Admiral Forrest Sherman, who had steered clear of the hearings. Congress recessed and the issue cooled. By the time elections came around in 1952, the Korean War had begun and drove the defense budget to quadruple, the draft had been reinstated, military programs were in full-swing and the Navy and Air Force were at peace with one another.

The Navy was getting its first super carrier, the Forrestal and the B-36 was in full production at Consolated-Vultee's (Convair) plant in Ft. Worth. The Forrestal was to be in the 76,000 ton class and five-times larger than anything in the Soviet fleet. Likewise, the B-36 was designed to replace the World War II B-29's and could fly 10,000 miles un-refueled while carrying a 10,000 pound bomb load. Congress authorized 446 B-36's to be built. The Soviets had nothing to match its size or strategic capability. The Air Force was also authorized to order 260 advanced versions of the B-29, dubbed the B-50.

By the time the Korean War broke out, SAC had its mission, most of its personnel and its new heavy bomber would soon be operational and prepared to fight a global war. The Soviets carefully monitored the U.S. military build-up along with the committed support to Korea. The response was a concurrent push by Stalin to match the Americans with their own arms race. Charles Morris, in his book, Iron Destinies, Lost Opportunities, described Stalin's war fighting strategy as archaic at best; stuck on World War II philosophy. With an insistence for military build-ups in infantry, artillery and masses of soldiers, the Soviet Union evolved into a military autocracy. Some predicted this single-minded and determined military strategy would eventually drive the Soviet Empire into a social and economic quagmire. History proved the prediction to be accurate, but it took several decades. While the Soviets feared the overt consequences of a nuclear war, they also believed that the greatest threat would mainly affect the civilian population since soldiers moving rapidly in the battlefield would escape the effects. The Soviet experience in holding off the Germans at Leningrad and Moscow likely reinforced Stalin's emphasis on ground forces theory. Accordingly, the Soviet Air Force took second chair to the armored tank forces in their build-up to face the West.

Stalin persistently played down the importance of nuclear weapons, stating once, "I do not consider the atomic bomb as a serious force as some politicians are inclined to do. Atomic bombs are meant to frighten those with weak nerves, but they cannot decide the fate of wars since they are quite insufficient for that."

Whether the Soviet leader actually believed this premise or if it was for Western consumption isn't clear. In any event, the Soviet scientists aggressively pursued a nuclear weapons program, perhaps even without the full knowledge of the Soviet leader; it progressed rapidly from their first successful chain reaction on Christmas Day 1946 to the detonation of a plutonium enriched bomb two and a half years later on August 29, 1949.

Stalin's doctrine also dictated that the Soviet air mission be limited to supporting the infantry. Until he died in 1953, the Soviet military doctrine continued to rest with the infantry and artillery. The Soviet military was also kept distant from training and handling nuclear weapons until after his death.

Meanwhile, the U.S. Strategic Air Command under the leadership and tutelage of General LeMay continued to grow in strength and weapons systems, eventually peaking in manpower to almost 283,000, operating the most sophisticated bombers, tankers, reconnaissance aircraft and ICBM's that any one could have ever dreamed. SAC adopted an enduring paradoxical slogan, "Peace is Our Profession." Contradictory, perhaps, because many found it inconceivable that the proprietor of the world's largest nuclear weapons arsenal and extraordinary delivery systems could characterize itself as a professional peacemaker. Time would tell.

At the heart of the long period of success of the United States in maintaining deterrence against Soviet aggression was a compelling national will, great leadership, innovative technologies, a superior industrial base and, most importantly, young American men and women. The United States clearly enjoyed the unsurpassed patriotism and loyalty of its Cold War military forces. They served, they trained hard and they performed incredible tasks and missions without fanfare and mostly without recognition by the rest of the world passing by. They worked long hours with short pay, their families sacrificed with them, weekdays blended with weekends, long absences from home were the norm rather than the exception and yet morale remained at an amazingly high level. The discipline was exacting, their commitments were unsurpassed, and the warriors of the late forties and fifties grew into older warriors and senior commanders of the seventies, eighties and nineties. With the passage of time, the strategic nuclear deterrent forces of SAC and the submarine Navy maintained a truly elite professional war-fighting capability.

In 1960, Department of Defense planners with full support of President Eisenhower created what became known as the Single Integrated Operational Plan—the SIOP—the first comprehensive plan for nuclear war. The SIOP became the most secret and sensitive issue in U.S. national security policy at the time, perhaps ever. The essence of the first developed SIOP was a massive nuclear strike on military and urban-industrial targets in the Soviet Union, China and their allies. U.S. war planners developed a complex organizational strategy involving the interaction of targeting, weapons delivery systems and their flight paths, enemy defensive measures, nuclear detonations over selected targets and direct and collateral damage measurements. When the first SIOP was created, DOD architects established a special information category—Extremely Sensitive Information (ESI)—to ensure that only those with exceptional "need-to-know" requirements would have access to the documents.

Significant features of the SIOP included retaliatory and preemptive nuclear attack options against designated enemy targets. Preemption could occur if the U.S. received strategic warning of a Soviet attack; a preemptive nuclear strike would have delivered over 3200 nuclear weapons to 1060 pre-selected enemy targets and a nuclear strike by the strategic alert force in retaliation to a Soviet strike would have delivered 1706 nuclear weapons against a total of 725 enemy targets. Targets included operational nuclear weapons systems and depots, government and military control centers and approximately 130 cities in the Soviet Union, China and their allies.

President Eisenhower approved the Single Integrated Operational Plan for implementation in fiscal year 1962 and that it go into effect on April 1, 1961. SIOP-62 was the U.S. government's first comprehensive nuclear war plan which would synchronize the nuclear forces of the Air Force, Navy and Army for potential attack on the Soviet Union, China and their communist allies. The SIOP-62 plan was designed to conduct a combined attack by strategic bombers, Polaris submarine-launched missiles and Atlas ICBMs. The SIOP, according to historian David Rosenberg, was "a technical triumph in the history of war planning!"

The SIOP remained fundamentally intact as it was originally developed with only minor adjustments as the Cold War evolved. The Kennedy

Administration, looking for "flexible response" and additional options available to the president, pressed the Joint Chiefs of Staff to make the Plan less rigid. The JCS were willing to introduce target withholds and create options to strike military targets only (counterforce) but were reluctant to change the essential character of the plan. SIOP-63 included some of the requested changes but resisted such huge attack options that someone characterized as "five choices for massive retaliation." The original SIOP evolved through additional modest changes, but the overall structure of attack options did not change in its basic construct until the late 1970s, after the Nixon and Carter administrations in turn pressed for limited nuclear options that would give the president an alternative to catastrophic massive attacks. In any event, even after the basic attack options became more 'flexible', they maintained the original premise of massive destruction against enemy targets.

An essential requirement to implementing the SIOP function was the creation of a joint strategic planning organization. The planning differences between SAC and the Navy had become even more significant with the advent of the sea-based Polaris ballistic missiles. General Thomas Power, succeeding General LeMay as CINCSAC, had previously recommended that SAC control all strategic weapons targeting. Even as the SIOP was being conceived and developed, Secretary of Defense, Thomas Gates recognized the need to coordinate nuclear weapons targeting and established the Joint Strategic Target Planning Staff (JSTPS). He appointed the Commander-in-Chief, SAC, supported by an integrated joint military staff, to assume the separate duty as Director of Strategic Target Planning. Gates further directed, "The JSTPS will be the planning agent for the Joint Chiefs of Staff in developing and keeping up to date the detailed plans which are necessary."

Chief of Naval Operations Admiral Arleigh Burke initially objected to the new arrangement, perhaps because the location of JSTPS at SAC Headquarters implied Air Force control. Secretary Gates encouraged Admiral Burke to argue his case with President Eisenhower. The president ultimately upheld Gates' decision. Thereafter, Admiral Burke fully supported the JSTPS and assigned exceptionally qualified nuclear submarine officers to staff the assigned positions. From this author's experience as Deputy Director, JSTPS, for three years, the Navy sustained its support by providing some of its best and brightest junior and senior officers to come to Omaha to serve in the JSTPS. The new joint staff became operational in time to prepare the first SIOP-62 with its specified various strategic nuclear attack options including the timing, weapons, delivery systems and targets to be used by U.S. strategic forces if executed. General Power became the first Director of JSTPS.

General Power initiated additional deterrent readiness programs, testifying before Congress in February 1959: "We in Strategic Air Command have developed a system known as airborne alert where we maintain airplanes in the air 24 hours a day, loaded with bombs, on station, ready to go to the target... I feel strongly that we must get on with this airborne alert... We must impress Mr. Khrushchev that we have it, and that he cannot strike this country with impunity."

The new tactic nicknamed "Chromedome" was employed sooner than anyone might have predicted when the Soviets triggered the Cuban Crisis. The new dimension in alert response capability challenged the B-52 combat crew force to new heights—the bombers took off fully loaded with fuel and nuclear weapons at gross weights of almost 300,000 pounds, two heavy-weight refuelings en route to pre-planned target areas and airborne sorties of nominal 24-hours in duration or until relieved by the next airborne alert crew. The key element of the Chromedome concept was to position the bombers in world-wide pre-planned stand-off orbiting patterns. From those planned positions, the crews could quickly respond to attack their designated targets in the Soviet Union if and when directed by the National Command Authority. Chromedome gave new meaning to flexible response. The concept also served to prove the overall ability to employ strategic weapons in a selective and controlled manner. The unique strategy still could not ignore the realities of force structure and performance provided by the steady influx of professional performers who came into the strategic forces to serve.

Several other initiatives were taken during those apprehensive Cold War years to enhance combat crew survivability and response. SAC achieved a one-third alert posture of the bomber and tanker force in May 1960 and followed in February 1961 with the continuous airborne command post operation, "Looking Glass". Looking Glass provided for a fully configured command and control center on board a converted KC-135 (Boeing 707) aircraft. These aircraft were designated EC-135's and were equipped with the latest and most advanced communications equipment. The flying command post remained in the air continuously 24 hours a day. This was accommodated by three EC-135 aircraft per day flying nominal eight to nine hour "shifts". The principle of the concept mandated that the airborne "on duty" aircraft could not land until properly relieved by a successor aircraft in the air and operationally ready to assume the command and control responsibilities. The procedure thereby insured the required unbroken communications link. Should the relief aircraft fail to takeoff due to maintenance, weather or other problems, the airborne Looking Glass aircraft would be refueled in the air by a stand-by alert tanker and then continue on for another full airborne shift. The staff aboard Looking Glass included a general officer and necessary operations, logistics and communications specialists to carry out any emergency contingency planning and response. The staff could communicate directly with SAC forces world-wide including the SAC underground command post, all SAC unit command posts and aircraft in the air or on the ground, as well as, the Pentagon Command Center. By April 1967, the Looking Glass airborne staff possessed the capability to launch selected Minuteman ICBM's via an Airborne Launch Control System (ALCS).

The SAC general officer aboard Looking Glass served as the airborne commander of the flight crew and operations staff and was certified with special training in nuclear Emergency War Order (EWO) implementation and command and control procedures. The onboard general officer carried the title of "Airborne Emergency Actions Officer," (AEAO), and was vested with the authority to act for and on behalf of the Commander in Chief, Strategic Air Command, in any confirmed wartime emergency situation. He also had the authority to act for the President of the United States and the National Command Authority should they become incapacitated. The AEAO responsibilities was an 'additional duty' for all generals assigned to Strategic Air Command within the Headquarters and those serving in positions away from Offutt Air Force Base. Those serving in positions away from SAC Headquarters were scheduled to fly into Offutt for three or four days at a stretch to perform their AEAO duties and thence back to their primary jobs. If the general officer was also a rated pilot, he was required to become qualified in the EC-135 Looking Glass aircraft and to log a specified number of take-offs approaches and landings periodically in order to maintain proficiency. This added 'requirement' delighted these particular AEAO's, since most of them were not in a position to actively continue flying after being promoted to general officer.

Closely coupled with Looking Glass was the Post-Attack Command Control System (PACCS) fleet of similarly equipped EC-135 command, control and communications aircraft. The PACCS crews stood ground alert at designated SAC bases to augment Looking Glass during national emergencies by launching and flying to preplanned orbit positions across the United States to form a 'daisy-chain' communications relay network.

On November 1, 1975 SAC was given the added responsibility of managing the President's National Emergency Airborne Command Posts (NEAC). This included four E-4Bs (Boeing 747) equipped with communications systems common to the Looking Glass as well as state-of-the-art capabilities well beyond the EC-135. The exceptionally large interior of the E-4B, roughly that of a 4,350 sq ft home, was divided into six separate working compartments. The space permitted a considerably larger crew of specialists to operate and maintain the equipment array and to support the President and his staff when they were airborne during national emergencies. The media promptly dubbed the E-4B the 'Doomsday Plane'. The E-4B was truly a dream for the SAC Looking Glass staff teams who periodically flew the aircraft for familiarization training, to fly aboard and to operate its systems.

The incredible smooth stability of the huge aircraft in flight and the spacious operating and living conditions were a far cry from the EC-135. No one at the time of implementation would have believed that the Looking Glass airborne alert operation would continue for almost thirty years which it did until July 24, 1990, when the United States became relatively confident that an impending Soviet threat of attack was no longer imminent.

The continuous airborne presence of the Looking Glass with a general officer and a war fighting command and control team on board added immeasurably to the deterrence posture of the United States by giving the Soviet high command a constant worry regarding its potential intent.

Other Cold War readiness enhancement initiatives were implemented in 1961 with the increase of the ground alert posture to fifty percent of the bombers and tankers combat-loaded and committed to a fifteen minute take-off response time. SAC combat crewmembers found even more demands on their lives with the escalating alert postures. The norm became 7-days on alert at either in their home base alert facility or at a deployed base. The crews would generally come off alert and promptly fly a combat training mission of 14 to 20 hours in duration which had been pre-planned during the week on alert. They would then enjoy a *few* days of free time and then repeat the routine often as soon as the next week. The routine continued for more than thirty years.

Looking back, the nation should marvel at how it was all accomplished. Thousands upon thousands of young men and women willingly stepped forward and served their country under the most trying stressful conditions; morale remained more than reasonably high and the retention of quality officers and enlisted personnel remained the highest ever for such a sustained period.

SAC had been charged with the greatest responsibilities in the history of warfare. The Free World will never know what the consequences may have been without Strategic Air Command. Richard Hubler in his book, SAC, speculated: "What other, more benign forces supplement or replace SAC in the future is none of the business of this history."

"You never let us down, you were always prepared, and the horror of World War III never came. You kept the peace, and the nation and the Free World will be forever grateful. Thank you, SAC."

General Colin Powell
Chairman, Joint Chiefs of Staff
June 22, 1992

Peace was their profession and they preserved it.

THREE

WEAPONS OF DETERRENCE

"The aggressor makes the rules for such a war; the defenders have no
alternative but matching destruction with more destruction."

Franklin D. Roosevelt

The Cold War witnessed the greatest development of arms and weapons systems
in history. The forty-five year period of competitive military weapons research
and force development can only be defended by the fact that the world did
not disintegrate as a result. It is doubtful that anyone could have envisioned
the extraordinary break-out in weapons, weapons systems technology and
the accumulated arsenals that would be developed and without a declared
war between the adversaries to drive the requirements. The "leapfrogging" of
technology was often so rapid that it was not unusual to have weapon systems
approach obsolescence before reaching full deployment. The respective
defense industries were challenged by ever-increasing demands to which they
responded with extraordinary technologies, including intercontinental ballistic
missiles, nuclear driven submarines, high performance heavy jet bombers,
cruise missiles, exotic command, control and communication systems, and
the list goes on. The net results were the largest and most powerful nuclear and
conventional arsenals that no one would have rationally or logically planned
outside actual warfare. They simply evolved out of an extreme challenge and
response atmosphere that pervaded the world for forty-five years, with the
U.S. and the Soviets each maintaining a remarkable degree of crisis stability

considering both had the overpowering means to attack, re-attack and destroy the other at any given time.

When the skills of diplomacy failed to resolve differences and the threat of potential war heightened, each side responded with revised policies of threatened force: mega-tonnage, unique delivery systems and innovative offensive or defensive tactics. Future historical analysts will have to determine if the result was because of, or in spite of, the respective creation of such arsenals. We will review in detail some of the more significant weapons systems provided the Cold War deterrent forces.

THE BOMBERS

B-29 SUPERFORTRESS

Developed by Boeing Aircraft Company during the war years, the B-29 gave the United States a "long-rifle" capability that the B-17 and B-24 did not have. The heavy bomber concept was consistent with American military thought from the earliest of air war-fighting developments—"fight the war on the other guy's turf whenever possible." Gen William "Billy" Mitchell had long argued that bombers could fly far out to sea and sink the enemy's ships or drop bombs on his capitals, a situation which would be far better than fighting the war in our own territory.

The bomber evolution was slow between the two world wars as several US aircraft companies—Boeing, Martin, Curtiss, Douglas, Lockheed, Consolidated Vultee (Convair)—attempted to develop the desired long-range bomber. The Air Corps had requested a bomber that could fly at speeds of 300 MPH, with a range of 3,000 miles and at an altitude of 35,000 feet. All too often, however, the contractor tried to sell the Air Corps what it thought it needed rather than what was asked for.

World War II brought the issue to a preliminary conclusion. While the Boeing B-17, first of the US heavy bombers, did not entirely fulfill the long-range military strategists' desires to "fly missions from the US mainland to foreign targets," it became the most famous bomber of the day. At the end of the war, 12,731 Flying Fortresses had been built. The B-17 was not the production leader, however; Convair built over 18,000 B-24 Liberators—more than any other aircraft before or since.

Meanwhile, back in 1940, Boeing had begun to design a "super bomber"—the XB-29. The aircraft's designers attempted to fully address the long-rifle bombing concept. The thinking was that European bases might not always be available to the United States. The XB-29 was dubbed the

"Hemisphere Defense Weapon." In designing it, Boeing looked ahead to the potential for the basic structural innovations of the B-29 to be applicable to the all-jet bombers of the future.

Other ideas under consideration were turbojet and pusher engines. The war was ongoing, however, and the "super" aircraft had to be completed as soon as possible—which it was. The first B-29 prototype flew in 1942; two years after the initial design, and the first production models came off the line in 1944. The new strategic bomber had the first pressurized crew compartment and was powered by four 2200 horsepower R-3350 Wright Cyclone engines. The aircraft was fitted with remotely controlled gun turrets, the APQ-7 radar bombing system, double bomb bays and an engine central fire control system. It also had the size and power to carry large weapons, such as the atomic bomb; the Air Corps ordered 1,660 B-29s. The aircraft's achievements in Europe and the Pacific Theater, including the bombings of Japan, set the stage for strategic bombers of the future. As a demonstration of the newly organized SAC's capability, 101 B-29s flew in the command's first "Max-Effort" mission launched on May 16, 1947, flying an extended navigation route and a simulated bomb run on New York City. SAC later had 187 B-29 bombers converted to airborne tankers—KB-29s—and more than 60 to reconnaissance platforms—RB-29s and F-2's. Earlier versions of the KB-29 were fitted with the British-developed in-flight refueling system, which used trailing hoses and grapnel hooks. Later, in 1950, the KB-29s were fitted with the telescoping "stiff boom" system. The Soviets, equally impressed with the large bomber, built a thousand unauthorized replicas—the TU-4. Some of the B/RB/KB-29s remained in the SAC inventory until 1956; the TU-4 remained in the Soviet inventory well into the 1960s.

B-50A ADVANCED SUPERFORTRESS

The B-50A was an enhanced version of the B-29, with more reliable Pratt & Whitney R-4360 3500-horsepower engines. The first B-50A aircraft was delivered to SAC on February 20, 1948. Over 250 of the newer bombers, equipped with an engine analyzer to diagnose engine problems and outfitted with a taller vertical stabilizer for improved maneuverability, were built. While the B-50A had a range of 4,900 miles (un-refueled) and an operational altitude of 36,000 feet, it had an air-refueling capability and was also configured as a long-range reconnaissance platform. The last B-50 was phased out of the active inventory on October 20, 1955.

B-36 PEACEMAKER

The B-36 holds perhaps the most unique place in military aviation history. The largest bomber ever built, it could fly in excess of 10,000 miles, un-refueled and carrying a 10,000-pound payload. The Army Air Corps announced the design competition for the bomber on April 11, 1941, eight months before Pearl Harbor and five years before the atomic bomb. In addition to its weight and range capabilities, the Air Corps wanted it to have airspeed of 300 to 400 MPH and an operating capability from 5,000-foot runways. Convair of San Diego won the contract to build two prototypes to be delivered in 30 months, or about May 1944. Even though the war shifted Convair's priorities to production of the B-24, work continued on building a mock-up of the XB-36. The partially finished mock-up was eventually shipped by rail to a new assembly plant at Fort Worth, Texas.

The development of the B-36 was not only an engineering challenge; it was a hard-fought battle within and between the services. The Navy set out to discredit strategic airpower in an attempt to get a larger share of the defense budget for its own fleet programs—large carriers in particular. A Naval officer anonymously created a document, ostensibly without the knowledge of his superiors, detailing 55 serious accusations against the development of the B-36 and its proponents. The document was traced to the Office of the Secretary of the Navy and, finally, to Cedric R. Worth, an assistant to the Undersecretary of the Navy. Worth admitted that he had largely made up the accusations. A lengthy investigation into the possibility that there had been higher-level direction to create and distribute the document ended with Mr. Worth accepting sole blame.

Within a short time, the infamous "Admirals' Revolt" erupted and the B-36 was targeted again. The furor was over money and global priorities. The Air Force, SAC in particular, had won most of the budget battles for strategic systems. In 1958, nine years after this brouhaha, defense budget summaries would reflect that aircraft and missiles had accounted for 58 percent of all DOD expenditures between the start of the Korean War and 1958. A whopping 67 percent had been allocated to the Air Force from 1954 to 1958. The admirals likely had reason to be frustrated and angry, but they simply had not made their strategic case strong enough or soon enough.

Congressman Carl Vinson, chairman of the House Armed Services Committee, called for hearings "to deal with all facts relating to matters involving the B-36 bomber." Vinson, who reputedly had a fondness for the Navy declared that he would, "let the chips fall where they may." He called 35 witnesses, among which were virtually every senior general officer in the Air Force and the leaders of every major aircraft company. General Kenney testified that he had at first favored the B-36. In 1946, after becoming commander of SAC, he became convinced that the bomber was not performing satisfactorily and recommended that production be halted.

By 1948, however, a dramatic turnaround had occurred and it suddenly became evident to the Air Force leadership that they had available in the B-36 a faster, longer-range, high altitude and heavy load-carrying strategic bomber. To a man, senior Air Force leaders testified that the B-36 was "the heart of any global air striking force."

General Henry H. "Hap" Arnold was called out of retirement to testify. He chastised the Committee and the detractors of the B-36 for attempting to disrupt the development of an immediate strategic deterrence requirement and for giving away secret performance information in open hearings. Arnold's testimony was powerful and sharp. He gave credit to Generals Kenney and LeMay for their candor and for taking the responsibility to build a believable strategic fighting force while others "whimpered" about what "ought" to be done. Arnold's appearance before the Vinson Committee was his last; he died shortly afterward.

There was an attempt within the Air Force to play the future B-47 against the B-36. LeMay said he would take the B-36 now and his chances with the unproven jet technology when the time came. Others testifying included Generals Carl A. Spaatz, Hoyt S. Vandenberg, Lauris Norstad, and Nathan Twining, along with the Secretary of the Air Force, W. Stuart Symington; each testified strongly for the B-36.

Finally, the Navy's Mr. Worth was called to testify before the Committee. During his testimony, he made a startling revelation that he had been a newspaper reporter and Hollywood script writer before being appointed to the Navy Department. The Navy was embarrassed, Worth was severely censured and the hearings were concluded. The battle for the B-36 was won.

Convair's initial design of the huge bomber called for six Pratt & Whitney Wasp major engines, with 19-foot three-bladed pusher propellers mounted on the trailing edge of the wing. Each 28-cylinder, 4-bank, radial engine had two super-chargers that could produce three thousand horsepower up to an altitude of 35,000 feet. The huge engines in the "pusher" configuration projected a distinctive and unique sound because it was virtually impossible to synchronize all six propellers at the same time with reasonable precision. The result was that the B-36 couldn't "sneak up" on anyone—it sounded like a flight of bass-throated bumblebees about to attack and projected its noise miles ahead and behind. Jokingly, wives living on or near the B-36 bases would comment that they could begin hanging their wash on the clothesline when they first heard the roar of a B-36 coming from far over the horizon and would finish hanging the clothes by the time its "moan" disappeared in the distance.

The initial mock-up design of the B-36 was fitted with a twin tail assembly, which was later changed to a single vertical stabilizer. The vertical tail was deemed more stable, but it measured 46 feet, 10 inches from the ground to the top. This latter feature of its large dimensions required special very heavy bomber (VHB) hangars to be built with a padded circular hole in the hanger doors to permit the tall tail to always remain outside. Each wing section had three rubber-coated self-sealing fuel tanks, for a total of six. Together, the six tanks could hold 21,053 gallons of fuel. Outer panel tanks added 2,770 gallons and auxiliary wing tanks added another 9,577 gallons. A bomb bay tank, added later, held approximately three thousand gallons of fuel. The B-36J, the last major modification, had a fuel capacity of 32,965 gallons or roughly 214,273 lbs, which gave the aircraft a takeoff weight of approximately 410,000 lbs.

The wingspan of the bomber from initial design throughout production was maintained at 230 feet, and the fuselage measured 163 feet. An unusual feature was a single wing spar that extended from wing tip to wing tip and supported 90 percent of the engine and wing fuel tank load. The bomber's electrical system operated on a 208/115-volt, 400-cycle alternating current system. DC converters were used to operate instruments and other components requiring direct current power.

The prototype cockpit in the Peacemaker had a much smaller canopy than the final "green house" version that was adopted for the production models. The cockpit was reasonably roomy, with a wide expanse between the two pilots and an equally wide console to house the six throttles, trim controls, and some radios. The flight engineer's console sat at an angle behind the pilots and contained all the engine operating controls and instruments, electrical power, fuel management systems, and environmental system controls, along with a duplicate set of throttles. The pilots had duplicate manifold pressure gauges for use in adjusting power settings for takeoff and landing. The bombardier-navigator compartment was another story—the three members of the bomb-nav team pretty well had to "muscle" for space. If a mission required instructors or evaluators, it was even more crowded. The radio operators, on the other hand, enjoyed a "living room," as did the gunners in the pressurized aft compartment. The B-36D, the 54th production model of the bomber, introduced a jet engine pod under the outer edge of each wing. Each pod contained two J-47 turbojet engines to assist in heavyweight takeoffs and to provide backup power for landings, climbing, and maintaining desired speeds at high altitude. The engine controls for the jet engines were placed above and to the left of the copilot's position. The earlier B-36s were all returned to

Convair for addition of the J-47 engines. Both the forward crew compartment and the aft gunner compartment were pressurized. The two compartments were connected by an 85-foot-long, 25-inch diameter pressurized tube. A small rail-mounted pull cart moved crew members between compartments.

The initial design underwent several major changes throughout the aircraft's development. The landing gear on the first prototype had two large single wheels measuring 110 inches in diameter, which limited the bomber to runways that had a concrete thickness of 22½ inches—and there were only three such military airfields in the United States. But the main problem with the oversized landing gear wheels was the enormous pressure exerted on the gear struts when the plane landed. One of the landing struts collapsed on an early test flight, which drove the development of a four-wheel truck unit that greatly reduced both the landing "footprint" and the stress exerted on the strut. The four-wheel truck configuration required a nominal 300-foot-wide runway to safely accommodate the aircraft's turning radius, although a skilled pilot could maneuver the airplane around with considerably less operating space. After several attempts to meet the Air Force's requirements for armament, Convair outfitted the bomber with an elaborate defensive weapons system consisting of sixteen 20-millimeter (mm) cannons mounted in pairs in eight remotely controlled retractable turrets. The protective armament provided a full 360-degree protection radius while the bomber was in flight. A built-in contour arrangement on the turrets prevented the guns from firing at the tall vertical stabilizer. The standard bomber crew consisted of 15 members: three pilots (aircraft commander, pilot, and copilot), three bombing-navigation specialists (radar bombardier, navigator, and co-observer), two flight engineers, two radio/electronic warfare operators, and five gunners.

In the forward compartment, the copilot, co-observer, and number two radio operator were trained to operate and fire the remote turrets. Flight crew requirements varied with the aircraft configuration, however. The RB-36D/F/H reconnaissance model, for example, carried a 23-man crew. In this version, the forward bomb bay was enclosed and pressurized for additional equipment and operating space.

On June 26, 1948, the first of the largest and heaviest bombers ever built up to that time, the B-36A, was delivered to SAC's 7th Bombardment Wing at Carswell Air Force Base, Texas. By the end of the year, 35 aircraft had been delivered. SAC celebrated the success of the program by staging a long-range navigation and bombing mission that extended from taking off at Carswell through dropping a 10,000-pound "dummy" bomb in the Pacific Ocean near the Hawaiian Islands and returning to Carswell. The un-refueled mission covered 8,100 miles in 35½ hours. The mission was, in a way, a "LeMay triumph" in that the bomber made an approach over Honolulu undetected by the local air defense system on December 7, 1948!

Early in 1949, another B-36 crew set a long-distance record of 9,600 miles. The B-36 covered the distance in 43 hours, 37 minutes. There was little doubt that the vast Soviet communications monitoring system was taking note of these and other similar demonstrations of long-range "strategic reach."

There were several follow-on test versions and modifications of the B-36. One such version was the proposed "C" model, which had six turboprop engines on the forward edge of the wings; each extended some ten feet from the leading edge. The variable discharge turbine (VDT) turboprops would have boosted the bomber's airspeed to 410 MPH and a service ceiling of 45,000 feet, enhancing its "over the target" dash speed. An initial order of 34 aircraft was canceled when the engine failed to deliver the promised performance. The overall B-36 program followed a precarious path of indecision even after it had won its political battles, budget costs being the persistent enemy. The Soviets, however, in their inimitable way, boosted the bomber program into new life with the Berlin Blockade, prompting Secretary Symington to direct full production of the original contract. Following the retrofitting of all B-36s with the J-47 engines, the B-36F, H, and J configurations came along. These included newer R-4360-53 engines with more power and reliability. The K-3A radar bombing system was added to provide for both precision radar and visual bombing capability. Some of the bomb bay systems were modified to carry the MK-17 thermonuclear bomb, the largest ever developed. It weighed 42,000 lbs and measured 24½ feet in length. The B-36J "Featherweight" modification program reduced the aircraft's weight appreciably by removing all of the 20-mm retractable turrets except the tail gun, thereby reducing the crew requirement to thirteen and reducing drag on the airplane by replacing the large gunner's blisters with flush windows or plugs. The "J" model had an increased range, higher speed (418 MPH at 37,500 ft), and a service ceiling of 43,600 feet. The FICON (Fighter-Conveyor) modification was made on 11 aircraft assigned to the 99th Strategic Recon Wing at Fairchild Air Force Base, near Spokane, Washington. Designated the GRB-36D/F, these bombers were modified to carry and retrieve the F-84E and, later, the RF-84K reconnaissance-fighter aircraft as an extension of the RB-36's reconnaissance capability. The GRB-36 could take off with the RF-84K "tucked" in its bomb bay, fly a nominal radius of 2,810 miles and launch the "parasite" fighter at 25,000 feet. The RF-84K, carrying five cameras and four 50-caliber guns, weighed 29,500 lbs at release.

The tactic added approximately 1,100 miles to the reconnaissance-fighter's radius of flight. It could fly to a target area, take pictures, and dash back to the "mother ship." In late 1955, after 170 successful launches and retrievals, the unit was declared combat-ready with 10 GRB-36s and 25 RF-84Ks. After a year, however, the program was suddenly canceled. A similar pilot program, called Tom-Tom, featured modified RB-36s and RF-84Ks mated with a wing-tip launch and retrieval system. The program proved workable but with considerable risk and fatigue on the part of both aircraft.

Convair developed the prototype YB-60, an eight-jet, swept-wing version of the B-36. Its performance was a quantum leap over the B-36, but it did not compete favorably with the performance of the prototype B-52. Between 1946 and 1961, the Air Force and the Atomic Energy Commission spent more than $7 billion developing a nuclear-powered version of the B-36—the NB-36H. It did not use nuclear power, but it carried an onboard nuclear reactor to test radiation shielding and the potential effects of radiation on the crew and the aircraft. The cumbersome 12-inch-thick cockpit window glass, radiation absorption system and closed-circuit television system designed to monitor the engines, all in all proved too costly, heavy, cumbersome and inefficient. After 47 test flights between July 1955 and March 1957, the program was canceled. In theory, the nuclear-powered bomber could stay in flight for weeks at a time un-refueled.

Lastly, a large-body passenger-cargo version of the B-36 configuration— the XC-99—was flown in 1947. Its oversized fuselage could carry four hundred combat troops or 50 tons of cargo. Only one XC-99 was built, but it was used extensively during the Korean War to haul cargo back and forth across the United States. After the war, it continued to operate under Military Air Transport Service (MATS) until 1957. The XC-99 was retired to its permanent "pedestal" at Kelly Air Force Base near San Antonio, Texas. Pan American Airways had placed an option to buy three C-99s for their Hawaii route, but they canceled it when it was determined that there was insufficient passenger traffic to support the aircraft's large capacity.

Maintaining and flying the B-36 took on a life of its own for the maintenance teams and combat crews associated with the complex bomber. While it was relatively easy, straightforward to fly and incredibly "forgiving" of human errors, it nevertheless required an inordinate amount of maintenance, care, and preparation to operate. The maintenance crew chief and team were required to be fully coordinated with the flight crew. The aircraft status and maintenance information "hand-off" from ground to flight crew was essential. The complex electrical, hydraulic, fuel, engine, avionics, communications, and flight control systems required that flight crew members be expertly knowledgeable in their operation. Consequently, B-36 combat crews tended to be highly stable with minimal crew changes over extended periods of time—often years. Crew coordination was critical to the success of every mission.

Like the long flights, operational preflight by the combat crew was also long and extensive. Preflight began four hours before the scheduled takeoff time. The pilots conducted their routine checks: walk around, struts, tire inflation, fuel and oil leaks, and propellers for nicks, control surfaces and general condition. The flight engineers had by far the most comprehensive preflight checks, allowing little time for weather interference or maintenance problems. They had to crawl into the wings and check for fuel and oil leaks and any signs of engine or flight control problems. Severe weather only added to the difficulty of their task. They also climbed into the cavernous wheel wells to check all of the control linkages and hydraulic lines. The copilot (3d pilot) was tasked to measure (dip-stick) all the fuel tanks against the planned fuel load for the mission. Since this was accomplished from the top of the wing, weather conditions could make it a "sporty" exercise. The remainder of the crew conducted their respective systems checks, ranging from routine to very complex; when practice bombs were to be dropped or the guns were to be practice-fired, then considerable detail had to be given to those systems. Engine start was initiated 45 minutes before the scheduled takeoff time. (Today's jet aircraft would already be airborne and at altitude.)

Taxiing and steering the huge monster was relatively easy, the main concern being wing tip clearance for moving through other aircraft. The pilots had excellent visibility, but they sat approximately 70 feet in front of the main gear, making it necessary to constantly ensure that the area 180 degrees around and at least 250 feet wide was clear to move the huge bird. Takeoffs in the B-36 were extremely pleasant and smooth. The power of the six pusher engines and the four jets provided all the thrust necessary to launch the airplane at any gross weight. For its size, it also handled extremely well in turns and during climb-out; its control pressures were exceptionally light. Likewise, both approach and landing were very straightforward and fun——"under most conditions!" Crosswinds constituted the obvious exception, given the B-36's wide wing spread and tall tail. The final approach was usually at about 125 MPH, with touchdown at 100 MPH for a smooth landing. Even with the cockpit "floating" at 40-feet above the ground at touchdown, visibility and control were excellent. Thunderstorms, a "few" engines out, or a fire, however, created an entirely different environment. No pilot or crew member who ever served aboard the mighty ten-engine aircraft had anything but respect for her capability and safety—but mainly for the unique pleasure of flying with her.

In the words of Lt. General James Goldsworthy:

"The public relations people dubbed the B-36, this gentle giant, the Peacemaker, a name that never caught on with the crews, and it droned through the skies of the world until February 1959 without dropping a bomb or firing a shot in anger. The jet age left the aircraft obsolete after a relatively short life span, and when it was flown to the bone yard, it was the end of a proud era of heavy bombers powered by reciprocating engines. Technology passed it by and left it outperformed, but never out-classed. The B-36 wasn't an agile bird—in fact, at times it could be downright ponderous—but it was honest. Crews had confidence that it would get there and bring them home. It was modified and abused, always pressed to come up with more performance. And it seemed to respond with more than anyone had the right to expect. If its crews did not always love it, they surely respected it. And perhaps the Peacemaker wasn't so bad after all. We will never know what the course of world events would have been without the B-36 standing ready to deliver its awesome load to any point in the world in a few short hours."

The B-36 never dropped a bomb in combat during its ten years of active duty, but it remained ready and capable; SAC owned over 150 B/RB-36s by the end of 1950. However, the bomber was held out of the Korean War as it continued to perform its nuclear deterrent role. In August and September 1953, after the Korean truce, SAC sent a flight of B-36s to the Far East; landing airplanes in Japan, Okinawa, and Guam to demonstrate US resolve to back peace in the region.

A total of 385 B-36s of various models and configurations were delivered to the Air Force. The last B-36, a "J" model Featherweight, was retired from the 95th Bomb Wing, Biggs Air Force Base, Texas, on February 12, 1959. Its final flight was made to Fort Worth, Texas, to be placed on permanent display. A few others were given to airports and museums around the country. The best-preserved B-36 resides comfortably, in "mint condition," inside the National Museum of the Air Force at Wright-Patterson Air Force Base, Ohio. Two other restored B-36 bombers are located in the Strategic Aerospace Museum, near Omaha, Nebraska and at the Pima County Air Museum, Tucson, Arizona, respectively.

B-47 STRATOJET

The Army Air Corps initiated a request in 1943 for the aircraft industry to study the feasibility of an all-jet bomber. The Germans had already begun work on jet propulsion engines (they were flying a jet fighter-bomber before World War II ended) and the British were far ahead of the Americans in developing jet fighter and bomber prototypes. In 1944, the Air Corps called for a bomber aircraft that would fly at least 500 MPH. Five manufacturers promptly submitted preliminary designs. North American offered the XB-45, which in the end became the first all-jet bomber to go into production. It operated successfully as a light bomber and reconnaissance aircraft in Korea and through the 1950s. Convair, which presented the most competitive bomber, was not considered because it had won the B-24 and B-36 contracts (the "wealth" had to be "spread around"). Martin and Northrop offered acceptable designs, but their aircraft were not large enough to perform truly strategic bombing missions.

Boeing won the competition with its XB-47, a six-engine aircraft having a swept-wing design and a bicycle landing gear configuration. Boeing engineers leaned heavily on their B-29 design concepts, although the B-29 had little in common, physically, with the B-47. However, the stressed webbed-wing design, landing gear struts, low-pressure hydraulic system, and 28-volt DC electrical system found places in the B-47 design. The early major shortfall in the bomber was the low technology of its jet engines. The excessively long "spool-up" time on the initial J-35 engine was critical in landing situations. And the total thrust of the six J-35s was rated at only 21,500 lbs for the planned 125,000-lb aircraft. Consequently, carrying high power on approaches mandated landing at higher than desired speed and with longer roll-out. A drag chute to offset the high power settings during approach and a brake chute to slow the aircraft after touchdown were added. An antiskid brake system provided an additional safety factor. As development preceded, J-47 GE engines, each having 5,200 lbs of thrust, replaced the underpowered J-35. The bomber began to look more practical to the designer and to the Air Force.

The final design gave the bomber a 107-foot fuselage and a 116-foot wingspan. The wing had an extraordinary flexible deflection of 17½ feet, tip-to-tip. The bicycle landing gear was chosen because the thin wings couldn't accommodate wheel wells. The gear was retracted into the fuselage section.

The three crew members—pilot, copilot, radar-navigator—were "tucked" into a small, pressurized cabin compartment, minimizing the need for a large pressurization and environmental system. In September 1948, the Air Force placed an order for ten B-47As for capabilities testing. The aircraft were assembled at Boeing's facility in Wichita, Kansas, adjacent to McConnell Air Force Base where the first Air Force B-47 crew training would eventually take place. This concept had proven successful with the Convair B-36 assembly facility collocated with the first recipient unit, the 7th Bomb Wing, at Carswell Air Force Base, Texas. The B-47's refueling capability was initially supported by the KC-97 "Stratotanker" and later by the KC-135 (a Boeing 707). "Fly Away" kits were designed and built, allowing the B-47 to deploy anywhere in the world, carrying along spare parts and equipment. The B-47 filled a large gap in the US strategic inventory and gave war planners broad flexibility in covering the Soviet target complex. SAC would eventually reach a peak of 1,367 B-47s and an additional 176 RB-47 reconnaissance aircraft.

The B-47, not unlike virtually all military weapons systems, was designed for one principal mission; and not unlike virtually all military weapons systems, it was employed in other, sometimes radical, ways to meet new threats. In order to attain greater distances with heavier payloads, the gross weight of the aircraft grew from the original 125,000 lbs to 230,000 lbs for taxi and takeoff, with a maximum in-flight weight of 226,000 lbs. These additional requirements placed considerable stress and fatigue on the airframe, shortening its life span. Additional strain was placed on the aircraft with the introduction of "pop-up" maneuvers designed to avoid Soviet antiaircraft missiles along SIOP flight routes and target areas.

In the "pop-up" maneuver, the B-47 flew into a defended area at 300-500 feet altitude and at high speed. The aircraft then climbed rapidly to about 18,000 feet, dropped a nuclear weapon on the target, made a sharp turn, and descended back down to treetop altitude. This maneuver enabled the bomber to avoid the blast effects from the released bomb.

In a similar maneuver Low Altitude Bombing System (LABS), the aircraft flew into the target area at low altitude and high speed but pulled up into a half loop just prior to the bomb release point. The pilot then released the bomb and rolled the aircraft out in an "Immelmann" maneuver to avoid the impact of the nuclear explosion.

Neither large bombers nor bomber pilots were well suited for these fighter-type aerobatics. They subjected the airplane to potentially severe "g" forces, inducing even further fatigue. SAC reported six B-47 crashes in a one-month period during the Spring of 1958, all attributed to wear and fatigue in wing skins and fuselage fittings.

Major General Earl G. Peck, former SAC Chief of Staff, and a B-47 aircraft commander as a young Air Force captain, described the experience of flying the B-47:

"The Boeing B-47, officially the Stratojet, was one of those airplanes that never seemed to acquire any sort of affectionate nickname. This probably stems from the fact that although it was often admired, respected, cursed, or even feared, it was almost never loved. In fact, I think it would be fair to say that it tended to separate the men from the boys! It was relatively difficult to land, terribly unforgiving of mistakes or inattention, subject to control reversal at high speeds, and suffered from horrible roll-due-to-yaw characteristics. Cross-wind landings and takeoffs were sporty, and in-flight discrepancies were the rule rather than the exception. All in all, the B-47 was a very demanding machine for her three-man crew. But, its idiosyncrasies notwithstanding, the

B-47 served as a mainstay of the SAC deterrent posture during the darkest years of the Cold War. A typical B-47 mission was comprised of all those activities that the crew had to master if the system was to serve as a credible deterrent. They were also the same things that would be required during a nuclear strike mission if deterrence failed: high- and low-level navigation and weapon delivery, aerial refueling, electronic countermeasures against air and ground threats, positive control procedures, exercising the tail-mounted 20-mm guns, emergency procedures, cell (formation) tactics, and others I am sure I have forgotten. Crew planning for a mission took up most of the day prior and was elaborately precise and detailed. The crew was expected to approach each training sortie with the same meticulous professionalism that would be required for an actual strike mission. And professionalism keynoted the mission attitude that prevailed from inception to completion. On the day of the flight, [there were] an exhaustive series of inspections—station, exterior, and interior...perusal of forms, equipment, and safety items...walk-around inspection of aircraft...system-by-system interior inspection. Finally finding the bird fit, we would leave it and wend our way to base ops for a weather briefing and to compute takeoff data and file a clearance. Taxiing the B-47 was relatively easy.

"Takeoff in a B-47 was, to my knowledge, unique in its day, for the airplane in effect was "flying" shortly after beginning the roll. This could be attributed to the flexible wings, which permitted the outriggers to lift off as soon as the airflow generated any appreciable lift. Somewhat ungainly on the ground, the B-47 assumed a classic grace in flight. Aerial refueling presented its own difficulties, stemming principally from incompatibility with the piston-driven KC-97 tankers then in use. Very-high-wing loading and associated stall speeds in the B-47 meant that the KC-97 was taxed to provide any respectable margin above stall while hooked up. The KC-97 more often than not had to maintain a continuous descent during air refueling with the B-47 and the B-52 in order for the heavy bombers to maintain sufficient airspeed to avoid stalling out. On one particularly dark night, in fact, my airplane stalled off the boom and fluttered gracefully down 5,000 feet of murk before it became a flying machine again! Looking back, although much of the flying I did in the B-47 was not particularly enjoyable—it was in fact tedious, demanding, even grueling at times—it was terribly rewarding in terms of professional satisfaction. I felt I was doing an important job and took great pride in doing it well in a machine capable of performing. As with most airplanes, the advertised performance figures (4,000 nautical-mile ranges, 600 MPH speed, 40,000 feet service ceiling) didn't mean much to the guys flying the B-47. It was only important that it would go fast and far enough to enable a group of professional, dedicated and gutsy SAC crews to provide the bulk of American deterrent strength during the middle and late 1950s. As the decade waned, the B-47 was gradually supplemented and later supplanted by the B-52 as SAC's mainstay bomber. But the stratojet had written an important chapter in military history."

B-52 STRATOFORTRESS

The B-47 created a success story for Boeing and big bombers. Walter Boyne, author of Boeing B-52, A Documentary History, credited Boeing's bold vision and several young Air Force officers (who were not overly inhibited by the existing bureaucracy) with the key decisions that led to the development of the B-52. "Similarly," Boyne said, "senior officers were still permitted to exercise the vision, imagination, and leadership which were then and are still the primary reasons for their existence."

A careful review of bomber histories, particularly the B-70, B-58, B-1, and, to some extent the FB-111, confirms Boyne's assessment. The B-2, to some degree, became a victim of the same syndrome of, "too many experts, too many built-in requirements, and too many politicians."

"The Congress," he lamented, "in its desire to know everything about a weapon system in real time, has put itself in the position of a restaurant customer checking in with the chef every step of the way, sampling, tasting, directing, changing his mind, and making decisions long before the menu is defined."

In 1946, Boeing was finishing off the B-29, had a few orders for the B-50, and was concentrating on the first true all-jet strategic bomber, the B-47. The Army Air Corps, anticipating the demise over time of the large reciprocating engine and the "experimental" XB-36, placed a requirement on the aviation industry for a "second generation" heavy bomber. Boeing engineers, however, could not produce a design that exceeded the B-36. The main shortfall was in turbojet engine technology. The B-47 had experienced the same problem in its initial development: insufficient power to fly the airplane at the desired gross weights. Finally, Pratt & Whitney agreed to build the largest jet engine they possibly could. The J-57 would be a quantum leap above the J-47, and would initially produce 10,000 lbs of thrust. The production model B-52B engines would be improved to produce 12,100 lbs thrust each, and eventually the "F" model J-57 would be rated at 13,750 lbs of thrust.

Convair attempted to meet the heavy jet bomber requirement with its jet-powered YB-36, but fell short. Boeing, however, presented a proposal for an eight-jet aircraft built along the lines of the B-47. The bomber would be much larger, having a gross weight of roughly 330,000 lbs, an eight-thousand-mile range carrying a 10,000-lb bomb, and a cruising speed of 570 MPH. The first prototype rolled out in November 1951. An ecstatic General LeMay went to work to get the necessary funding to produce the bomber. He also directed changes in the design. He did not like the B-47 tandem seating for the pilots. Boeing changed the cockpit to a side-by-side configuration for better crew coordination.

The news media weighed-in on the prospects of acquiring the new bomber. Following a visit to the Soviet Union in 1956, Hanson Baldwin, New York Times reporter and self-proclaimed military expert, reported: "The United States is still clearly superior to the Soviet Union in air power today. It would be a mistake to put too much money into the production of the big B-52 long-range jet bombers, since overstressing these planes might force a curtailment in research funds. In any case, in a few years, the B-52 may be technically obsolescent."

It would be interesting to receive Mr. Baldwin's revised assessment of the B-52 in view of the fact that the resilient bomber continues to currently play an important role in the Air Force's strategic air operations almost sixty years later!

Soon after flight tests began to show progress, LeMay directed that range and gross weight be increased. The later "G" and "H" models eventually reached takeoff gross weights of 488,000 lbs, and the B-52H would be powered by a state-of-the-art TF33-P-3 engine having a flat-rated thrust of 17,000 lbs.

The first production B-52 was the "B" model, delivered to SAC on June 29, 1955. It was indeed a large jet aircraft with a 185-foot wingspan and a fuselage measuring 140 feet in length. The bomb bay, measuring 28 feet by 6 feet, could accommodate any of the nuclear weapons in the inventory. The flexible wing, similar in design to the B-47, has an incredible deflection of 32 feet! This feature was at first very disconcerting to the pilots when they glanced back at the wings during considerable turbulence; the wings would be slowly flapping. The top of the original tail section was 48 feet from the ground. In the first B-52s, the two pilots were seated in the upper cockpit with the navigator and radar-navigator (bombardier) directly below them. The electromagnetic countermeasures officer (ECM), later renamed the electronic warfare officer (EWO), sat behind the pilots at the rear of the pressurized compartment. The tail gunner was tightly fitted in a pressurized compartment located in the rearmost end of the fuselage tail section.

The tail gunner's was not a happy position—particularly due to the cramped quarters, but also because of the bomber's twisting movement and "see-saw" motions even in the lightest of turbulence. Egress by the tail gunner from the aircraft in an emergency also presented a special problem: he had to pull an ejection handle to remove the tail section and then manually bail out. This would normally work if the aircraft had not rolled into a nose-down dive, in which case he could have difficulty in overcoming the 'g' forces enough to pull himself out. Air sickness was common and morale amongst tail gunners was terrible—yet, amazingly, they flew on! Later, in the "G" and "H" models, the gunner was moved to the forward pressurized compartment and positioned in an ejection seat side-by-side with the EWO. There, the tail gunner became a "happy camper."

The earlier bombers were equipped with four 50-caliber machine guns in the tail. The later "H" model was fitted with a six-barrel M-61 20-mm Gatling gun. The fire control system, with either gun configuration, has the capability to search, detect, acquire, track, and compute the angle of attack of an incoming aircraft. The gunner also is equipped with a periscope gunsight for manual aiming and firing; in the "G" and "H" models, he has a rear-projection television monitor. The original B-52 bombing-navigation system was a rudimentary radar tracking and plotting device with a visual optics backup.

Modifications and enhancements, however, have kept the B-52 current with state-of-the-art technology. The MA-6A serves as the bomber's baseline bomb-nav system. The later B-52G and H models were equipped with an Electro-optical Viewing System (EVS)—forward-looking infrared (FLIR) and low-light-level TV sensors integrated into bombing, navigation, and pilot directional systems. Like the B-47, the B-52 is equipped with a bicycle landing gear, but the B-52 version is considerably more complex. The "quadricycle" landing gear, which consists of four wheels in front and four in rear, retracts into the fuselage. The front wheels are steerable for taxi and takeoff, and both front and rear can be canted on final approach to accommodate a crosswind. The pilot can then land the aircraft in a "crabbed" position, touching down with the aircraft at an angle to the centerline of the runway. It takes some getting used to, but it works.

The electrical system consists of four gear-driven constant-speed generators providing 200/115-volt AC power and transformer rectifiers for DC requirements. The B-52 was initially outfitted with 1,000-gallon wingtip fuel tanks. Three-thousand-gallon tanks were added later. The tanks provided wing stability as well as additional fuel. The later "G" and "H" models were equipped with smaller 700-gallon tanks, mainly for wing stability. Within two years of first delivery, three B-52s flew nonstop around the world—24,235 miles—in 45 hours and 19 minutes.

The B-52G and H models, virtually "new" airplanes, were "Cadillacs" compared to the "B" through "F" model predecessors. They were some 15,000 lbs (dry weight) lighter, but the aircraft's gross weight was increased to 488,000 lbs. The fuel was stored in a "wet wing," rather than the now discarded rubberized fuel cells. Fuel capacity was increased to over 310,000 lbs. Ailerons were removed, and lateral control was shifted to the wing spoilers. Crew comfort was enhanced by the addition of more comfortable seats and an improved air conditioning system. The EWO position was upgraded with more sophisticated tracking and jamming systems. The pilots were initially given the advanced capability radar (ACR), which provided terrain avoidance, anti-jamming, and enhanced low-level mapping capabilities. The ACR system employed small (5-inch) television monitors at each pilot's position and at the navigator's station. The ACR was followed shortly by the EVS, which generated greater confidence and provided greater comfort for a night-weather, low-level flying mission.

B-52 systems underwent constant upgrades and major modifications to keep up with potential enemy threats and evolving technologies. The G and H model bombers had little resemblance to the first production aircraft, except in overall profile appearance. That also changed when the vertical stabilizer was shortened to 40 feet and a growing array of radar and sensor antennas began to "crop-up" around the outer fuselage surfaces. Over its life, the B-52 has accommodated an ever-increasing volume of weapon systems:

- Free-fall and chute-retarded nuclear bombs;
- GAM-72 Quail missile decoy (which with its 13-ft length and 5-ft wingspan replicated the image of a B-52 to an enemy radar);
- GAM-77/AGM-28 Hound Dog air-launched attack missile, one carried under each wing of the Gs and Hs, and equipped with a nuclear warhead;
- GAM-87 Skybolt nuclear warhead air-launched ballistic missile also carried and launched from under the wing;
- AGM-69A short-range attack missile (SRAM) air-launched missile up to 20 carried under the wings and in the bomb bay;
- air-breathing turbojet air-launched cruise missile (ALCM), launched from under the wing and from the bomb bay.

Additionally, the bomber had the incredible capability to carry 108 five-hundred-pound conventional bombs, which it did routinely in Vietnam. The last of 744 B-52s was an H model, Serial Number 61-040, delivered on October 26, 1962—forty-six years ago as of this writing. And many of the "H's" are still flying!

Unlike its SAC predecessors, the B-36 and B-47, both of which were held out of combat, the B-52 performed in Vietnam—and performed well.

Taxiing a fully loaded B-52 out onto the runway, setting the brakes, and pushing the throttles forward to full power for takeoff had a feeling of exhilaration like no other. I am sure fighter pilots experience the same feeling, but for a "much shorter time." Flying the reliable B-36 had its special feeling of power, mass, and control; but the B-52 had it all...and speed to go with it. It was easy to taxi at all gross weights, directional control during takeoff was excellent, and climb-out was very straightforward and smooth. Landing in a crosswind could be "sporty," due to the tall vertical stabilizer (either 40 or 48 feet); but the crosswind landing gear feature, once taken into confidence, compensated very well. Flying at high altitude was a routine procedure, with the exception of large air refueling operations, which required a determined skill.

The 24-hour Chromedome sorties required taking on approximately 110,000 lbs of fuel—an operation that demanded 20 to 30 minutes of 'sheer flying skill and determination'. At relatively light gross weights and high altitude (30,000 to 35,000 feet), the airplane tended to 'float' through the air; a small power adjustment while you were approaching and connecting with the KC-135 tanker would move you about rapidly.

Once the fuel began to fill the wings and the aircraft took on more weight, it became very controllable—except in turbulence, of course! Turbulence required another feat of skill to manage the "flapping wings." Flying the B-52 at extremely low levels—which the B-52 was not originally designed to do—placed the pilots and crew into another challenging dimension. Dropping from 35,000 feet to 500 feet—300 feet on some routes—at night, and maintaining that flying environment for several hundred miles required every ounce of confidence in the airplane and faith in its flight and navigation instruments that one could muster.

There was hardly a minute during a tightly planned and coordinated 14 or 20-hour training mission when the majority of the crew were not interacting with each other. High-altitude navigation, low-level navigation, bomb runs, air refueling, electromagnetic countermeasure testing against simulated radar sites, gunnery practice, fighter intercepts—each activity required attentive concentration. The redeeming consequence of these long training missions was the traditional "wagging home" of the carefully prepared (but undisturbed) flight lunch box which had been delivered fresh to the aircraft by the in-flight kitchen just before takeoff. This was more often than not the norm rather than the exception. The kids were always delighted to see what marvels of "goodies" (and soggy sandwiches) dad brought back from his flight.

One of the reasons that the B-52 remains with us yet today is the quality of design, engineering and durability. A story about the resilience of the venerable bomber is worth telling here:

January 10, 1964, started out as a typical day for the flight test group at Boeing's Wichita, Kansas aircraft plant. Test Pilot Chuck Fisher took off in a spanking new B-52H with a three-man Boeing crew to fly a low-level profile mission to obtain airframe structural data. Cruising over Colorado at 500 feet above the mountainous terrain, the B-52 encountered some turbulence. Fisher climbed to 14,300 feet looking for smoother air. At this point the "typical day" ended. The bomber suddenly flew into severe clear-air turbulence. The crew said that they felt as if the plane had been engulfed in a giant high-speed elevator, shoved up and down, and then hit by a heavy blow on its right side. Fisher was convinced that he had lost control of the giant bomber and told the crew to prepare to bail out. Maintaining as near level flight as he could, he eased back the throttles, slowed the aircraft's speed and descended to approximately 5,000 feet to make it easier for the crew to bail out. As the aircraft leveled-out, he regained some flight control and decided to climb back to a comfortable altitude to put some room between the plane and the ground while he tried to figure out the problem. He informed Wichita about his situation...that although flight control was extremely difficult, he believed he could get the bomber back to the Boeing plant runway. "It's still flyable," he said.

An emergency control center was mobilized in the office of Boeing Wichita's Director of Flight Test. Key Boeing engineers and other specialists were summoned to provide their expertise and advice. Federal Aviation Administration air traffic control centers at Denver and Kansas City cleared the air around the troubled plane. A Strategic Air Command B-52 flying in the area maintained radio contact with the crew of the stricken Wichita B-52.

As Fisher approached the Wichita area, a Boeing chase plane flew up to meet him to visually report any visible damage. When Dale Felix, flying the F-100 fighter chase plane, came alongside Fisher's B-52, he couldn't believe what he saw. The B-52's vertical stabilizer, the entire tail, was missing. Felix broke the news to Fisher and those gathered in the control center.

The crew aboard the damaged B-52 and those in the control center took the news calmly. Both groups were trained and experienced to address emergency situations, perhaps not as dramatic as this one, but nevertheless disciplined. The Boeing engineers immediately began making calculations and suggestions regarding the best way to get the plane down safely. Another Air Force B-52, just taking off on a routine flight from adjacent McConnell Air Force Base which shared runways with Boeing Company, was employed to test the various flight configurations and procedures suggested by the engineers before Fisher was asked to try them.

As gusty winds began to roll into the Wichita area, the decision was made to divert Fisher and his crew to Blytheville Air Force Base in Northeastern Arkansas. Boeing specialists from the emergency control center took off in a KC-135 and accompanied Fisher to Blytheville, serving as an airborne control center. Six hours after the incident first occurred, Fisher and his crew brought in the damaged B-52 for a safe landing at Blytheville. The flight crew and those on the ground stood in awe as they stared up at the rear empennage of the bomber with its tail shorn off at the base.

"I'm very proud of this crew and this airplane," Fisher said. "Also we had a lot of people helping us, and we're very thankful for that. The B-52 is the finest airplane I ever flew."

The B-52 first flew in 1952, fifty six years ago as of the publication of this book, and the Department of Defense has decided to continue to employ the bomber for at least another decade. Not unlike the Energizer Bunny, the sturdy bomber continues to fly—and fly close air support missions in the war in Iraq and Afghanistan. The Air Force has retained some sixty of the venerable old bombers and some predict that it could be flying until 2040. That would make the latest built bombers 80 years old!

B-58 HUSTLER

While the B-52 is the oldest and longest living bomber in US military history, the B-58 had one of the shortest "active duty" tours with fewer than a hundred production aircraft rolled off the assembly line. But it was the only supersonic strategic bomber to enter the Western world's operational inventory. As B-36 production at the General Dynamics-Convair facility at Fort Worth came to a halt, the company offered a competitive proposal to develop and build a supersonic medium bomber as "gap filler" for the anticipated phase-out of the B-47. The Air Force and SAC accepted the proposal, and the first B-58 was delivered at Carswell Air Force Base, Texas, on August 1, 1960. The relatively small bomber, 96.8 feet in length with a 56.8-foot wingspan, was powered by four J-79-5A engines, each producing 10,000 lbs of flat-rated thrust—15,600 lbs in afterburner. The pilot, navigator, and defensive systems operator (DSO) were positioned in separate tandem cockpits that were in fact encapsulated seats for ejection. The bomber was 'all airplane'. It carried a 62-foot-long pod—which had the appearance of an afterthought—beneath its underside to accommodate a nuclear weapon and additional fuel. To safeguard against a blowout or a flat tire causing the aircraft to crush the pod, the landing gear included smaller steel wheels inset between the sets of tires.

The B-58 also suffered from other problems, including one that required the pilot to continuously transfer fuel during taxiing to prevent the airplane from tipping on its tail. Another required the installation of water-filled cooling tanks through which fuel and hydraulic oil were routed to prevent evaporation caused by the extraordinary heat generated within the plane at high speeds. General LeMay was never really satisfied with the B-58; it required an extraordinary number of in-flight refuelings to complete a mission, and it severely taxed a disproportionate share of other SAC resources to maintain its combat readiness. As one story had it, LeMay flew the bomber, declared that it was too small and added, "it didn't fit my 'arse'."

SAC reached a peak of 94 assigned B-58s in 1964, just one year before the Johnson Administration directed phase-out of the aircraft. Having had a record-breaking career, the last B-58 was retired on January 16, 1970.

FB-111A AARDVARK

The F-111 with the unlikely nickname, re-designated as a fighter-bomber, became an equally unlikely addition to the strategic nuclear force. The FB-111A, a relatively small two-man bomber version of the swing-wing F-111 fighter, was built by General Dynamics at its Fort Worth facility. The two-man side-by-side fighter-bomber was literally forced into the SAC scheme of manned-bomber capabilities. By 1965, the B-47s had been retired to the "bone yard," the B-52Cs and Fs were being retired rather than refurbished and the B-58 was programmed to phase out by the end of the decade. The future of the manned bomber was largely in question. Defense Secretary Robert S. McNamara, with the cloud of Vietnam lingering heavily over military decisions, budgets, and emotions, stated in 1964:

"Various options are open for replacing the B-52s if a replacement requirement exists at that time. In case supersonic speed and high altitude are needed for the future strategic bomber, the experience gained from three different Mach 3 planes, currently in the research and development stage, will be available—the XB-70, the A-11 and the SR-71."

In actuality, the B-70 materialized only in the form of two prototypes, the A-11 was not pursued (it could not have been seriously considered as a strategic bomber in the first place), and the SR-71 (a derivative of the A-11) became a productive reconnaissance platform.

McNamara went on to say, "In case low-level penetration capabilities turn out to be the key to future bomber effectiveness, the lessons being learned from the F-111, for example, will be applicable." (Perhaps of no small significance, the F-111 was being built in Texas, the home of President Lyndon B. Johnson.)

The following year, Secretary McNamara announced that all B-58s and the B-52Cs, Ds, Es, and Fs would be phased out by June 1971. The announcement would mean the eventual disposal of 449 B-52 bombers, but continued employment of the "D" models in Vietnam delayed their retirement and the remaining "F's" until 1978.

Reflecting on Secretary McNamara's December 8, 1965, projection to replace the B-52 in the 1970s, some forty years later, the venerable and durable B-52 is still flying and a vital part of US war-planning and war-fighting strategy. Sixty-six of these bombers, equipped as ALCM carriers, are projected to be around until at least the year 2020!

On December 10, 1965, Secretary McNamara announced that the Department of Defense would budget for the purchase of 210 FB-111 fighter-bombers for SAC's use. Two months into the Nixon administration, Secretary of Defense Melvin Laird announced that the FB-111 procurement would be limited to 60 operational aircraft and a few replacement aircraft. He said the FB-111 did not meet the requirements for a strategic bomber, but the government was committed to purchase 60 of them to salvage the invested cost.

The first FB-111 was delivered to SAC's 43d Bomb Group at Carswell Air Force Base on October 8, 1969. Preceded by the B-36 and the B-58, the FB-111 became the third type of bomber delivered to the SAC from General Dynamics. The new medium strategic bomber had two Pratt & Whitney TF-30-P-7 engines capable of delivering 20,350 lbs of thrust with afterburner. The aircraft was relatively small, with a fuselage length of approximately 73 feet, a fully extended wingspan of 70 feet, a fully swept wingspan of 33 feet, 11 inches, and a gross weight of 100,000 lbs. It was designed to fly at speeds up to Mach 2.5 at 36,000 feet. It had a service ceiling of 60,000 feet and a range of 4,100 miles (with external tanks). The bomber's delivery capability included up to four SRAM air-to-surface missiles on external pylons and two in the bomb bay, or six gravity nuclear bombs, or a combination of missiles and bombs.

Having no alternative to back up the rapidly depleting manned bomber leg of the TRIAD, SAC reluctantly accepted the FB-111 as a strategic bomber. General LeMay had fought the suggestion to buy the aircraft from the time it was made. He argued that, "It is not a long-range bomber and with only two engines, it lacks the payload-carrying capacity to deliver an adequate number of weapons for the incurred operating cost...too many refueling tankers to support its combat missions."

To partially mitigate the aircraft's range limitations, SAC positioned them on the northeast coast of the U.S. which would require shorter missions and fewer tankers to reach Soviet targets.

B-1 LANCER

Soon after his inauguration, President Ronald Reagan directed the "resurrection" of the controversial B-1 strategic bomber that had been canceled by President Carter. The Carter administration had opted to shift U.S. deterrent strategy in favor of the more survivable standoff cruise missile. The Reagan decision was undoubtedly more internationally political than militarily practical. He wanted to send a strong message to the Soviets that his pre-election declarations were more than rhetoric.

Unfortunately, Rockwell International and dozens of supporting industry contractors had all but dismantled the tooling and the organization that had been designed to build the bomber. Four preproduction B-1 bombers had been built, however, and all original design requirements had been met. Operational test flights had demonstrated its ability to fly at Mach 2, fast-react for base escape, penetrate at high and low altitudes and at high speeds, fire and control both gravity and cruise missile weapons, and maintain a stable air refueling capability. The B-1's defensive avionics, frequency surveillance, and warning and electronic countermeasures were, at the most, modern state-of-the-art level. The bomber's four General Electric F101-GE-100 afterburner turbofan engines were capable of delivering 30,000 lbs of thrust. The crew consisted of two pilots and two offensive systems operators (navigator-bombardier and electronic warfare controller).

The bomber had a fuselage length of 150 feet, 2½ inches, a fully extended wingspan of 136 feet, 8½ inches, a fully swept-back wingspan of 78 feet, 2½ inches, and a gross weight of 389,800 lbs. The B-1 had a design speed of Mach 2.1 at 50,000 feet and an un-refueled range of 6,100 miles. Its weapon delivery capability included three internal bomb bays, which could accommodate either 24 SRAMs on rotary dispensers or 75,000 lbs of gravity bombs.

The revived B-1 program called for essentially the same configuration and performance requirements as the original versions, which were based on early 20-year-old design technology. The revised production program encountered serious problems, including: Cost, which rose exponentially with the retooling and reorganizing required by industry after the four-year hiatus as well as fuel leaks, electronics, and overall performance.

The B-1 was integrated into the SIOP for only a few years before being negotiated out as part of a nuclear arms reduction program.

THE AERIAL TANKERS

A major contributor to the concept of flexible response and extra-long-range bomber planning was the development of aerial refueling. SAC moved rapidly from the "probe and drogue" flexible hose concept passed on from the Royal Air Force (RAF) to the largest, most reliable, and most efficient air refueling force in the world. The venerable World War II B-29 became the first air refueling "tanker." It was followed by KB-50A and finally, an aircraft fully developed as an aerial tanker—the KC-97. Described briefly below are the various configurations of the SAC tanker fleet subsequent to the modified B-29 and B-50.

KC-97 STRATOTANKER

SAC's first designed tanker, the KC-97 evolved from the Boeing Stratocruiser commercial airliner of the 1950s and the Air Force transport version, the C-97. The Air Force purchased 780 KC-97 tankers which remained in service until 1965. The KC-97 had an operating range of 4,300 miles—an excellent range, considering that the aircraft had to burn 115/145 aviation gas in its engines while carrying JP-4 for off-loading to the B-47 and B-52 bombers. The tanker had its limitations in altitude and airspeed; the bombers had to descend to low altitudes in order to rendezvous with the KC-97 and had to fly much slower in order to "hook-up" with the sluggish tanker. These restrictions resulted in the bombers burning considerably more fuel than they used at their normal operating altitudes and higher speeds.

KC-135 STRATOTANKER

Also derived from a Boeing-built commercial airliner (the 707), the KC-135 became SAC's first all-jet tanker. First test-flown as a tanker in August 1956, Boeing delivered a total of 820 KC-135 tankers to the Air Force. Several of the aircraft were converted to RC-models (for reconnaissance) and EC's (for airborne command and control and electronic warfare operations).

This author's experience with the KC/EC-135, having logged over three thousand hours in the two models, was a pleasant one: I thoroughly enjoyed flying the airplane; it was a joy to make instrument approaches and landings and as the improved engines came along, it became an even greater pleasure. The 135 has become the latter-day C-47 "Gooney Bird" of the Air Force, having flown actively and in large numbers for forty years—and it has a projected life of another 25 years or more!

KC-10 EXTENDER

McDonnell Douglas won the competition to develop and produce an extended-range tanker for the Air Force. The KC-10 is once again a derivative of a commercial airliner, the DC-10. The KC-10 can carry a total of 367,847 lbs of jet fuel within its bladder tanks in the lower fuselage bay area and in the wing tanks. The tanker is capable of off-loading 200,000 lbs of fuel up to 2,200 miles from its launch base and then returning home. The basic aircraft was also modified to take on fuel from another tanker, thereby extending its range for refueling, cargo delivery or passenger missions. The first of fifty KC-10s was delivered in September 1982. No complaints were heard from the fortunate young tanker warriors who received assignments to fly the new airplane.

STRATEGIC RECONNAISSANCE

Keeping a vigilant eye on the enemy—by whatever means—is the oldest form of intelligence collection. Strategic reconnaissance becomes necessary when access to the enemy's borders or direct contact within its territory is denied. Aerial reconnaissance by specially equipped aircraft or satellites is the essence of strategic reconnaissance. Aerial reconnaissance dates back to the Civil War, when crude balloons were used to spy on the enemy from above. Balloon reconnaissance came into its own in World War I, as did airplane reconnaissance. Ground activity below could be observed and information about that activity could be brought back to the field commander.

During World War II, the British and the Germans used aerial photography to document, confirm and report enemy movements. From their airborne platforms, they could also hear radio transmissions more clearly. These were the earliest forms of photo intelligence (PHOTINT) and communications intelligence (COMINT). The Cold War and the emerging technologies that accompanied opened a new frontier. Signals intelligence (SIGINT), which includes telemetry intelligence (TELINT) and electronic intelligence (ELINT), entails the monitoring and collection of non-imaging electromagnetic radiation.

Telemetry guidance signals emanating from missiles and rockets are picked up by TELINT; radar emissions are the main signals picked up by ELINT. Technological advances and refinements in each of these disciplines have continued to escalate, which has generated a growing demand for better and more precise information. Major diplomatic, policy, strategic, and tactical decisions are based on collected and interpreted information derived from strategic reconnaissance. Strategic reconnaissance "grew up" with the

Cold War. The United States and the Soviet Union matched wits throughout the Cold War period, each developing ever-increasing improved means of surveillance and detection.

SAC and the Navy began developing greater strategic reconnaissance capabilities immediately after World War II. Better reconnaissance capabilities were needed to support their strategic charter, which in turn, increased their planning requirements. By 1948, SAC had two strategic reconnaissance groups of converted bombers, including 24 RB-17s and 30 RB-29s, (F-2's), for long-range aerial surveillance and information collection. Later, the RB-36 and the RB-47 joined the reconnaissance mission. Specially stripped "light-weight" RB-36s could range over areas of interest at altitudes of 55,000 feet, well above the Soviet MiG-15's ceiling. Each of the converted bombers utilized pressurized compartments in the bomb bay areas to accommodate specially trained SIGINT and PHOTINT operators and their equipment.

SAC took delivery of its first RC-135 reconnaissance platform in 1962. Thereafter, several KC-135s were converted to RC-models in various configurations. The RC-135 provided ample space for equipment installations, external antennas and working areas for operators. It also had the range necessary to accomplish its missions from operating bases around the world.

The RC-135 was a welcome relief for the crews that had flown for years in the cramped and cold RB-47 bomb bay "pod." The Navy began reconnaissance activities in Europe and the Far East, flying converted PB4Y Privateers (an outgrowth from the Air Force B-24), along with Lockheed P2V Neptunes and Martin P4M Mercators. Later, the Navy operated the Lockheed EC-121 and EP-3B Orion in a variety of ocean and overland surveillance, photo, and signals collection roles. The EA-3B twin-jet reconnaissance aircraft operates from both carriers and land-based runways, primarily for SIGINT operations.

Suffice to say, reconnaissance missions were and are remain highly classified, including the various types of onboard collection equipment and capabilities. Therefore, these unsung aviators did not receive the publicity or recognition accorded the other war-fighting forces. These "intelligence warriors" often encountered more of a "Hot War" than a Cold War in carrying out their assigned missions. We will discuss several of their extraordinary exploits later.

U-2 DRAGON LADY

The first worldwide awareness of the U-2 came when Gary Powers was shot down over the Soviet Union in 1960. Six years earlier, in 1954, the Central Intelligence Agency (CIA) had given the legendary "Kelly" Johnson of Lockheed Aircraft's "Skunk Works" the task of developing a high-altitude, extremely long-range reconnaissance aircraft. Richard Bissell, the agency's "spy plane guru," worked closely with Lockheed and Johnson in designing the new aircraft. It was dubbed "U" for "utility" to disguise any particular interest in the engineering development and manufacture of the airplane. By August 1, 1955, the first U-2 was ready to fly. It had a short fuselage and a wingspan of 80 feet, which made it difficult to keep the aircraft on the ground during the takeoff roll. Its bicycle-type landing gear was designed to retract into the fuselage. It had outrigger "pogo stick" wheels that were used for takeoff, and then dropped when the plane became airborne. The U-2 was fully conceived under the auspices of the CIA and was developed from scratch to be a spy plane.

The initial program called for 30 airplanes at a cost of $35 million. The first U-2 pilots, recruited from the Air Force and the Navy, resigned their commissions and became Lockheed employees to protect their military backgrounds and their mission. Also, they had been "sheep dipped" by the CIA to expunge their military backgrounds. The initial intended use of the U-2 was to support the Eisenhower "Open Skies" initiative, which Khrushchev rejected.

Given the resources to conduct surveillance of Soviet ICBM developments, however, and with persistent assertions of a "missile gap," CIA Director Allen Dulles, supported by Secretary of Defense Thomas Gates, convinced the president that over-flight missions ought to be conducted anyway. When he approved the first deep-Russia U-2 over-flight, President Dwight Eisenhower gave a prophetic admonition to CIA Director Dulles and U-2 manager Bissell: "Well boys, I believe the country needs this information and I'm going to approve it. But I'll tell you one thing. Someday one of these machines is going to get caught and we're going to have a storm."

On July 1, 1956, the first U-2 intelligence-gathering flight flew over Moscow, Leningrad, and the Baltic Seacoast. The Soviets detected the U-2 but could not intercept it at its extreme high altitude. Its vast PHOTINT capability photographed a seven-mile-wide path and brought back phenomenal "real-time" photographic coverage of Russia. The Soviets at first lodged secret protests with the State Department. Later, they were more vocal with the US Embassy in Moscow, demanding that the United States stop the intrusions. Nikita Khrushchev continued to protest thereafter—until the Powers incident.

The first U-2 platforms were delivered to SAC in June 1957, at the 4028th Strategic Reconnaissance Squadron, Laughlin Air Force Base, in far Southwest Texas, where transition training took place. The Air Force's initial experience with the U-2 was a near disaster—five SAC pilots and two Lockheed pilots killed in the first year of operation. Eventually the U-2's mechanical defects were worked out and the aircraft became a reliable collection platform. It continues to operate today, along with its advanced successor, the TR-1.

This author was privileged to enjoy a couple of "dollar rides" in the U-2 while serving as commander of the 12th Air Division, to which the U-2 reconnaissance aircraft wing was assigned. The thrill of the "slingshot" takeoff and the climb to 80,000 feet was an exhilaration I had never before experienced—nor ever after—not to mention the several "porpoising" touch-and-go landings that followed. Flights such as this by senior commanders were mostly symbolic, demonstrating to the "troops" their interest in the systems. But they were also important from the point of view of "living" in the environment, if only briefly. Each event in the U-2 experience deepened my respect for the young fellows who squeeze and contort their pressure-suited bodies into the cramped cockpit and sit routinely for   12-plus hours, flying incredible missions.

SR-71 BLACKBIRD

The success of the U-2 prompted the CIA to contract the same team to develop a collection platform that could cruise at even higher altitudes and at supersonic speeds. The initial A-12, created by Kelly Johnson's team, was completed in January 1962. The huge delta wing twin-engine aircraft was generations ahead in design, material technologies, and engine propulsion. These factors combined to revolutionize aircraft speed and altitude. The CIA bought fifteen of the A-12s, single-seaters with sensor equipment operated by the pilot. The Air Force gave some consideration to buying the A-12 (YF-12) for use as an interceptor, but they opted instead for the SR-71, a two-seat reconnaissance platform version. The addition of the second cockpit and the reconnaissance systems officer (RSO) greatly relieved the pilot's workload and further amplified the aircraft's capabilities. The SR-71 program and its operations remain highly classified, with most of the aircraft now resting on display pedestals around the country.

THE INTERCONTINENTAL BALLISTIC MISSILE (ICBM)

The Air Force and SAC won the battle for management, deployment, and command and control of the land-based strategic ICBM programs. The first missile program assigned to SAC was the Snark, a tactical ground-to-ground system. It was followed by the Thor, also a ground-to-ground intermediate range ballistic missile (IRBM) with a 1,900 nautical mile nuclear warhead delivery range. The Thor was later provided to the United Kingdom's Royal Air Force, Italy and Turkey, as part of NATO's nuclear deterrence strategy with SAC conducting Thor crew training for the NATO Allies. SAC and NATO eventually jointly operated 30 Thor missile squadrons across Europe during the 1960s.

SM-65 ATLAS

The first Atlas squadron was activated in February 1958 at Francis E. Warren Air Force Base, Wyoming. Atlas was the first truly intercontinental ballistic missile, having a range of five thousand miles. It was also very large and cumbersome, measuring 75 feet in height and 10 feet in diameter. With a single warhead, it had a liftoff weight in excess of 300,000 lbs. President Eisenhower, in response to the pressures of the "missile gap" hysteria, put a high priority on developing and deploying the Atlas which became the personal project of Major General Bernard Schriever.

The system moved rapidly from research and development to operational in just three years—a phenomenal feat, considering the technologies required to field such a mammoth system. By 1962, SAC had 142 Atlas ICBMs deployed, with Titan I and II and Minuteman ICBM moving quickly to keep pace with rapid technology developments. The Atlas weapons systems were all retired by June 1965. The Atlas remained for years thereafter as an important heavy-payload launch vehicle for the Air Force and NASA.

LGM-25 TITAN I AND TITAN II

The two-stage heavy ICBM development program, begun in 1955, followed the success of Atlas. The Martin Company won the contract to build the Titan system and launched the first missile in February 1959. The Titan, which measured 110 feet in length with the warhead attached, was 10 feet in diameter at the first stage and 8 feet in diameter at the second stage. The missile's Aerojet XLR91-AJ liquid propellant engine burned a mixture of hydrazine and nitrogen tetra oxide. With a one-minute countdown sequence from launch initiation, it lifted a weight of 300,000 lbs with a thrust of 530,000 lbs, sending it toward its target at 17,000 MPH with a range in excess of six thousand miles. Its four-megaton nuclear warhead, the largest in SAC's arsenal, had a target strike accuracy of less than a mile. The SAC inventory reached a peak of 63 Titan ICBM's in 1963. As the Minuteman ICBM system came on line, the last Titan complex was deactivated in 1985. This brought an end to liquid-propelled, heavy ICBMs in the US war plan.

LGM-30, MINUTEMAN I, II, AND III.

Boeing's Minuteman ICBM was designed specifically as a strategic weapon system, unlike Atlas and Titan, which were basically space launch vehicles first and weapon systems second. The Minuteman system used solid propellant which eliminated the requirement for the crew to handle volatile liquid propellants. The design of Minuteman with its remote operating system and instantaneous launch response permitted combat crews to monitor ten missiles concurrently and moved SAC into "push-button warfare." The dispersal of the missile silos and launch control centers along mostly rural roadways contributed to security and ease of maintenance response. The basic Minuteman design was simpler, lower in cost and considerably safer than the earlier liquid-propelled engine systems, and it will not become obsolete in the near future.

SAC eventually deployed one thousand and fifty Minuteman missiles within six wing complexes in the western and mid-western United States. The basic missile, which measures 54 to 60 feet in length and 6 feet in diameter, operates with a continuously running inertial guidance system. Reaction time from launch initiation is less than 60 seconds. With a 120,000 lb thrust, the missile can project its warhead 5,500 miles to the target. ICBM systems brought a new and different dimension to SAC's combat crew force.

LGM-118A PEACEKEEPER

Initially dubbed the MX missile, also a land-based ICBM was deployed by the Air Force and SAC beginning in 1986. A total of 50 missiles were finally deployed to the 90th Strategic Missile Wing at F.E. Warren Air Force Base, Wyoming. Under the conditions of the START II treaty, the Peacekeeper systems were to be removed from the U.S. nuclear arsenal in 2005. In spite of the fact that START II was never placed in force, the last of the Peacekeeper ICBMs were decommissioned on September 19, 2005.

The Peacekeeper weapons system was a MIRV'ed missile with each ICBM carrying up to 10 re-entry (R/V) vehicles and each R/V armed with a 300-kiloton W87 nuclear warhead. Each warhead had twenty times the destructive power of the atomic device dropped on Hiroshima in World War II.

THE CRUISE MISSILE

To provide a multiple mission capability to its war-planning strategies, the Air Force developed and deployed several types of air-to-ground attack missiles with the bomber force. The GAM-77/AGM-28 "Hound Dog" was designed as a standoff weapon to "soften" defenses or target complexes up to seven hundred miles away as the bomber penetrated enemy territory. The Hound Dog, operational with the B-52G and H models from 1961 to 1976, was equipped with an internal navigation guidance system that was updated to its actual position and its intended course of flight just prior to launch from the B-52. The missile could be programmed to fly to its target at speeds up to Mach 2.1 and at altitudes from treetop level to 55,000 feet. It was also unique in that its J-52 engine could be used to augment the bomber's power in flight and its fuel tanks could be topped off from the B-52's fuel system prior to launch. The GAM-87 "Skybolt" air-launched ballistic missile, developed by Douglas Aircraft Company, Aerojet General, General Electric, and Nortronics, came into the inventory in 1959. Programmed to be carried by the B-52 and the British Vulcan bomber, the missile consisted of a two-stage solid propellant engine that could fly at hypersonic speeds to targets up to 1,000 miles from the launch point. Similar to the Hound Dog, Skybolt was designed to be a "roll-back" weapon for the penetrating bomber force. The Skybolt, never a favorite of Secretary of Defense McNamara because of its checkered development tests and cost overruns, was canceled just as the Air Force had concluded it was proving to be a reliable weapon.

As Soviet air defenses proliferated, making bomber penetration more of a concern, the Air Force turned to another air-to-ground missile, the AGM-69A "SRAM," to support the B-52s and FB-111s. Developed by General Dynamics, SRAM was selected to follow the defeated Skybolt. The SRAM was developed as a semi-ballistic air-launched missile with a Minuteman III equivalent warhead capability. The B-52 could carry up to 20 SRAMs mounted externally and internally, and launch the missiles up to one hundred miles prior to a planned target. Its exceptionally short flight time of nominally three minutes made the SRAM virtually invulnerable to radar tracking and interception by air defenses. SAC ultimately integrated 1,500 SRAMs into the SIOP bomber mission.

Shortly after his inauguration in 1977, President Carter canceled production of the B-1 bomber in favor of developing a air-launched cruise missile (ALCM). The ALCM was given the highest priority for weapon system program development in the Carter Administration which clearly indicated that no new strategic bombers would be built. The B-52 would become the ALCM delivery vehicle just as it had been for the Hound Dog and SRAM. The major difference, the ALCM would be a "long-range" missile capable of low-level flight to its target after being launched outside enemy air defenses. A competitive fly-off between an airborne version of the already operational General Dynamics AGM-109 Tomahawk sea-launched cruise missile (SLCM) and a long-range version of Boeing's AGM-86A resulted in a win for the AGM-86. Boeing set out to develop a small unmanned vehicle powered by the 600 lb static thrust Williams F107-WR-100 turbofan engine, fitted with retractable wings. The ALCM's guidance system relied upon both inertial and preprogrammed navigation systems. The preprogrammed terrain matching and comparison system (TERCOM) could fly the missile at 500 MPH at extremely low altitudes, avoiding traditional radar detection en route to its target 1,500 miles into enemy territory.

The B-52G was the first bomber to be equipped with the ALCM (12 missiles, fitted externally under the wings). This allowed the bomber to launch its missiles well away from enemy radar detection and penetrate at low level and deliver its internally carried gravity bombs. The B-52G and later, the B-52H, was modified to carry a rotary launcher within the bomb bay with an additional eight ALCMs in place of gravity weapons. The strategy permitted the bomber to carry 20 ALCM nuclear weapons, launching them outside enemy territory and substantially reducing the risk to aircraft and crew.

While Carter's decision to rely more heavily on the cruise strategy than on the manned penetrating bomber was contentious among bomber advocates, the ALCM later proved to virtually overwhelm Soviet defense strategies. The small missiles, when launched in massive numbers, were capable of saturating Soviet target areas, virtually negating any reasonable cost-effective defense measures.

Close behind the ALCM came the development of the ground-launched cruise missile (GLCM). Utilizing the ALCM's basic design features, navigation systems and engine, the GLCM could be launched from a transporter erector launcher (TEL) and fly 1,500 miles to a target. SAC was given the GLCM mission and was authorized to purchase 464 GLCMs for deployment with NATO's theater nuclear forces in Europe. The Soviet defense structure was complicated further and the balance of power considerably skewed toward the west; a factor that provided an important SALT "bargaining chip" in the 1980s.

Joining the Strategic Air Command deterrent forces in the call to duty, professionalism, discipline, hard work, and sacrifice was the nuclear submarine Navy. The nuclear submarines, which came along in the early 1960s, also met the challenge—first with Polaris, then Poseidon and finally Trident sea-launched ballistic missiles (SLBM). Their alert posture called for remaining submerged at sea for periods of 60 days or more, constantly ready to launch missiles.

As highlighted earlier, the Strategic Nuclear Navy became the third leg of the TRIAD. The Navy had begun work on nuclear-driven submarine technology as early as 1947 under the leadership of Captain Hyman G. Rickover. Four years into the design phase of a nuclear submarine, the Electric

Boat Company of General Dynamics was placed under contract to build the first reactor-powered submarine. The Mark II thermal reactor power system was chosen as the propulsion unit. The keel for the first boat, the Nautilus, was laid in June 1952; the submarine was launched on January 21, 1954.

The first sea voyage test of the new submarine commenced a year later under the command of Captain Eugene Wilkinson with a pensive Rear Admiral Rickover anxiously watching the proceedings. The nuclear-powered submarine performed perfectly, quickly proving that the new power source could drive submarines of virtually any size to unlimited distances. In the first two and one-half years, the Nautilus traveled 62,000 miles on its first uranium reactor core. In July 1958, four years after it was commissioned, Captain William R. Anderson guided Nautilus from Seattle, Washington to Portland, England, transiting under the Arctic ice pack.

With the proof-of-concept for a nuclear-powered submarine solved, the Navy set about investigating the possibility of launching IRBMs and ICBMs from the undersea platform. The Navy began to develop its own submarine compatible sea-launched ballistic missile (SLBM).

UGM-27 POLARIS A1 AND A3

Sea-launched ballistic missiles kept pace with nuclear submarine technology with the first Polaris A1 developed in the late 1950s. The two-stage missile was 31 ft 6 inches long with a 54-inch diameter, weighed 35,000 lbs, and had a range of 2,900 nautical miles. The Polaris systems have now been retired and are no longer operational—with either the US Navy or the British Royal Navy.

UGM-73 POSEIDON C3

The Poseidon C3, a 65,000-pound, 34-foot by 74-inch, two-stage missile was capable of reaching targets up to 3,230 miles with a payload of ten 50 kiloton (Kt) Reentry Vehicles (RVs) or 2,485 miles with 14 MIRV weapons. The C3 has the same relative range as the Polaris, but with twice the payload and a 100% improvement in accuracy. The Poseidon gave way to the Trident weapon system in the late 1980s.

UGM-93 TRIDENT I C4/TRIDENT II D5

With relatively the same dimensions as the Poseidon, the Trident I C4 weighs 70,000 lbs. It is a three-stage solid propellant missile capable of delivering eight Mark 4 100Kt MIRV weapons to targets up to 4,400 miles from its launch point.

Concurrent with the development of the nuclear-powered submarine and appropriately sized SLBMs, the Atomic Energy Commission (AEC) continued work on smaller nuclear warheads for use by Air Force fighter-bombers and the Army's missiles. The defense electronics industry was perfecting miniature inertial navigation units for ballistic missiles while Dr. Charles Draper at MIT was developing a precise navigation plotting system for submarine use. The Ship's Inertial Navigation System (SINS), when finally installed in the Nautilus, could accurately pinpoint the geographic location of the submerged submarine at any place under the ocean, a factor critical to a missile's onboard inertial guidance system.

While Rickover was managing the SSBN development, Rear Admiral William Raborn became the Navy's chief SLBM developer; he skillfully guided the creation of the entire Polaris system until it became a reality. The Navy launched into the full production of SSBN boats with emphasis on deeper operational submarines and quieter engines.

LAFAYETTE CLASS

Thirty-one boats were built during the 1960s and 1970s. The first eight were equipped with 16 Polaris A2 SLBMs; the remaining 23 could carry 16 Polaris A3 MIRV SLBMs. All were later converted to carry the Poseidon C4 missiles. The huge submarines, which measure 425 feet in length and 33 feet across the beam, have a submerged displacement of 8,250 tons. The boats have four 21-inch torpedo tubes for defensive operations. The 15,000-horsepower nuclear propulsion engine provides power through a single propeller shaft to achieve speeds of 20 knots on the surface and 30 knots submerged. The normal crew complement of the Lafayette class boats is 140. The last 12, referred to as Benjamin Franklin class boats, were enlarged in size and given improved underwater stealth features. The crew size was increased to 168 and can deliver the Trident C4 SLBM.

OHIO CLASS

The Navy launched the USS Ohio in 1979. Much larger than its predecessors, it measures 560 feet in length and 42 feet across the beam and it displaces 18,700 tons submerged. Like the Lafayette, the Ohio's 60,000-horsepower nuclear engine delivers power through a single propeller shaft. The Ohio's submerged speed is in excess of 30 knots, and it carries a crew of 133. It also carries 24 Trident I C4 or Trident II D5 SLBMs.

Richard Hubler's rhetorical appraisal cited earlier was prophetic. With the end of the Cold War came the demise of Strategic Air Command, and much of its mighty weaponry either retired or dispersed without an apparent specific force supplement, replacement or weapons management as the Air Force reorganized itself for an uncertain future. The weapons management aspect eventually proved to place a black mark on Air Force leadership for the apparent lack of attention the imperative discipline required to maintain, secure and manage nuclear weapons. The tried and true nuclear weapons management disciplines carefully developed and honed by SAC deteriorated within a short time with disastrous results to the careers of a number of senior Air Force officers and leaders. The result is the creation of a new near Strategic Air Command 'look-alike' "Global Strike Force' to bring back into the fold, the remnants of the critical weapons and weapon systems once maintained by Strategic Air Command; a hard lesson learned.

HUMAN EVENTS

"The laws of necessity, of self-preservation, of saving our country when in danger, are of higher obligation."

President Thomas Jefferson

FOUR

THE COLD WAR LEADERS

"Here's my strategy on the Cold War; we win, they lose."

Ronald Reagan

The remaining chapters of this project will focus on the human element of effectively protecting the nation against an aggressor regime. The national leaders dealt with the ever-present roller coaster politics in America while the military commanders addressed the persistent threats and the men and women in uniform carried-out the challenging heroic deeds.

Nine presidents served the United States during the Cold War era, and seven leaders held dominant power over the Soviet Union during the same period. From Truman to Eisenhower, to Kennedy-Johnson, to Nixon-Ford, to Carter to Reagan and finally George H.W. Bush, the broadly prescribed Cold War policies of the United States remained reasonably consistent: avoid direct engagement with the Soviet Union, contain communist expansionism, and maintain an acceptable quality of life for all Americans.

The variances in leadership and policy mainly had to do with the "how," which was always largely politically driven, and the perceived requirements for a sufficient defense posture while balancing social and domestic programs. Each Cold War presidential campaign required candidates to create new and different ways to address these fundamental issues. Hence, the mood of the American people followed a consistent cycle of shifting from Democrat to Republican president and back again throughout the Cold War years. The Congress, on the other hand, remained for the most part Democrat until after the Cold War subsided. George H. W. Bush's election to succeed Ronald Reagan was a notable exception as the Cold War slowly came to an end, resulting in large part from the persistent efforts of his predecessor, Ronald Reagan. But even Bush, with the highest performance approval ratings of any previous president a year prior to his expected re-election after the Soviet Union collapsed, fell victim to post-war doldrums and American politics. This resulted principally from political campaign economic down-turn rhetoric and a fickle electorate.

In this writer's view there were two truly heroic Cold War presidential leaders: Harry Truman and Ronald Reagan—the Alpha and Omega—of the period. This opinion by no means diminishes the commitment and demonstrated performance in varying ways of the other seven. In the simplest examination, Harry Truman promptly recognized the Soviet threat in its most severe and menacing terms, and he began to posture the nation to confront this newest evil. Ronald Reagan came into office in the 34th year of the Cold War stalemate, re-energized a lagging nation to address the threat once and for all, skillfully devised a plan to bring down the Iron Curtain and succeeded.

The following brief abstracts attempt to provide a perspective review of each of the nine Cold War presidents.

HARRY TRUMAN

The first Cold War president, Harry S. Truman, had served as vice president for only 82 days before being thrust into the office of the presidency. He was promptly confronted with more pressing foreign policy decisions in a shorter period of time than any previous president. During his first three months in office, Germany surrendered; he learned for the first time about the existence and development of the atomic bomb and about the terms agreed to by Roosevelt concerning Europe at the Yalta Big Three Conference. The determined resistance of the Japanese to not surrender and to fight to the end was a troubling key issue. He ordered the Secretary of Defense to organize a military force of at least one million men to mount an assault on Japan, even acknowledging that a direct engagement of the entrenched and fanatical Japanese Army would result in horrendous losses of American fighting men. He crammed to get up to speed for a scheduled meeting with Stalin and Churchill at Potsdam for a third and final Big Three Conference. The post-war disposition of Germany and Europe would be the key issue at the conference. He had never met Stalin, but in any case, would attempt to petition him to join the United States in the war against Japan. His down home Missouri upbringing sustained him and gave him courage and confidence through the initial days as president.

Prior to his arrival at Potsdam, Winston Churchill rode Truman hard on Roosevelt's concessions to the Soviets regarding Europe and a perceived premature withdrawal of U.S. military forces from the region. "I am profoundly concerned about the European situation," he telegraphed Truman. "I learn that half the American Air Force in Europe has already begun to move to the Pacific Theater. The newspapers are full of the great movements of the American Army out of Europe...Meanwhile what is to happen about Russia?"

The wise and wily old warrior warned, "An Iron Curtain is drawn down upon their front," invoking the term for the first time and, "we do not know what is going on behind."

Prior to departing for the Big Three, Truman was briefed in detail about the new atomic bomb technology ongoing at Los Alamos and the optimism for its near-term successful testing "within weeks," he was told. Arguments from all sides within the Administration ensued——from "What if it doesn't work when it's dropped?" to "We shouldn't find ourselves being blamed for outdoing the Japanese or Nazis in atrocities." The media had already begun to condemn the B-29 fire bombings as inhuman and barbaric. Many of the prominent scientists at Los Alamos, although directly working to perfect the bomb, disagreed with using the bomb against an adversary, opting to showcase it as a demonstration for the world to see its potential devastating effects.

General George Marshall, who held Truman's highest confidence, made the most convincing argument: "We have just been through a bitter experience...losing thousands of lives...at Okinawa. This was preceded by a number of similar experiences in other Pacific islands. The Japanese have demonstrated in each case they would not surrender and they will fight to the death. In one night in Tokyo we killed one hundred thousand people with our bombs and it had seemingly no effect whatsoever....We have to end the war; we have to save American lives." Further, he reminded the President and those inside the Administration that the Japanese had rejected numerous offers of surrender.

Truman handled himself well at Potsdam to the surprise of the seasoned bureaucrats who accompanied him. He recalled being surprised by the small stature of Stalin——no more than five feet five inches tall. "A little bit of a squirt," he commented to his confidants. He attempted to charm and humor the Soviet leader as had Roosevelt and to Churchill's dismay, he did not attempt to renege on his predecessor's prior commitments. Churchill fighting his own internal political battle back home and outnumbered by Truman and Stalin, groused but went along with the realignment plan forfeiting large portions of Germany and the City Berlin, Eastern Europe and the Baltic's to the newly constituted Soviet Union.

During the midst of the conference the President received word of the test of 'the bomb' in New Mexico. It had been even more successful than anyone hoped. Truman was buoyed by the news and promptly notified Churchill...both agreed that Stalin should not be told. Churchill wryly commented, "This atomic bomb is the Second Coming in Wrath." Before the Big Three Conference ended, Churchill would be replaced by Clement Attlee who had won the election for Prime Minister back home.

The Potsdam Conference concluded and President Truman boarded the USS Augusta en route back to the United States. Before departing, he had issued the order to drop the new bomb on Japan. The two additional bomb devices built at Los Alamos were hastily shipped aboard the USS Indianapolis to the Pacific. Major General Curtis LeMay, in command of Air Force bomber operations on Tinian Island, quickly prepared the two B-29 bombers and crews to deliver the bombs.

President Truman notified the American people and the world via a message released by the White House at 11:00 a.m. Washington DC time on August 6, 1945: "Sixteen hours ago an American airplane dropped one bomb on Hiroshima...It is an atomic bomb. It is a harnessing of the basic power of the universe...We are now prepared to obliterate more rapidly and completely every productive enterprise the Japanese have above ground in any city. We shall destroy their docks, their factories, and their communications. Let there be no mistake; we shall completely destroy Japan's power to make war...If they do not now accept our terms they may expect a rain of ruin from the air, the like of which has never been seen on this earth..."

Stalin did not capture everything he sought at the last Big Three meeting—Italy's holdings in Africa, control of the German Ruhr Valley industrial complexes or the naval base on the Bosporus. But, seizing virtual occupation of Eastern Europe was more than sufficient to satisfy the Russian bear. Stalin had agreed at both Yalta and Potsdam that Korea would become independent and unified at the end of the war. But, he did not hesitate to move in and mop up the Japanese occupiers when it became apparent that they would encounter little resistance from either the weakened Japanese army or the Allies. The Soviets quickly set up a communist style government north of the 38th Parallel and installed a strong sympathizer, Kim Il-Sung, as their puppet leader. Attempts by the U.S. and the Allies to reunify the two Koreas never materialized while the Soviets persisted in organizing and heavily arming a North Korean military force. An agreement to separate Indochina at the 16th Parallel, giving China the North and British control of the South, would also have far reaching consequences.

It would only be six months later that Stalin made his address to the Russian people on February 9, 1946, declaring that communism and capitalism could not peacefully co-exist. Stalin's speech was followed a month later by Churchill's own famous proclamation at Westminster College. The Cold War was unofficially declared and would persist for four and a half decades. The dismantling of U.S. World War II forces had proceeded with lightening speed, and the president and his military advisors had to move fast to stem the downsizing. Truman had already determined to bring major changes to the U.S. military, and the advent of the Soviet threat hastened the work. In the interim, he directed General Carl Spaatz, Army Chief of Staff, to organize a special strategic air arm with a capability to deliver atomic bombs. Strategic Air Command was established on March 21, 1946, with General George C. Kenney as its first commander. He also directed numerous other organizational changes within the services pending the study and completion of a massive national security strategy study at work in the War Department and Congress.

When National Security Council Directive-68 (NSC-68) was completed, it galvanized the results of several comprehensive studies to unify foreign, military and budgetary policies within the government which had begun in

1947. NSC-68 was the turning point in addressing U.S. foreign policy. It recognized the Soviet threat, articulated foreign policy, military objectives vis-à-vis the threat and how the objectives could be achieved.

In the face of the many post-World War II recovery and economic challenges, and an even more frightening concern with a growing belligerent Soviet Union, Truman endorsed a monumental plan for the recovery of Western Europe. Secretary of Commerce Averell Harriman worked with corporate, labor and academic leaders to sell what became known as the Marshall Plan to the President and the American people. As a result, the Plan's $13 billion ($80 billion in today's dollars) set a course for recovery of Germany, France, Italy and the United Kingdom to some degree. The Soviets invited to participate in the Marshall Plan recovery program walked out of the initial meeting as if no doubt by design to send a further signal that "they would not take handouts from America" and would go it alone. President Truman hailed the program as "an investment in security that will be worth many times its cost." No doubt he was right.

As President Truman prepared to run for reelection in the summer of 1948, he received word on June 24th that the Soviets had blockaded all highway, rail and river traffic in and out of Berlin. Hawks in the White House and Congress called for an immediate assault by land into Berlin. On the other side there were suggestions that the U.S. pull out of Berlin and "Let the Soviets have the city."

General Lucius Clay, U.S. Commander in Berlin, began an immediate airlift of supplies from bases in West Germany. His initiative caught on quickly, and Truman ordered the organization of a massive airlift of supplies and additional troops. General Curtis LeMay was brought back from the Pacific Theater and sent in to direct the aerial re-supply effort. The Berlin Airlift was hailed as one of the most brilliant moves since the Cold War began. The U.S. had 3,000 troops stationed in Berlin; the British and French had a combined 3,500. The Soviets had positioned 18,000 in the Soviet Sector and moved 300,000 into East Germany. The President countered, ordering two B-29 bomber squadrons to the UK. The B-29, still famous for dropping the atomic bombs on Japan, disturbed the historically paranoid Soviets. They nevertheless held their ground and the blockade continued. They made veiled attempts to use propaganda to demoralize the West Berliners, but the endless supply of food, coal and supplies sustained their hopes. When Stalin finally dropped the blockade on May 12, 1949, the Berlin Airlift operation had fully matured, achieving a daily delivery rate of 10,000 tons of cargo. Before the year of airlifting was over, Soviet officers became a common sight slipping into the Western Sectors to buy food and goods. Stalin conceded quietly, but continued to use his propaganda element extensively within the Soviet

Bloc and with communists world-wide to denounce the Allied aggressors and to extol his generous leniency in allowing them to remain in Berlin and Germany.

The next major Soviet backed incursion in the Cold War occurred on June 24, 1950, with North Korea invading the South. The U.N. Security Council agreed that General Douglas MacArthur could take command of the UN forces in South Korea. He immediately requested thirty thousand American troops into the war. Truman was ambivalent about the "war" thousands of miles away from America and avoided using the term in his speeches, but he felt strongly that the United States had no choice but to support the honor of the United Nations to defend South Korea. "Such obligations are a part of the nation's burden for a long time to come," he said.

The conflict would witness a doubling of U.S. military forces, unprecedented defense budgets, the firing of the most revered officer in the United States Army, Douglas MacArthur, and the loss of over fifty thousand American men before Truman left office at the end of his term. Eligible for a second elected term, Harry Truman decided that it was time to step down. Adlai Stevenson became the Democrat candidate to run against retired General Dwight D. Eisenhower. Truman and Stevenson were not that close and he stood his distance during the campaign. On the other hand, he professed to like Eisenhower "As a general," he said, but didn't particularly care for him as a politician. He still had bitter thoughts of his experience with MacArthur's attempts to engage in political policy rather than sticking to his military job in Korea.

President Truman stood tall in the face of some of the most difficult and diverse challenges of any president in history up to that time. His complex and soul-searching decision to end the war with Japan with atomic weapons, the creation and implementation of the Marshall Plan, relieving General MacArthur of command in Korea, his strong and unyielding stance against the Soviets in the early days of the Cold War and his many legislative achievements in preparing the U.S. military posture for the long haul he knew lay ahead rank him as one of the all time great world leaders.

"IKE"

Dwight D. Eisenhower had been dubbed with the nickname, "Ike", by the GI's during the war who revered him as one of them, "a soldier's soldier." The moniker stuck with the American people. He chose a young senator from California, Richard Nixon, as his running mate and campaigned for the presidency against Adlai Stevenson in 1952, winning the election easily, becoming the 34th president of the United States. During the campaign he appealed to Democrats, Republicans and all Americans to choose him as the ideal leader to take the nation forward as it became stagnated in Korea and more embroiled in the Cold War. He vowed to "go to Korea personally" and bring the war to an end and to continue to stem communist adventurism wherever United States interests exist, and he did. "Communism, corruption and Korea," swept him into office. Josef Stalin was still around at the time but was seriously ailing.

Awaiting the new President was a dramatic and unwanted development arising from the investigations of post-war communist influence in the government. An FBI report linked Robert Oppenheimer, who had two years before forcefully and vocally distanced himself from the development of the H-bomb, with communist affiliations. This revelation followed on the heels of the Rosenberg case, which was still in disposition when Eisenhower took office. On April 5, 1951, Judge Irving Kaufman in sentencing the pair condemned them harshly: "Putting into the hands of the Russians the A-bomb years before our best scientists predicted Russia would perfect the bomb has already caused, in my opinion, the communist aggression in Korea, with the resultant casualties exceeding 50,000 and who knows but what that millions more innocent people may pay the price of your treason. Indeed, through your betrayal, you undoubtedly have altered the course of history to the disadvantage of our country."

Appeals for leniency were denied all the way to the President, and they were executed on June 19, 1953. Hailed as martyrs for years by communists around the world, the rigors and the emotions of the United Rosenberg trial also served to further inflame the anti-communist mood throughout the States.

Beset by the ongoing war in Korea on the one hand and with a goal of establishing a business environment in the White House, Eisenhower chose Charles Wilson as his Secretary of Defense and John Foster Dulles as Secretary of State. Wilson was president and CEO of General Motors, and it was thought he would bring a corporate business environment to the Department of Defense. Quickly though, he became too absorbed with trivial activities and was unresponsive to the attention and needs of the Joint Chiefs and the military. Next he named Neil McElroy, president of Proctor and Gamble, a delightful personality, but poor defense chief. Finally, the President appointed Thomas Gates, former Secretary of the Navy, who as a "workaholic" fared much better with an understanding of operational matters, but according to many critics, put the DOD budgeting system into a "tailspin." Without regard to special mission needs, he allocated an equal share of the "pie" to each military service causing unprecedented feuding.

Eisenhower inherited the Cold War and a by-product, the Korean War. Troubled by the fact that thousands of World War II veterans had been recalled to fight in another war, he plunged into the complex issue as he had promised during his presidential campaign. He promptly visited the war torn predicament to see for himself and to bolster the morale of the soldiers. He was greatly bothered that veterans of the past war were the only ready source of reasonably trained military manpower that was available to the Truman Administration when he responded to the invasion from the North. During the early phases of Korea, Truman had successfully abolished segregation in the Armed Forces and greatly improved morale and unit efficiency in all of the Military Services. But in virtually every other way, Korea had become a disaster: politically, economically and with the tragic loss of human life. There were an estimated 2 million casualties in the war with Korean civilians suffering the brunt with over 1,000,000 killed or severely injured as the battles moved back and forth up and down the peninsula. The U.S. suffered over 36,000 fighting men killed in action, 300,000 wounded and another 15,000 or more in unrelated deaths. There were an additional 300,000 South Korean military casualties.

The president considered the use of atomic weapons to end the stalemate in Korea as had Truman. He believed that selective use of tactical adapted atomic weapons would be much more 'cost effective' than the continued loss of lives—on both sides. The National Security Counsel endorsed a Pentagon suggestion to even go one step further—use atomic weapons against China—"All the way to Beijing," someone allegedly suggested. In lieu of carrying out the plans, he allowed his considerations to be leaked to the Chinese, and then ordered concentration bombings of major dams in North Korea which resulted in major floods throughout the region. The Chinese retreated; the Soviets pulled back their direct support and the North Koreans agreed to a cease-fire. A truce was signed in July 1953. The end of hostilities did not close the chapter on Korea; well over a thousand soldiers and airmen remained missing and never accounted for. The Chinese and the Soviets denied having anything to do with captured American fighting men although there was ample evidence that both may have been directly involved in the internment and torture of prisoners.

Eisenhower made a much better choice in Dulles as Secretary of State to address the Soviet situation. Dulles found little fault with Truman's containment policy and continued to push for keeping the Soviets and communist movements within their boundaries. He convinced the President that Communist China's claim to the islands of Quemoy, Matsu and Tachen, off Taiwan, amounted to an invasion of Nationalist China. The Nationalists, with U.S. aid and backing, defended the possessions. Dulles lectured that ideology was the major determinant of Soviet policy, stating, "It may be that Lenin and Stalin are dead. So they are. But, their doctrine is not dead ...they continue to practice it throughout the world." George Kennen, to the contrary, had argued earlier in 1949 that: "Communism ideology was the instrument, not the determinate of Soviet policy."

These diverse differences of opinion between the back-to-back administrations are highlighted to demonstrate the often meandering path of U.S. policy directions. In defense of both, each believed that containment was the most effective measure of control of the Soviets and communism. Dulles, like Kennen, was a student of political history and communist-Soviet ideology.

Eisenhower's "New Look" strategy of collective security through treaties provided, in his view, "maximum deterrence for minimum cost." The President was economic-minded and urged the government and industry toward business and consumer products. The New Look strategy was coupled with a "massive retaliation" warning to the Soviets and a reduction of over-all defense spending and military strength requirements to support small or limited wars. In the President's view limited conflicts were not necessary and should be avoided. He felt that a strong and visible nuclear deterrent capability out-weighed the potential for such conflicts and the requirement for additional military spending.

Americans were awakened on the morning of October 4, 1957, to the news that a 194 pound Russian-launched satellite, dubbed "Sputnik", was "beeping" a signal as it orbited the earth at a speed of 18,000 miles per hour and at an altitude of 560 miles. This was a wake up call for confident America. A year earlier, the Soviets had successfully flight-tested an ICBM, the SS-6. It was the SS-6 rocket engine configured into a cluster of 20 which was used to launch the satellite from test facilities at Tyuratam. Following the SS-6 test flight, TASS announced on August 27, 1956: "The results obtained show that it is possible to launch rockets to any region of the globe. The solution of the problem of creating intercontinental ballistics rockets will make it possible to reach distant regions, without resorting to strategic aviation."

The policies of "containment" and "new look" and their potential for endurance suddenly paled in the realization that the Soviets had not only broken-out of their imposed boundaries, but had done so in a highly sophisticated manner. This was a characteristic normally expected "only of the United States." Less than a month later, the Soviets launched an even larger satellite weighing 1,120 pounds, but "dragging" the five thousand-pound third-stage booster rocket which failed to separate. Sputnik II contained a sealed life-support system and carried a dog named Laika, which was wired for electronic monitoring. There was no provision for recovering the dog, which would eventually die after its oxygen and heat was exhausted. This latter cruel revelation shocked many in the world and also served as another confirmation of Soviet insensitivity to even the most basic concerns. Americans had been content up to then and not particularly worried about Soviet technology beyond their development of nuclear weapons. That had been worry enough.

The frightening specter of "space vehicles" circling overhead caused great concern for the status of U.S. space and missile technology development. The "missile gap" wail by the media and partisan political pundits was activated: "If the Soviets were so advanced in missile technology, then they could easily strike the United States from Russian ground launch sites!"

Two of the early critics were Senators John Kennedy and Lyndon Johnson, both aspirants to the White House. President Eisenhower had been provided intelligence information discounting the high state of Soviet missile technology and that a "gap" was more illusory than real. Adversaries of the President, including Senators Kennedy and Johnson, argued that his persistent efforts to reduce defense spending had placed the United States in a position of vulnerability. Others such as Professor Henry Kissinger and General Thomas Power, Commander-in-Chief, Strategic Air Command, stated publicly that a missile gap existed. General Power testified that the Soviet Union could "wipe out the United States in thirty minutes."

The advent of the Soviet space program flew in the face of Eisenhower's optimism to begin dealing with Soviet Premier Khrushchev to cool the differences between their two governments. He had halted the surveillance over-flights of the Soviet Union sixteen months earlier as a peace initiative and although Khrushchev was scheduled to visit the U.S., the President yielded to pressure to resume U-2 flights. The Premier visited the United States in October 1959 and rekindled the acrimony by boasting that the Soviets possessed an all new ICBM force. During Khrushchev's visit, the State Department arranged for the special train taking him from Los Angeles to San Francisco to transit through Vandenberg Air Force Base where the Air Force put on display two ATLAS missiles with oxygen plumes streaming from the erected ICBM's—apparently "ready to launch."

As Eisenhower's term began to close, the Democrats and the media jumped on the missile gap band-wagon with greatly exaggerated "evidence of Soviet capability." Respected journalists such as Stewart Alsop wrote an article claiming that the Soviets were ahead in operational intercontinental ballistic missiles "100 to 1" and by 1961 would be ahead "1000 to 70". This implied that the Soviet's missile production was at least hundreds of times ahead of the United States. Aviation Week reported that the Soviets were turning-out: "fifteen ICBM's per month." The liberal weekly, Reporter, published the most bizarre statistics of all in 1959: "The Soviets have 20,000 ICBM's with ranges from 150 to 6,000 miles; Khrushchev had reported within the Kremlin the completion of a 'super missile' with a range of 14,000 miles; and the Red Army had a capability to fire thermonuclear missiles in salvos of six at a time up to 1,200 miles radius." There were equally wild eyed stories about the advances in Soviet submarine launched ballistic missile (SLBM) advances and "long-range" aircraft that could fly in the stratosphere and drop weapons from over 100 miles altitude. U.S. politicians enthusiastically contributed to the hysteria.

Seven months after Khrushchev's visit to the U.S., President Eisenhower was scheduled to make a return gesture to Moscow. Prior to his trip, he yielded to mounting missile gap rhetoric from Democrat presidential hopefuls and the usual compliant media and ordered what was to be a fateful U-2 surveillance flight over the suspected Soviet missile test site at Tyuratam. Gary Powers took off from a base in Pakistan; he was shot down in the vicinity of Sverdlovsk and was taken prisoner. The U-2 event doomed the planned summit meeting between the two leaders and as some lamented, re-energized the Cold War. We will discuss Powers' flight and several other reconnaissance incidents in detail later in the journal.

Eisenhower, while fiscally disciplined and deeply committed to keeping the country economically viable and militarily strong, also relied heavily upon his intelligence advisors regarding real versus implied Soviet strategic and defensive capabilities. He directed the creation of the National Reconnaissance Office to coordinate the collection and data reduction of all intelligence gathered by aircraft and satellites. The U-2 flights, along with numerous other collection platforms, continued to the end of the Cold War and trouble spots around the world until this day. He approved the development of a massive CIA headquarters to provide the agency with the facilities and security to accomplish their work. He established the Joint Strategic Target Planning Staff at Omaha and under the direction of the JCS coordinated strategic nuclear planning and execution of forces in time of war. Additionally, to his credit, when Eisenhower left office the country was not in a shooting war; he had created the most ambitious national highway system in history and had placed the country on a strong economic path, including a viable national defense posture.

"JFK"

John F. Kennedy began campaigning for the presidency in 1958, two years before the election. His platform focused on the Eisenhower Administration's lack of attention to the Soviet threat—"weak on defense, military spending and the missile gap." Senators Kennedy and Johnson admonished the President for failing to recognize that the country's "most pressing technological problem...is the missile lag..." which was "certain to grow for the next five years." The unusual strategy for a Democrat won Kennedy the nomination and the presidency over Vice President Richard Nixon who had touted a "secret plan," without specifics, for peace with the Soviets. Kennedy chose his arch rival for the office, Lyndon Johnson, as his vice presidential running mate.

Nikita Khrushchev fueled the U.S. debate over strategic balance and claims of Soviet dominance in an interview in Izvestia on May 5, 1959, in which he was quoted: "Certain American generals and admirals...allege that the Soviet Union has few intercontinental rockets....But this, after all, is what the American military men assert. It should be said, however, that it is always better to count the money in your own pocket than that in the other fellow's. I might say, incidentally, that we have enough rockets for America, too, should war be unleashed against us." The U.S. actually never fell behind in strategic capability at any time during the Eisenhower Administration; to the contrary it stayed well ahead in total strategic systems.

The youngest elected president entered the White House as Eisenhower, the oldest at the time, departed. The "New Frontier" replaced the New Look. The youthful John F. Kennedy, as Eisenhower had been before him, was quickly dubbed by the media with a responsive nickname, "JFK." He represented a new and younger generation to:" Take charge of America and address our enemies face to face."

Kennedy followed his predecessor by also choosing a Secretary of Defense from the automobile industry, Robert McNamara, president and CEO of Ford Motor Company, and a Republican. Dean Rusk, a career State and Defense Department official became Secretary of State. The President began an early shift in Soviet deterrence strategy, moving from the Eisenhower "all-out" strategic response force of bombers, ICBM and SLBM "massive retaliation" to a "flexible and balanced" response force. The RAND Corporation-inspired "flexible response" theory suffered through several incarnations as McNamara sought to work it into other RAND-produced doctrines:

"counterforce" and "countervalue". It became painfully obvious within days of the new Administration that the traditional Pentagon planners under the new Secretary of Defense and the RAND "whiz kids" began suffering acutely from a familiar Washington syndrome, "paralysis via analysis". McNamara added further confusion to the Pentagon planning mix, by calling for an immediate build-up of the Navy, Marine Corps and Army to address tactical contingencies and limited wars. He believed in spite of the afore-alleged missile gap, that strategic deterrence or retaliation was not a high priority.

For other reasons not entirely clear, Kennedy entered the office placing his immediate attention on two international fronts, Cuba and Southeast Asia. Three months after his inauguration, he succumbed to the advice of his White House staff and the Pentagon, and installed the "whiz kids" to rescue Cuba from Castro's communist takeover. Eisenhower had considered the same move shortly after Castro's guerilla takeover of the country but rejected the temptation. Without as much as consulting his National Security Council, the President directed his inner office and the CIA to coordinate an invasion of Cuba utilizing a loosely organized band of Cuban-American civilians and military refugees left over from the Batista regime. The Bay of Pigs assault was a disaster from the very beginning of the ill-thought-out brain storm. Over half of the 2,500 ragtag Cuban rescuers were killed when they stormed the beach; the remainder were captured and imprisoned by Castro's army. Kennedy would eventually pay $53 million to Castro for the release of the remaining imprisoned invaders. An uncoordinated air strike by surplus B-26 bombers operating out of Nicaragua also ended in disaster when they were shot down. U.S. Ambassador to the UN, Adlai Stevenson, reported to the Security Counsel that the United States—"had no part in the Bay of Pigs invasion."

The miscue embarrassed the President but did not deter his zeal to pursue his second quest, Southeast Asia. Accepting the blame for the ill-fated Cuban invasion, he promptly ordered the CIA to launch an aggressive guerilla operation in Vietnam. Consistent with McNamara's military tactical buildup plans, he concurrently directed the dispatch of four hundred Army Green Berets to South Vietnam where there was a—"gathering storm of a communist takeover." Within two months there were 1,200 American soldiers on the ground in South Vietnam. In a rare criticism of his predecessor, former President Eisenhower cautioned the Administration on getting "bogged down" in Southeast Asia as did retired General Douglas McArthur. By the end of 1961 there were over 7,000 U.S. military in the area and the escalation continued as we will see.

When Kennedy came into office, the missile gap controversy continued to persist, especially with the media. After all, some reported that he had used it convincingly in his campaign. James Baer, Editor of Military Affairs, greeted the new president with an article on February 13, 1961, with—"the Soviet Union has a three to one advantage over the United States in ICBM's" and questioned whether the U.S. had enough bombers to avoid a "deterrence gap." Secretary McNamara earlier in the same month, however, had let slip in an off-the-record discussion with members of the press that likely there was no missile gap after all. The New York Times leaked McNamara's remark with a front page article entitled: "Kennedy Defense Study Finds No Evidence Of A Missile Gap." The White House reacted immediately by denying the story, but a cascade of unraveling truths began. Shortly after Kennedy's inauguration, the House Policy Committee had also released a report to the Times which printed excerpts in two issues on January 25th and February 9, 1961, that provided comparative combined strategic missile and bomber capabilities of 648 U.S. systems versus 235 for the Soviets. One must wonder why the Eisenhower Administration or Nixon in his campaign did not make the same argument.

By November of 1961, McNamara, touting the requirement for U.S. tactical military forces in Southeast Asia, attempted to quell the strategic forces issue by telling the media, "I believe we have nuclear power several times that of the Soviet Union." Quoting the Secretary, Newsweek Magazine in the November 13, 1961, issue went on to ask: "Was there ever a 'Missile Gap' or just an Intelligence Gap?" Perhaps further, was there a "credibility gap?"

With the missile gap issue more or less dying and the monkey shifted, the Administration moved on to conduct drastic cutbacks in strategic defense appropriations. McNamara and his Pentagon analysts outlined a four-part basic mission force structure for the Military Services, but they were also careful to prioritize the objectives for public consumption as follows: "Strategic Retaliatory Forces, Continental Defense Forces, General Purposes Forces and Airlift and Sealift Forces." The Strategic Retaliatory Forces were to include the present number of B-47, B-52 and B-58 strategic bombers, the KC-135 airborne tankers, the Atlas, Titan and Minuteman ICBM's, the Army's Jupiter IRBM and the Navy's Polaris SLBM's. The revised force structure also initiated a cut-back in strategic systems. The first to go was the B-70 supersonic heavy bomber development program and a $525 million outlay for production of 45 new B-52's. The B-58 medium bomber production line was suspended. General Curtis LeMay, by then Chief of Staff of the Air Force, went public with his criticism of the Administration's drastic cut-backs particularly and said, "In view of the four-years of rhetoric about the missile gap."

Kennedy supported McNamara in cutting back on the production of the Minuteman and Polaris ballistic missiles, but he elected not to take on the Service Chiefs or the "vociferous strategic lobby" in Congress which supported LeMay. One writer characterized the missile gap era as, "The years of high theory" and an attack by "defense intellectuals." McNamara stood by his "whiz kids", most of whom he had recruited from RAND Corporation and key universities such as Harvard, Princeton and Yale. The defense intellectuals had begun their movement outside Washington during the Eisenhower Administration and easily captured the attention of the media and other intellectuals in the Departments of Defense and State when they came into their own in the Kennedy Administration.

Khrushchev, having won the final power struggle over Malenkov, had begun a campaign of teasing the new president soon after the U.S. elections. Employing a carrot and stick strategy, he first congratulated Kennedy on his promise of "peaceful intentions toward the Soviet Union." Following a cordial meeting with him in Vienna in June 1961, he returned to Moscow and ordered the building of a permanent wall separating the eastern and western sectors of Berlin. The Berlin Wall quickly evolved into a physical barrier, more than 300 yards wide and extending across the entire city of Berlin and into the countryside. The various detectors in the no-cross zone followed the traditional pattern of Soviet treachery; plowed ground, barbed-wire, electrified fencing, land mines and tethered dogs, along with East German sharp-shooters manning watch towers. The flow of immigrants fleeing East Germany had become a large embarrassment to the Soviet leader. Hence, in crude but effective style, he sent a strong message to the German people captured within in the Soviet sector and to the West. The Soviets moved 300,000 Red Army troops into East Germany to fortify the migration flow. The provocative moves shocked Kennedy and the Western Allies, but fearing what Khrushchev might be capable of doing next, protested only mildly.

Next, the Soviets renewed open-air nuclear testing despite a prior agreement with the Eisenhower Administration. In August 1961, they detonated an unprecedented thirty plus atmospheric weapons tests, the largest ever at the conclusion which measured an estimated 58 megatons. Kennedy, hoping for the best, delayed renewing U.S. testing for eight months.

The Soviet leader, enjoying his success with a seemingly supple administration in Washington and with confidence following the earlier Bay of Pigs debacle, moved on to the next step with Cuba. His attempt to introduce tactical fighter-bombers and offensive ballistic missiles into Caribbean Island, however, brought an abrupt and shocking response from the American President that startled the Soviet Premier. Within hours of the detection of ships bearing ballistic missiles and U-2 reconnaissance observations of missile launch site and aircraft runway preparations, Kennedy ordered a quarantine of all Soviet shipping into Cuban ports. Shortly after issuing a stern personal warning to Soviet Foreign Minister Andrei Gromyko and the subsequent shooting down of a U.S. U-2 reconnaissance plane over Cuba, he placed U.S. military forces into a DEFCON-2, the highest state of readiness to go to war since the Cold War began. As an operational part of DEFCON-2, Strategic Air Command implemented its airborne alert plan, sending some sixty B-52 heavy bombers into the air, fully loaded with nuclear weapons.

The bombers remained in airborne orbits near the Soviet borders, recycling around the clock until the Soviets recanted. The crisis brought the United States and the Soviet Union to the closest brink of open warfare during the Cold War period. The clarity and boldness of President Kennedy's actions toward the Soviets during the Cuban crisis was the toughest stance by any world leader since World War II. The President was also careful not to close the door throughout the crisis, allowing his counter-part both an opportunity to withdraw and to save face with his people. Public communication and awareness was near non-existent among the Soviet people, but the Free World and Castro knew.

Cold War tensions lowered after the Cuban Crises. The Soviet leadership had tested the United States once too often and failed. Kennedy exhorted his staff not to gloat publicly over the Soviet retreat and lauded Khrushchev publicly in a television broadcast, for his "statesman-like decision...an important and constructive contribution to peace." The President initiated a series of conciliatory message exchanges with Khrushchev. Both parties agreed to install a "Hot Line" between the Kremlin and Washington should further 'misunderstandings' arise. Teletype communication systems were chosen to allow both sides more time to review and properly develop well-thought-out responses. By the summer of 1963, the exchanges had reached the point of negotiating a nuclear test ban treaty prohibiting atmospheric testing. The treaty was ratified in September of that year. France and China were invited to join in the agreement but refused.

The clarity and boldness of President Kennedy's actions toward the Soviets during the Cuban crisis was the toughest stance by any world leader since World War II and redeemed his potential legacy. General Maxwell Taylor, Chairman of the Joint Chiefs of Staff, had bolstered the President's confidence during the crisis by sending a brief assessment to McNamara: "We have the strategic advantage in our general war capabilities; we have the tactical advantage of our moral rightness, of boldness, of strength, of initiative, and of control of this situation. This is no time to run scared." The President had also been careful not to close the door throughout the crisis, allowing his counter-part both an opportunity to withdraw and to save face with his people.

On November 22, 1963, while visiting Dallas, Texas, President Kennedy was assassinated, becoming the fourth such tragedy to befall a U.S. president while in office. Lyndon B. Johnson, sworn in hours after the assassination, became the 35th president of the United States.

"LBJ"

Lyndon B. Johnson's entering theme to the American people was "let us continue." As vice president and an avowed anti-communist, Johnson had attempted to involve himself deeper into the Cold War issues and more directly with the Soviets, but he was distracted considerably by Kennedy's Southeast Asia strategy. When he became president himself, his strong southern leanings led him to find more comfort in addressing domestic and social problems. He succeeded Kennedy at a time when there was a lull in global conflicts—the Cuban missile crisis had been resolved safely, the nuclear test ban seemed to be working and the United States continued to enjoy a decisive balance of power with the Soviets. Only the Vietnam situation loomed over his inherited legacy. The investigation into the assassination of John Kennedy and the subsequent Warren Commission, for the most part, pre-occupied the news.

Johnson kept virtually all of the Kennedy Administration cabinet and staff. He reasoned that his earlier bid for the presidency himself was lost because of the skill of the Kennedy team. As a result, the Kennedy followers continued to concentrate on Southeast Asia and Vietnam in particular. McNamara had continued to feed the increasing requirement for military forces to thwart the ever-defiant North Vietnamese Army and the Viet Cong. In contrast to addressing the war in Vietnam, Johnson began his own social actions agenda, civil rights and the Great Society. Eventually the three would clash over the priorities for funding the government. Also competing for attention, time and funding was the space program which Kennedy had deeded to Johnson early on to "put a man on the moon" by the end of the decade. Even though support for the war by McNamara's Defense Department led the way in requirements for funding, NASA successfully landed a lunar module and Neil Armstrong on the moon on July 20, 1969. Meanwhile, Vietnam escalation continued and by 1968 was absorbing over 10% of the GDP.

The President decreed that the country could succeed with all the programs on his agenda. He pressed the Allies for more support and troops to help out in Vietnam, but most responded with only token military forces. Meanwhile, China continued to send aid and eventually an estimated 400,000 troops to North Vietnam over the period of the war while the Soviet Union used the opportunity to test vital anti-aircraft missile systems, fighter aircraft and tanks. The Washington strategy for fighting a "controlled and limited" war against North Vietnam provided virtual immunity to both the Chinese and the Soviet troops in the North. U.S. military commanders lived a life of frustration, their hands tied by Johnson and McNamara, preventing them from pursuing the enemy beyond the 17th Parallel while the North Vietnamese and the Viet Cong infiltrated the South at will. Neither the White House nor the Secretary of Defense consulted the Joint Chiefs on war strategy; they dealt directly with General Westmoreland in Saigon. This caused a great strain on overall military relationships within Washington and with commanders in Southeast Asia. By 1965, U.S. military troops numbering 185,000 had been sent into the war zone. The military draft had been reinstituted with quotas being increased monthly. By 1968 there were upwards to 600,000 military forces, Army, Navy, Marines and Air Force on duty in Southeast Asia with casualties averaging 5,000 each year. Westmoreland believed in a strategy of attrition to wear-down the enemy, throwing massive numbers of ground troops against the opposing enemy only to lose more casualties as the North Vietnamese and Viet Cong, more often than not, vaporized into the dense jungles. Air strikes by the Air Force and the Navy were equally unproductive with a "selective target" stratagem that limited effectiveness against important North Vietnamese installations, particularly, the harbors and re-supply ships in and around Hanoi and Haiphong.

Doris Kearns Goodwin in her book, Lyndon Johnson And The American Dream, described Johnson's dilemma in his words: "I knew from the start that I was bound to be crucified either way I moved. If I left the woman I really loved, the Great Society, in order to get involved with that bitch of a war on the other side of the world then I would lose everything at home. But, if I left that war and let the communists take over South Vietnam, then I would be seen as a coward and my nation would be seen as an appeaser."

In attempting to accomplish both, Johnson had concealed the price of the war in Vietnam as long as he could. In the end, inflation, raising taxes to combat the rising costs of Vietnam, domestic programs coupled with losing the war on the battlefield and trying to stabilize the Cold War, brought him down. The majority of his administration, finishing out Kennedy's term and his own election in 1964, would deal with his personal quest for civil rights until the steady escalation and failures in Vietnam policies forced him to not seek reelection in 1968.

RICHARD NIXON

Richard M. Nixon made a successful second run for the presidency in 1968 following Johnson's decision not to run for reelection. Vietnam had become too much. Nixon, as had Eisenhower, entered the White House with the legacy of an on-going war. He believed that his forte' was foreign relations and set an early goal to deal with Vietnam and normalize relations with China. If he was successful with the latter, he thought, it might be a first step toward driving a wedge between the two bastions of communism and fundamentally shift the pattern of the Cold War. Meanwhile, he had inherited the dark cloud of Vietnam hanging heavily over the United States. As soon as he assumed the presidency in January 1969, he made the Vietnam War one of his top priorities and to end it as quickly as possible on terms favorable to his administration. By mid-1969, he and his national security adviser, Henry Kissinger, had come to favor a strategy that combined international diplomacy with threats and acts of force to induce the Democratic Republic of Vietnam (DRV) to bend to their will. Considering different approaches, they settled upon issuing dire warnings to leaders in both Hanoi and Moscow that if by November 1, 1969, North Vietnam did not agree to compromise on American terms to end the conflict, Nixon would, "take measures of great consequence and force." Further, they decided that if these threats failed to move Moscow to persuade Hanoi to compromise, then a second phase of the military escalation option would begin. This would include a dramatic multifaceted campaign against the DRV consisting mainly of heavy air attacks in the far north of Vietnam and mining operations on coastal ports.

Kissinger and his staff went to work developing a secret and highly sensitive contingency military plan codenamed "Duck Hook". Concurrently, he established a special NSC committee dubbed the "September Group" to evaluate the secret plans prepared by members of the Joint Staff in Washington and the military planners in Saigon. "I refuse to believe that a little fourth-rate power like North Vietnam does not have a breaking point," Kissinger lamented. "It shall be the assignment of this group to examine the option of a savage, decisive blow against North Vietnam," he directed. "You start without any preconceptions at all." The president, he told them, wanted a "military plan designed for maximum impact on the enemy's military capability" in order to "force a rapid conclusion" to the war. Leaks out of the September Group alluded to the fact that nuclear weapons options might be "on the table" for consideration. Responses by staffers to a "nuclear weapons" option, however, played down the notion with the exception that a nuclear device might be considered for certain targets such as dams.

Even before Duck Hook planning was completed, Nixon began to doubt whether he could maintain public support for the three- to six-month period the operation might require. Another concern was that the three major antiwar demonstrations previously scheduled for October 15 and November 13, 1969——the period that coincidentally bracketed the launch of Duck Hook——might erode public confidence in his leadership and expand into larger demonstrations, thereby blunting the psychological impact of the operation upon Hanoi. He had also come to the conclusion that the North Vietnamese had been unmoved in the face of the military threats he had communicated to them since taking office. Further, the attempted linkage diplomacy with Moscow had thus far failed to leverage Soviet cooperation vis-à-vis North Vietnam. This prompted further doubt for Duck Hook's prospects for success.

After canceling Duck Hook, Nixon believed, "It was important that the Communists not mistake as weakness the lack of dramatic action on my part in carrying out the ultimatum." In an apparent surprise move to compensate for the aborted Duck Hook operation, he set in motion the "Joint Chiefs of Staff Readiness Test," an elaborate and secret global military exercise to be carried out between October 13 and 30, 1969, that for all intents and purpose was tantamount to a nuclear alert.

One of the largest secret military operations in ever conducted, the exercise included: the stand-down of all military training flights in order to raise operational readiness of Strategic Air Command ground alerts, heightened readiness postures for overseas aircraft units, stepped-up surveillance of Soviet ships en route to North Vietnam and a nuclear-armed B-52 "show-of-force" flight over Alaska. The purpose of the exercise was to "spur" the Soviets and North Vietnamese into making negotiating concessions; perhaps even indicating to that the increase in readiness posturing was the preparatory phase of Duck Hook. The nuclear alert exercise failed to achieve its objective of intimidating either the North Vietnamese or the Soviets.

Nixon sent National Security Advisor, Henry Kissinger, on a secret mission to Beijing in July 1971 to discuss American recognition of the Mao Tse-tung government. Staunch anti-Communists, members of Congress and many in the public were shocked when the White House revealed Kissinger's China visit and that the President himself would also meet with Mao in early 1972. The President spent eight days in China, an unprecedented lengthy visit for an official head of state. The war in Vietnam was still raging and yet he was able to walk a narrow path of mutual respect with his hosts. The strategy was shrewd; after all, the United States had entered the Vietnam fray to curb expansionism by China. The major agreements resulting from the China visit were that the U.S. would remove its military units from Taiwan, not Vietnam and continue a dialogue toward unspecified mutual interests. China, it appeared, was eager to join the new relationship; in early 1973, liaison offices were opened in Washington and Beijing, respectively.

A rift between China and the Soviet Union had previously erupted in 1963 following the Cuban Crisis which served to fuel their ideological differences in the communist world. Khrushchev had reversed Stalin's anti-west dictum and weakly argued that coexistence was necessary, contending that the threat of nuclear war was too great a risk to continue to antagonize capitalist nations. The Soviet policy shift at the time was confusing to the Chinese leaders, who asserted that fear of war should not inhibit either government from taking whatever steps necessary to defeat the forces of western imperialism. The fracture between the two communist governments had grown even more acrimonious after the Soviets capitulated in Cuba. In his last act as the Soviet leader, Khrushchev denounced China as an uncooperative ally in a speech at the December 1964 communist international conference. Six and a half years later, President Nixon would capitalize on the fortuitous situation.

In the Soviet Union, the communist leadership was apoplectic with the Nixon move toward China. They no doubt believed that they should have been the ones courted by the United States, not by China. Nixon, by now confident in his role as an 'internationalist', seized the opportunity to appease the Soviets and their new leader, Leonid Brezhnev. He flew to Moscow in May 1972, three months after the meeting with Mao, to meet personally with Brezhnev. The Soviets had carefully observed Nixon's welcome to China, and it was thought they would make every effort to out-do their communist antagonist's reception. Upon arrival, however, the initial mood of the Soviet leader was surprisingly cool, as was that of Premier Aleksey Kosygin. Nixon had ordered the B-52 bombings on Hanoi and the Port of Haiphong only a few days before he departed for the visit and the Soviets claimed to have lost four cargo ships.

The timing of the visit, nevertheless, spoke to the bravado of Richard Nixon, stridently walking into the 'jaws of the tiger'—first visiting China and then the Soviet Union at a time of perceived critical conflict when most leaders would have likely hunkered-down and waited for expected reactions, vis-à-vis. According to those accompanying the President, the Soviets also demonstrated their own style of boldness during the visit. Brezhnev, Kosygin and Nikolai Podgorny, it was alleged, cleverly separated Nixon from his aides and secret service detail into a locked room in the Kremlin. There they lectured and berated him crudely (according to Nixon later) for three hours on Vietnam and American foreign policy. Also according to his staff, once the harassment session ended, the Soviet leaders turned on the charm adjourning to an all-evening affair of dinner and heavy toasting accompanied by flowing compliments to their American guests.

[Author's note: Many would have considerable difficulty believing that the President's staff and security detail, in particular, would permit such a bizarre breach; nevertheless, the story is told.]

Nixon inherited the Vietnam yoke, cancelled Johnson's bombing embargo and redirected the war effort toward the North, giving the field commanders unlimited authorization to bomb military targets in and around Hanoi and Haiphong. Operations Linebacker I and II, and Arc Light unleashed concentrated B-52 bomber raids of magnitudes never before seen. We will discuss several of those operations later.

Concurrent with the saturation bombing missions, Nixon began to withdraw from the 543,000 plus Nixon-Johnson in-country troop levels. This was in part to attempt to quell the negative press and protests in the U.S. as well as to eventually begin bringing the long-drawn-out bloody war to some sort of ending. The troop withdrawals had a two-fold effect—neither would prove positive. First, the initiative coupled with the heavy bombing brought the North Vietnamese to a shaky negotiating table in Paris. But, the withdrawals also demonstrated just how weak and ineffective the 1.2 million "trained" South Vietnamese would become. The forces literally melted away as the American forces downsized. The bombing of the North, however, resulted in the negotiated release of some 1,500 American prisoners of war held in animal-like conditions in Hanoi. Some had been in captivity for upwards to seven years. By the time the prisoners were released and safely home; only about 25,000 American troops remained in the rapidly decaying South Vietnam. The last year of the war remained vicious with six hundred and fifty Americans killed and fifteen B-52 bombers shot down over North Vietnam. In short order, the Hanoi government took control of all of Vietnam as the last Americans evacuated. Perhaps the most devastating result of the U.S. departure from Southeast Asia was the rampage of the Khmer Rouge in Cambodia. Pol Pot, rising from the same fraternity as that of Stalin, Mao, Castro and Ho Chi Minh, and no longer fearful of American intervention, set out to 'cleanse' the region. His militia methodically murdered millions of their own people as well as left-over Chinese who had sought refuge.

Richard Nixon's China policy literally removed a chess piece from the Soviet side of the board and repositioned it on the U.S. side, or at least neutrally. The recognition of China 'cracked' the image of a monolithic communist family and exacerbated Soviet paranoia over its Southern border with China. The new relationship with the Soviet Union became known as "détente" or "razryadka," and provided for a "more orderly and restrained competition" in the nuclear arms race. For the United States it meant strategic parity and balance and stability. U.S. and Soviet negotiators had been unsuccessfully working on a Strategic Arms Limitations Talks (SALT) agreement for three years prior to the May meeting.

Once they met, Nixon and Brezhnev each signed the first draft. The SALT Interim Agreement (SALT I) and the ABM Treaty, discussed later, were by no means "end all" agreements. They did, however, set limits on the respective numbers of ICBM's and curtailed the construction of anti-ballistic missile (ABM) systems. The Soviets were permitted to actually maintain a greater number of ICBM's, with more destructive capability, while the United States retained a larger number of warheads. There was no agreement on the development of new weapons. The negotiations with the Soviets, according to the Nixon team, were at best, bizarre.

In typical Soviet style, the discussions were obsessively secretive. Russians, by historical nature, are paranoid. In these meetings, the Soviet civilians had no idea what Soviet nuclear weapons numbers were. When the U.S. participants began to openly discuss weapons capabilities, the Soviet negotiators were called aside by their senior military members and asked not to discuss weapons capabilities or numbers. In a side discussion, Kissinger was admonished for mentioning Soviet weapons figures to Andrei Gromyko, the Foreign Minister. Negotiations with Russians are more often than not, un-structured and even disorderly, usually without a firm objective. It is traditionally their nature and very disconcerting to the 'officious, orderly and ever-prepared' American.

Charles Morris summarized the climax of the Nixon Administration's strategy: "A two-year period of American diplomacy marked by rare imagination, boldness and sustained success." No doubt Nixon's visit to China concerned the Soviets and reordered their priorities regarding negotiating nuclear weapons limitations with the United States.

Further commenting on negotiating with the Soviets, Averell Harriman once assessed: "The Soviet leaders have great respect for U.S. presidents, more so than any other world leader. They look upon such meetings as great events and doing everything possible to avoid failure, risking embarrassment amid meetings until results can be favorable."

[Author's note: Serving as my corporation's senior negotiator for several joint venture agreements in the 1990s—obviously several levels below the previous Cold War Washington-Soviet talks—and engaging with numerous former Soviet high level bureaucrats, I witnessed the difficulty in coming to closure even on the most mundane of issues. Chronically paranoid and suspicious of our objectives or motives, they would frequently call a halt to discussions and huddle in secrecy for hours before returning to the table to continue the talks. Never predictable, it was not unusual for a negotiating group to agree to the terms on an issue, shake hands and then later show up for an after meeting dinner haughty, irritable and wholly inhospitable; their interpreter told me we would readdress the issue in the morning. It was equally difficult to interpret the subdued quiet that might precede one of these social dinners when the entourage arrived; neither was unusual after considerable libation that the evening turned into a jolly, back-slapping party. In the end, agreements were almost always signed with minor niggling changes and we moved on to the next bout.]

The beginning of the end of the Nixon Administration unfolded with the embarrassment of the disclosure of the misdoings by Vice President Spiro Agnew. Agnew resigned and he appointed Michigan Congressman Gerald Ford as vice president. Watergate became the final blow to Richard Nixon's presidency. Fraught with paranoia and assisted by several former CIA operatives, Nixon allegedly personally orchestrated a break-in of the Democratic National Committee election campaign headquarters in an apparent attempt to foil the candidacy of the acknowledged underdog, George McGovern. A landslide election followed in November 1972 and, subsequently, the unfolding of the Watergate caper drove the president to resign from his office.

In retrospect, the legacy of a potential great Cold War leader, who daringly opened concurrent dialogues with China on trade and the Soviet Union on arms limitations talks, brought the Vietnam War to a close and continued to sustain a mighty deterrent force, was suddenly destroyed.

GERALD FORD

President Gerald R. Ford brought Congressional savvy to the White House; he retained Henry Kissinger as Secretary of State and James Schlesinger as Secretary of Defense. Both were vital to the continuance of the requirement to address the Soviet threat, particularly in light of the visible turbulence within the U.S. Government. Schlesinger, considered by many as intellectually bright, but bumbling scientist, however was soon replaced by Ford's former vice presidential chief of staff, former congressman and Navy pilot, Donald Rumsfeld. The aggressive Rumsfeld made the case to move forward with cruise missile development, newer bombers and ships for the Navy in order to sustain the only thing the Soviets understood—massive strength and power.

Gerald Ford's "caretaker" Administration witnessed an unraveling of stability in Africa, Angola and Ethiopia in particular. Dealing with non-communist dictatorships was ever-present during the Cold War, and Ford elected to pull out of Angola leaving the country wide open for Fidel Castro and the Soviets to move in. The case was the same for Ethiopia; once the U.S. backed away, the Soviet Union continued to establish strongholds in the region. Those extensions of aid and force would eventually take their toll on the over-extended communist regime.

Ford's brief tenure as U.S. President can be attributed in great part to his pardon of Richard Nixon. In spite of the fact that he had persisted in keeping the Soviet threat and deterrence as his major goal, the pardon issue would haunt him through his loss of the 1976 election, which he had narrowly edged-out Ronald Reagan for the nomination.

JIMMY CARTER

Following Watergate and the subsequent untimely pardon of Richard Nixon by Gerald Ford, a veil of political apathy settled over most Americans. The election of James Earl Carter in 1976 recorded one of the smallest turn-outs of registered voters in history. As one reporter commented, "Neither Ford nor Carter won as many votes as Mr. Nobody." The political issues and the lackluster candidates kept the majority of voters home. Jimmy Carter came to the office of the Presidency without the depth and breadth of a Richard Nixon or Gerald Ford. He also lacked the substantive support of a Kennen, Nitze, Dulles, Kissinger or Eugene Rostow, each of whom had capably guided previous leaders through their respective Administrations on international policy, strategic issues and beyond. While Carter brought Zbigniew Brzezinski in as his National Security Advisor, and who possessed an academic background similar to Henry Kissinger, there is where the comparison ended. Even the revisionists have characterized Brzezinski's performance on critical issues as "frenetic superficiality," coupled with eccentricity.

Fortunately, Carter's penchant for "group decision-making" did not permit Brzezinski to exercise exceptional influence or to impose a mandate on U.S. policy. The result was an obvious vacuum in the Carter national security forum. Initially, Carter attempted to follow the Nixon-Ford-Kissinger policies and strategy (having no other plan to go by) toward negotiations with the Soviet Union, but his cabinet and chosen advisors being of fundamentally different persuasion, led him away from the reasonably well-established philosophy. His advisors sought a visible perception of change in dealing with the Soviets. Consequently, his administration failed to ever develop a coherent foreign policy, mainly due to the personalities involved and a failure to benefit from the experience of the previous administrations.

The Soviets seized the opportunity and further complicated the anemic Carter foreign policy by invading Afghanistan in December 1979. This provocative move left hands wringing in Washington, but would in the end, become an untimely and disastrous decision by the Kremlin. The aggressive move was clearly a 'break-out' on the part of the Soviets, entering a sovereign country for the first time since World War II. SALT II negotiations had been on-going for six years at the time of the Afghanistan invasion, and Carter and Brezhnev had signed the final draft of the treaty the previous June. The SALT II ratification already had a slim chance in the Senate, so Carter postponed submitting it indefinitely in reaction to the Soviet invasion.

Fulfilling a campaign promise, Carter canceled the B-1 bomber production program as one of his first acts in early 1977. Kennedy had done the same 16-years earlier with the B-70.

Once again, this left the U.S. Strategic Forces with only the B-52, then entering its 25th year of operation as the main bomber deterrent. The Soviets, hoping to capitalize further on a perceived "weaker" Washington to make headway in weapons negotiations, were dismayed at the postponement of the ratification of the arms treaty by the United States. The shelving of SALT II for all practical purposes also ended détente with the Soviets. Their Afghanistan venture soon bogged-down into old-style Russian trench-fighting and proved to be an obvious miscalculation.

Meanwhile, Carter, in announcing the B-1 program cancellation, also lauded Defense Secretary Harold Brown for his courage in supporting the cancellation of the B-1 bomber and announced that the United States would concentrate on a cruise missile strategy using the B-52 and submarines as launch platforms, as well as to develop a "mobile" MX ICBM concept. He argued that a cruise missile launched from the aging B-52 bomber would be more cost-effective. Several reasons were cited for canceling the B-1: (1) More than 100 cruise missiles could be built for the price of a B-1, (2) that they could be launched from either a "mother plane", a submarine or from peripheral land-based launchers, (3) a "swarm" of cruise missiles would saturate Soviet defenses, permitting manned bombers to penetrate more safely, and (4) the progress on stealth aircraft technology would quickly make the B-1 obsolete.

Other of Carter's foreign policy initiatives also caught him in the crossfire. In an attempt to bolster alliances with the Western Europeans, the Germans in particular, the United States announced the development of the "neutron bomb." The enhanced radiation weapon was, in fact, an artillery round which would be fired at approaching Warsaw Pact ground forces, killing-off ground troops and tanks without causing as much destruction as traditional bombs. The announcement served only to enrage the anti-nuclear protestors in Germany. Chancellor Helmut Schmidt was able to partially quell the situation by voicing his support of the initiative as one that signified the U.S.'s continued military support to NATO. Within weeks of Germany's commitment and NATO's acceptance of the neutron bomb concept, Carter abruptly changed his mind about the weapon. U.S. credibility in Europe reached an all-time low.

George Kennen had previously postulated correctly that the Western Europeans, although much more economically stronger than the Soviet Union, would allow the United States to carry the burden of their protection as long as possible. Carter's "flip flop" was partially mitigated by Kennen's thesis along with a previous warning by the President; the NATO Alliance would have to increase their defense spending contributions by at least 3% a year if they expected the United States to continue its level of support.

Carter had another problem with his credibility and consistency. He had vowed shortly after his inauguration that "the soul of our foreign policy" should be the defense of human rights around the world. The high-level 'moralizing' strategy did not fit well with those who saw the declaration as a detachment of national interests and others who pointed to the White House's inconsistency in applying a standard. Very similarly, his decision to relinquish control of the Panama Canal came under severe attack from all quarters. The greatest criticism cited the surrender of American authority in a strategically significant part of the world. Lastly, in his restoration of formal diplomatic relations with China which was begun earlier by Nixon, he agreed to sever diplomatic relations with the Taiwan government. This move, as with the others, was condemned by most conservatives and many Americans.

Speaking for the Soviet Union, Marshal Nikolai Orgakov, Chief of the General Staff, told his senior military leaders in June 1980: "In fact what is happening is the creation of a military alliance between the USA, China and Japan similar to the 1930's Rome - Berlin - Tokyo axis of sad memory." Orgakov was used later to berate the United States for its attempts to undermine, by any means, the influence of the Soviet Union and their Socialist Allies to gain military superiority. I have found it interesting that it was quite often more successful for the United States to manage the Soviets during the Cold War era by indirect means rather than confrontation.

The Soviets intensified saber-rattling by introducing the SS-20 MRBM: a mobile, three-warhead nuclear weapon that could strike any target in Western Europe. They had initially deployed 160 SS-20's with a total of 480 warheads in 1971 to replace their 20-year old SS-4's. With no active SALT treaty they let it be known that they would have 423 SS-20's with 1,269 warheads in place by 1985. They also maintained roughly 100 MRBM's totaling 300 warheads, directed toward China.

Meanwhile, U.S. Administration policy planners had been preoccupied with trying to determine the most suitable and reliable basing option for the proposed MX missile: a powerful, but considered light-weight ICBM, capable of carrying up to ten re-entry vehicles (RV's), or warheads. SALT II provisions had allowed both sides the option to develop "one" new ICBM to replace older systems on a one-for-one basis. Another provision permitted a new ICBM to carry up to the number of RV's with which the missile had been tested. It had been rumored that the Soviet SS-18 could conceivably carry up to 40 RV's but had not been tested with more than ten. It appeared that both the U.S. and the Soviet Union would continue to abide by the

SALT II accords in principle, even though the United States refused to ratify it.

The MX basing issue kept strategic planners in Omaha and the Washington "Beltway Bandit" contractors busy for several years attempting to satisfy White House and DOD staffers by determining the most efficient and survivable basing mode. Literally $$ millions were spent addressing truck-mobile, train-mobile, deep underground (cavern) launchers, as well as a "dense pack" shell-game mode. Finally, logic prevailed by deciding that the MX would fit fairly well into existing retro-fitted Minuteman silos since a one-for-one missile trade-out had to be made anyway. While all of the various basing concepts should have likely been considered non-starters after only preliminary reviews, the in-depth and costly analysis and planning proceeded anyway. The persistent MX basing mode exercise was a mild embarrassment to the Carter Administration, eventually drifting into Reagan's first term where the existing Minuteman silo mode was selected. Although not amusing, there were strong liberal backers of the various creative modes described earlier who encouraged the analytical efforts, knowing full-well that the end cost of any of the impractical options would cause the MX program to collapse.

The Carter Administration pressed-on with the cruise missile development attempting to address the SS-20 threat in Europe. Finally, in direct contrast to an earlier highly criticized Kissinger notion to place tactical nuclear weapons in Europe, the decision was made to deploy 108 Pershing II nuclear missiles to Germany, replacing the older Pershings. They also announced that 464 ground-launched cruise missiles (GLCM's) would be deployed when they were built. The hope behind these announcements was that the Soviets would back-down on their deployment of the SS-20's. The Soviets didn't budge, perhaps believing that something might change before actual deployment took place. Nevertheless, the Soviets had great concern for the Pershing II with its 1000 mile range, 5 to 50 kiloton variable yield and an exceptional accuracy of 30 to 50 meters. There was no question in the Soviets' minds that the Pershing represented a virtual no-notice first strike capability.

Carter's foreign policy initiatives did include some successes. His best achievement, which even the most outspoken critics applauded, was the arrangement to a peace agreement between Israel and Egypt. The Israelis agreed to vacate the Sinai and, in turn, the Egyptians agreed to recognize the legitimacy of the Israel state.

A final devastating blow to the Carter Administration came on November 4, 1979, when an organized mob stormed the American Embassy in Tehran and placed the diplomatic staff under house arrest. The revolutionaries operating with the encouragement of Ayatollah Khomeini, a Muslim religious zealot, had earlier deposed the Shah of Iran. The Khomeini regime held the fifty-three American Embassy staff members hostage and demanded the return of the Shah from exile in the United States along with all his wealth. The embassy and hostage take-over, which lasted 444 days and into the first days of the Reagan Administration, was a great embarrassment to the United States and the Carter Administration. An ill-fated rescue attempt by U.S. Special Forces during the siege further aggravated the situation. Carter lost the presidential election of 1980 to Ronald Reagan, in great part to the ineptness of an administration to deal consistently with both foreign relations and domestic economic policies.

A period of malaise began when Jimmy Carter entered the White House. The Soviets promptly sensed the change in Washington and began to ratchet up the Cold War in their favor. Vietnam and Cambodia had fallen to the communists; Mozambique, Angola and Ethiopia had fallen under Marxist control. Carter, on the other hand, went out of his way to dismiss principled anticommunism as foolish paranoia.

"We are now free of that inordinate fear of communism which once led us to embrace any dictator who joined us in that fear," he spoke in a 1977 Notre Dame Commencement address.

Instead of acting in any manner to block further expansion of communist power, he sought to appease it. He began cutting billions of dollars out of the defense budget, including the aforementioned cancellation of the B-1 bomber development and ordering the removal of defensive missiles from South Korea. He seemingly welcomed the Sandinista takeover of Nicaragua, providing the junta with $90 million in aid. He began diplomatic relations with Fidel Castro's dictatorship, unperturbed by the thousands of Cuban troops fighting with Marxist forces in Africa. As the Soviets continued vast military buildups and cultivated international terrorist networks, the Administration eliminated hundreds of positions at the CIA. In direct contrast to his predecessor Democrat presidents, Truman, Kennedy and Johnson, who became hawks after dealing with the reality of the Soviet threat, Jimmy Carter capitulated. He became a poster boy for ideological revolution in the West. He embraced the philosophy back in Plains and retains it yet today. Evil really does not exist; people are basically good; America should embrace perpetrators and castigate the victims.

RONALD REAGAN

Ronald R. Reagan followed Jimmy Carter into the White House after a landslide election capturing 44 of the 50 states. He brought with him a belief that the United States had fallen behind the Soviets in both nuclear and tactical weapons systems during the malaise of the previous Administration. Almost immediately, he embarked on a program to close the "gap" which he claimed had developed as a result of the United States complying explicitly with arms limitations agreements. Reagan attacked the arbitrary cancellation of major defense programs, the B-1 bomber in particular, and an Administration that stood by while the Soviets continued on a path of planned aggression around the world. Détente had all but collapsed during the Carter Administration.

Reagan showed little initial interest in SALT; the faltering of SALT II by Carter was a campaign issue and he could not reverse his position and become an advocate. The SS-20 deployment by the Soviets was of considerable concern, however, so the first attempt was to play hard ball by challenging them with a "zero option" policy announcement on November 18, 1981. The U.S. would not deploy the Pershing II's or GLCM's if the Soviets would deactivate their SS-20's. The Soviets totally rejected the zero option concept. The long-time U.S. arms negotiator, Paul Nitze, attempted to find a middle-ground option acceptable to the Soviets. Peace demonstrations that had begun earlier in Western Europe quieted for awhile, but with the media's 'help' it was becoming a fact that Reagan was serious about carrying-out the deployment plan for IRBM's into NATO and they returned with intensity. Soviet propagandists aligned themselves with the peace protestors to influence the public that the United States was exploiting its European Allies: "Putting potential war fighting in their backyards."

The Soviets alleged that Reagan's zero option was nothing more than a smoke screen to conceal the real intentions of the United States to "arm-up" Europe. In the U.S., the European cause was taken-up loudly by the fragmented Catholic Bishops Movement and other 'peace-nik' movements, prompting dissent and peace protests around the country: in Washington DC, SAC bases, Minuteman launch complexes and Department of Energy weapons development laboratories.

I wish to note here that the late John Cardinal O'Connor, then Rear Admiral O'Conner, Chief Chaplain of the Navy, played a key role in articulating the issue and quieting the protests among Catholics around military facilities. To the contrary, and curiously so, Peter Oppenheimer, the eldest son of Robert Oppenheimer and father of the atomic bomb, became an activist in the anti-nuclear protests at Los Alamos and Sandia Laboratories in the mid-1980's.

After almost two years in office, and seeking an alternative to SALT, which he called "fatally flawed", Reagan announced his START (Strategic Arms Reduction Talks) initiative on March 23, 1983. This new proposal advocated deep cuts in both U.S. and Soviet land-based ICBM's. He also introduced an INF (Intermediate-range Nuclear Force) Treaty initiative to the Geneva negotiations. The thesis of an INF Treaty would eliminate all land-based nuclear missiles with a range of 500 to 1,500 kilometers thereby reducing the tension in Western Europe. The Soviets would remove their SS-20's targeted against NATO, and the U.S. would not deploy the Pershing II's and GLCM's. The Soviet negotiators, Yuli Kvitsinsky and Vladimir Pavlichenko, at first completely rejected the notion.

Paul Nitze, the senior U.S. negotiator, finally got Kvitsinsky aside and struck a partial deal whereby the Soviets would remove an unspecified number of SS-20's, and the U.S. would deploy a lesser unspecified number of GLCM's and no Pershing II missiles.

President Reagan flatly denounced the agreement, calling for "all or nothing at all." While the Soviets were absorbing the nuances of START and INF, the Administration also announced the Strategic Defense Initiative (SDI), the 'Star Wars' program. The Administration appeared to be 'steam-rolling' the Soviets and none of these new initiatives soothed either them or the peace protestors. Conversely, the provocative moves, coupled with the schedule for deploying the Pershing II's and GLCM's in November 1983, only incensed the situation in Western Europe and in the Kremlin, and all but ended any further arms control talks with Moscow.

The Reagan Administration, in spite of the sporadic peace protests, felt the momentum and encouragement of the American people to pursue a much stronger defense against the Soviet threat. Congress felt the same impetus. According to David Stockman, Reagan's budget director, the Administration moved with such initial haste that the defense initiatives of the latter days of the Carter Administration's political campaign were not taken into account. Reagan had promised during his campaign that the government required at least an 8 to 9 percent real growth in defense. Stockman and Casper Weinberger, the new Secretary of Defense, agreed to a budget that would generate a 7-percent real growth in defense capability. As it turned out, Carter's lame duck budget coupled with independent initiatives in the Congress had already amounted to a 15-percent increase before Stockman and Weinberger's seven percent was added. For the Secretary of Defense to retreat from briefings already given Congress would have reflected "Carter vacillation" all over again. They stayed the course.

The results were overwhelming in favor of the hawks—an almost 50 percent increase in military spending during the first five years of the Reagan Administration. During the same period the military share of the gross national product (GNP) grew from 5.7 percent to 7.4 percent—an increase of $330 billion. Over half of the increase went for procurement and research and development, with the remainder spent on readiness. The B-1 strategic bomber program was revived with a planned production of 100 airplanes. 100 MX ICBM's were also planned for deployment, conventional bomber capabilities were improved, enhanced command, control, communications and intelligence (C3I) systems ordered and the Navy received a long overlooked share to proceed with the Trident Class submarine and the D-5 SLBM. Arms control at that point was given a low priority in the Administration.

The down side of the flush of available money came with the traditional over-pricing and fraud and waste by zealous military procurement specialists and the eager contractors always ready to take advantage of an opportunity. Consequently, the Administration was embarrassed time and time again by $500 toilet seats for airplanes, $600 coffee makers and $100 hammers. The Wall Street Journal commented: "The real crisis in defense is not defense input, but the downward spiral in defense output. What America really 'can't afford' is to keep paying more and more for defense while getting less and less of it."

The cost over-runs of the resurrected B-1, its design and redesign and the resultant poor performance in its maintenance and upkeep are a present-day example. Likewise, the MX ICBM program, initiated by Carter and came into production under Reagan, suffered similar technical problems. Too much money thrown at opportunities more often than not resulted in lesser quality of the product. On the positive side, the military services were able to drastically improve the quality of their forces. Service morale improved with the recruiting of better educated and brighter young men and women, and the retention rate jumped. Accordingly, combat readiness of the major war fighting organizations was greatly improved. However, the country continued to rely heavily upon the thirty-plus year old B-52 as its main penetrating bomber and the equally dated Minuteman missile as its main nuclear deterrent ICBM. The addition of the token number of B-1's with its electrical and avionics problems, the MX and the yet to be delivered B-2, had no effect on the outcome of the Cold War.

The Navy, on the other hand, benefited somewhat better from the defense spending spree with the introduction of the Ohio-class submarine, with improved navigation systems and SLBM accuracy's. John Lehman, Reagan's

Secretary of the Navy for six years, took advantage of the defense budget watershed and successfully sold the Congress on the 600-ship concept, a 125-ship increase, including a procurement program for the Los Angeles-class nuclear attack submarine. The Navy also gained approval of the first Nimitz-class nuclear-propelled carrier with a ninety aircraft deployment capability. This procurement alone, including aircraft, amounted to $5 billion. The budget initiatives also permitted the pursuit of the expensive SDI program. While 'Star Wars' was treated with a great deal of pessimism by many and scoffed at by influential members of the technical and scientific communities, the Soviets viewed it as an ominous and sinister weapon.

Charles Morris summed it up best: "Star Wars perhaps stands as a fitting monument and symbol of forty years of arms competition. It is huge, dangerous, ambiguous, fiercely expensive, born of uncertain and complicated intentions, some of them undoubtedly peaceable, and with a gathering technological momentum that will engulf its original motivations, whatever and however various they may have been."

It soon became apparent to the Soviets that Reagan's campaign and post-election anti-Sovietism was more than rhetoric. Brezhnev was already locked-into a no win situation in Afghanistan. The Red Army had failed to contain the rebels, and the political pacification was completely unsuccessful. Communist control in Poland was, likewise, coming apart. The Administration had imposed severe economic sanctions on Poland: suspending Polish air flights to the United States, terminating export-import bank credits, suspending imports of agricultural and dairy products and barring Polish fishing boats from U.S. waters. The Soviet Union fared little better. On December 29, 1982, Reagan suspended Aeroflot flights to the United States, severely limited cultural and scientific exchanges, and suspended licenses for the sale of high-tech products and curtailed the sale of oil and gas support equipment. The Soviet leadership had carefully observed the 1980 election campaign and truly believed that they could accept Reagan if he were elected, and simply "wait him out."

In 1982, Professor Georgi Arbatov, Director of USA and Canadian Studies, Moscow, and Chief Advisor to the Kremlin on American Affairs, wrote a lengthy article entitled, "American Policy in a Dream World." In the piece, he accused the Administration of engaging in "periods of uncontrollable political lunacy," and President Reagan as being surrounded by "a highly ideological group of people, holding what are perhaps the most right-wing views in the West today." In the latter sense he was probably right! Later in an August 30, 1986, statement recorded in the Current Digest of the Soviet Press, Arbatov attempted to agitate the Soviet leadership toward a belief that

President Reagan and the United States was directing a policy which would undoubtedly lead to a nuclear war.

Toward the end of the Nixon-Ford Administrations, a growing conflict had erupted among the Intelligence Community, but mainly between the CIA, and a new group of defense intellectuals regarding intelligence estimates of true Soviet capabilities and intentions. In contrast to the Whiz Kids and the RAND-produced thinkers of the Kennedy Administration, these were "Conservatives!" These Cold Warriors of the right consisted of Richard Pipes, a Harvard professor and Soviet expert, and the most outspoken, Edward Luttwak, Colin Gray, Fred Ikle' and Fritz Ermath, amongst others. They concerned themselves with what they believed to be basic flaws in U.S. strategic doctrine and policy. Pipes was highly critical of 'erratic' U.S. intelligence interpretations, so much so that he was appointed chairman of a group of analysts called "Team B", which CIA director George Bush created to conduct a competitive assessment between the intellectuals and the CIA ("Team A").

The Team B group, having a more public voice than the CIA, claimed several victories in their contest for analyses of Soviet capabilities and intentions. Pipes concluded that the Team B assessment was that the Soviet initiatives reflected a war fighting doctrine, "a set of strategic preferences that were in contrast with the American search for stable mutual deterrence." He further concluded that Soviet objectives were "not deterrence, but victory: not sufficiency in weapons, but superiority; not retaliation, but offensive action." If one is to believe the tough rhetoric in Soviet writings and chest-pounding speeches, this might be believable. But, if you recall George Kennen's summation, wherein he felt strongly that the Soviet's bark was much louder than his bite and would only resort to military action if they perceived that the odds were greatly in their favor. If they could win by intimidation, then they would not hesitate to move on the enemy. Afghanistan had both of these ingredients.

It appeared that the conservative defense intellectuals were not intent upon lecturing the government about Soviet intentions; these were clear enough in every word spoken or written since World War II. But, Pipes, Gray and Paul Nitze challenged the Intelligence Community's and DOD analysts' assessment that nuclear superiority translated directly into "actual power". They asserted that an "assured destruction" strategy was, in fact, not a strategy at all, but a "measurement device" for analysts. The conservative analysts also concluded that the United States did not have the nerve to engage in a nuclear war, in spite of their nuclear policies. And, that any war involving nuclear weapons on the United States would in effect be suicide, which the country could not tolerate, much less recover from such devastation. It is not surprising that Fred Ikle' and another RAND conservative, James Schlesinger, found themselves inside Republican Administrations, and Pipes and Gray continuing to provide collegial advice and consent on nuclear war-fighting strategies and options.

The Soviet Union was never prepared for a change of leadership of their own; there was never a succession plan, and no Soviet leader ever left his seat of power willingly or voluntarily. Planned retirement or being "voted-out" of office was never an option. Brezhnev might have become the first Soviet leader to electively retire. He was 75 years old, suffered from heart disease, was an acute alcoholic and had been in office 18 years, longer than any Soviet leader except Stalin. But, like his predecessors, except for Khrushchev who was unceremoniously ousted by his 'peers', he remained and he died in office on November 10, 1982. At the time of his death, there were two rivals for the Soviet leadership, Yuri Andropov, the head of the KGB and Konstantin Chernenko, thought to be Brezhnev's choice. Andropov however was endorsed for the position of General Secretary of the Communist Party. If there was a power struggle for the post, it was not apparent outside the Kremlin. Andropov had headed the KGB for 15 years and had the backing of Demitri Ustinov, the Minister of Defense, and the reliable Andrei Gromyko, Soviet Foreign Minister.

While Washington was busy evaluating and sizing-up the new Cold War leader, Andropov fell ill with kidney failure and died after only fifteen months in office. But, during his brief stint at leading the Soviet Union, Andropov, a tough disciplinarian, initiated a crackdown on worker absenteeism, corruption and alcoholism. He warned his colleagues in his first speech that discipline in every facet of Soviet life would be expected, especially from government bureaucrats. He warned: "Slogans alone won't get things moving."

When President Reagan announced the Star Wars program, Adropov was livid, stating that the initiative represented a "bid to disarm the Soviet Union in the face of nuclear threat from the United States." The new Secretary took an active part in attempting to block the deployment of the U.S. IRBM's to Western Europe, but with no success. When the U.S. began deploying the Pershing II's and GLCM's in November 1983, he responded by increasing the SS-20's on alert to 441 and placing 270 Backfire bombers on alert against NATO targets. He had even less success with settling the situation in Afghanistan, and in Poland the anti-Soviet control sentiment was literally bound within a powder keg and about to explode.

In August of 1983, the Reagan Administration, in an unusual gesture of goodwill to the ailing leader, signed a five-year grain pact committing the Soviets to buy up to 12 million metric tons of desperately needed American grain. The two governments also reopened the scientific and cultural exchange program, and opened consulates in New York and Kiev. The Soviets had obviously recognized that Reagan's popularity in the United States was continuing to gain strength and that they would undoubtedly be dealing with him for another four years after 1984.

It appeared that U.S.-Soviet relations might be ripe for substantive negotiations when Korean Airline Flight 007 was shot down by a Soviet SU-15 when it allegedly strayed over Soviet territory. This incident has been the subject of numerous written accounts, suppositions and documentaries; therefore, there is no need to pursue the details further herein. Suffice to say, however, that the blatant act by the Soviets suddenly awakened the senses of the Free World to the fact that the President's characterization of the Soviet Union as an "Evil Empire" bore some actual semblance truth. The shock and outrage were universal throughout the world. First, there was a clear reflection of the callousness of Soviet law and policy that permitted the shooting down of an airliner which drifted into sovereign airspace. And, second, the fact that the blame was placed at a very low military level, implying that Soviet command and control had become extremely eroded. Incredibly, the Soviet leader, Andropov, did not make a public comment on the incident until a 'month' later. Equally incredible, but consistent with old style Soviet conduct, the propaganda machine kicked-in attempting to lay the blame on the United States for being implicated in spy tactics and using the airliner as a decoy or even as an intelligence collector itself. During the initial days following the disaster, the Soviets offered no rescue or recovery assistance, and in the end they refused to make any restitution to the victims' families. This conduct, as we were vividly reminded, was consistent with Soviet behavior and goes back to Lenin's tenet of 'infallibility of the Party'. This might be characterized as real-time revisionism. But, importantly, it reflected the whole of communist or Soviet ideology; the State cannot admit to being in error or wrong. The entire Soviet regime is historically rooted in the question of its legitimacy of power and authority. Andropov, an "old school" communist and Leninist, immersed in the dogma, conducted himself accordingly. To his credit, however, before he died on February 9, 1984, Andropov had begun a difficult task of removing many of the older bureaucrats from influential positions and replacing them with younger and healthier politicians, many with formal education degrees. He succeeded in replacing 44 of the 300 or so deeply-rooted hard liners before he died. It was a modest but important beginning.

When Andropov died, many within the Politburo felt it was time to select a younger leader to head the Party and deal with the growing concerns with the United States, and Mikhail Gorbachev was strongly supported by several of these. But instead, the Central Committee gave the position to

Konstantin Chernenko, mainly due to his loyalty to Brezhnev, although there was evidence of a bitter disagreement within the Party ranks before the final vote. Chernenko was 72 years old when elected and not in good health. Again, as Washington and the world evaluated the unsettled Soviet situation, Chernenko died after only thirteen months in office. Much like his immediate predecessor, Chernenko had little time to make a major impact on Soviet policy or foreign relations. He did attempt to normalize relations with China by agreeing to several trade and cultural agreements, but the more substantive issues were not resolved.   China, mainly wanted an accord that would promise the Soviet withdrawal from Afghanistan, removal of North Vietnamese troops from Cambodia, and the reduction of Soviet forces along the border with China. None of these were acceptable to the Chernenko government. Chernenko died on March 10, 1985. The evidence that some important changes had occurred in selecting successors of a younger breed was revealed when in just a few hours of Chernenko's death Mikhail Gorbachev was announced as the Secretary-General.

During the first half of the eight-year Reagan Administration, three elderly and sickly leaders were in charge in the Soviet Union. And, often it was thought, especially during Brezhnev's latter days and through the brief stints of Andropov and Chernenko, that none of them were actually in command of the Soviet regime. Gorbachev was a breath of fresh air and reflected considerable relief to the United States and the Free World.

On October 12, 1985, two days after Gorbachev took over as the Soviet Union's newest leader, nuclear and space talks began in Geneva. The U.S. reiterated the Reagan "zero option" on European nuclear weapons and the Soviets remained non-specific with regard to counter-proposals, vaguely stating that any progress in negotiations would be contingent upon the U.S. constraining its SDI research program. The U.S. negotiator, Max Kampelman, stated that they had literally begged the Soviets to offer concrete counter-proposals, but they only responded in lengthy rhetoric.

Undoubtedly, the Soviets were buying time while Gorbachev was getting up to speed. The Soviets finally responded with their proposal for arms cuts in September 1985. It called for a fifty-percent reduction in IRBM's capable of "reaching the territory on the other side". That in effect, would limit only the U.S. weapons positioned in Western Europe and not the Soviet SS-20's. A bolder proposal called for a complete removal of all U.S. nuclear weapons under NATO's control, while the Soviets would retain an equal number of SS-20's to the IRBM's of the French and British. Further, the latter proposal called for a total ban on scientific research, testing and deployment of the U.S. SDI program. Their response was completely unacceptable to the Reagan Administration.

On January 15, 1986, the Soviets countered with an initiative directly from Gorbachev: "As a first step in arms reduction, the Soviet Union and the United States should agree to a 50-percent reduction of all their respective strategic systems, total elimination of Soviet and U.S. IRBM's in Europe, freeze French and British nuclear missiles at present levels, prohibit U.S. transfer of nuclear technology to NATO countries and a ban on all research and development of strategic defense weapons as a precondition to any offensive arms cuts."

The proposal contained all of the details that the United States had previously rejected. But, the Gorbachev message also included a postscript, proposing a reduction of all nuclear armament thereby "freeing all mankind from the threat of nuclear weapons world-wide." The latter statement set the stage for a new assault of Soviet propaganda which was initiated at the Twenty-seventh Party Congress during February-March 1986. The Communist Party leadership, including Gorbachev, presented the Soviet Union as a savior of all mankind through its initiatives in nuclear arms reduction proposals. The Soviet leaders called for an alliance to do away with nuclear peril and to provide for mankind's survival in a world free of violence.

The United States and NATO were condemned for their failure to join the Soviet Union in its quest for a nuclear-free world. Gorbachev began to sense a change in the west——the United States and Western Europe in particular——in view of the anti-nuclear protests and signs of a move toward 'mutual assured survival' on the part of the Reagan Administration with its potential SDI security. He sought to polish the Soviet Union's image by announcing a "new thinking", perestroika, and "reform" in the old Soviet ways.

Gorbachev, buoyed by perceived feelings of accomplishment, sent a letter to President Reagan in mid-September 1986 proposing an informal meeting during October 11 and 12 in Reykjavik, Iceland. The proposal caught the Reagan Administration by surprise, which was Gorbachev's intent. Soviets were known to seldom act on impulse, not even the more pleasant Gorbachev. The Soviet leader made it clear in his invitation that he continued to be unhappy with the attitude of the United States; therefore, the meeting could only be "informal and preparatory" in an attempt to remove the obstacles for a summit later on. President Reagan found himself suddenly at a disadvantage to the Soviet leader. After all his rhetoric denouncing Soviet intentions, he could not refuse to meet with him. Gorbachev had also appeared to have gained considerable popularity in the media in several Western countries, including the United States. This applied additional pressure to the White House to demonstrate interest in any Soviet overture to lessen tensions. The Gorbachev ploy worked. He had prepared for months for such a meeting, and then when he felt comfortable, he gave the U.S. president less than three weeks to be ready to talk. With a world audience watching and a news media ready to pounce, Reagan blinked.

On the first day of the meeting, Gorbachev laid-out three issues on which he sought U.S. agreement: First, all land-based IRBM's would be removed from Europe; second, the Soviet Union and the United States would promptly reduce their respective nuclear weapons by fifty-percent, with an ultimate goal of eliminating all nuclear ballistic missiles (according to the U.S. interpretation) or all nuclear weapons 'period' (according to the Soviet version) by the year 2000, and; third, establish a need to "strengthen" the terms of the ABM Treaty of 1972. This was made without reference or apparent reference to the U.S. SDI program. Reagan, felt comfortable with the proposals and agreed to issue a directive to the U.S. negotiators in Geneva to work-out the details. Gorbachev had achieved his 'first' objective. On the second day of the meeting the Soviets hit the "nerve" for which they had planned. With the world watching, Gorbachev demanded that the U.S. immediately stop all work associated with SDI technology. The President rejected the demand without any further discussion. The meeting took on the appearance of another Soviet charade; the unusual short notice and the first day's apparent conciliatory approach, then only to be scuttled when they made a move to go for their real goal, the SDI program.

Less than a hour after the meeting broke up, Gorbachev gave an obviously well-thought-out and upbeat press conference in which he denounced the United States' sincerity for world peace. There was later speculation that Gorbachev had not wanted to follow this line of reasoning with the United States, but he was pressured into it by the hard liners who felt that the Soviet image was suffering unfairly at the hands of Western propagandist. The Soviets returned to Moscow and continued to take advantage of the perceived failed Reykjavik conference and played the Reagan rhetoric of warmongering back to the United States. They also continued to work the anti-nuclear protest movement card, using the peace groups to carry-out their anti-U.S. nuclear challenges. The Kremlin gave complete support in a Moscow Peace Forum during February 14-16, 1987. Their theme was: "For a Nuclear Free World, for the Survival of Humanity".

The forum brought anti-nuclear ideological and religious, as well as political, radicals from all over the world. Gorbachev addressed the forum, calling the movement "new thinking" in the Soviet Union and "fresh impetus" in the struggle against nuclear weapons. The Soviets brought Andrei Sakharov, the former nuclear weapons genius turned pacifist, out of imposed exile to participate in the forum. Their sudden turn to embrace an anti-nuclear weapons and peace-movement stance puzzled many but succeeded convincingly so that the Soviets had finally come to their senses, and that the United States was the real war-minded culprit.

President Reagan clearly understood the importance of strategic deterrence and held great respect for the men and women serving in uniform during the Cold War struggle. So much so, during the critical negotiations with Gorbachev and the Soviets, he took time out to honor and laud the SAC combat crews on October 9, 1987 on the 30th Anniversary of alert force operations:

"In October 1957, air crews of Strategic Air Command went on alert for the first time. From that historic day forward, SAC's demonstrated readiness has been a cornerstone of peace and security for the free world. Today, strategic deterrence is still the foundation on which rest the peace of the world and the protection of freedom.

"We look with pride on SAC's 30-year alert history. The men and women of SAC mastered the growing challenge presented by the intercontinental ballistic missile, burgeoning technology, and by an expanding Soviet threat. You who serve in SAC today share with your predecessors a noble tradition of dedication to the unrelenting demands of constant watchfulness, instantaneous readiness, and unyielding professionalism.

"On this, the 30th anniversary of SAC's first alert, I extend to every member of the Strategic Air Command family the appreciation of a grateful nation along with my personal congratulations on a job well done."

[Author's note: My B-36 combat crew went on alert on that first noteworthy day of October 1, 1957 and this acknowledgement and tribute to SAC combat crew members by the President of the United States on the 30th anniversary speaks volumes to the young men and women then and those of us who look back at the "glory days" of Strategic Air Command and those who honorably served.]

In the end, importantly, neither Reagan nor Gorbachev gave up on the prospects of substantive arms reductions. Gorbachev was immediately recognized as being by far the most reasonable and progressive leader in Soviet history. This feeling endured with President Reagan, in spite of his conduct at the Reykjavik meeting. After persistent negotiations by both sides in Geneva, Reagan and Gorbachev signed an accord on the INF Treaty in Washington on December 8, 1987. Under the terms, the United States would withdraw 859 nuclear weapons from Europe, including the Pershing II's and GLCM's, and the Soviets would withdraw 1752 nuclear weapons, including the SS-20's and the Backfire bombers off NATO targets. During these cautious negotiations President Reagan did not concede, surrender or diminish any of the day to day strategic deterrence posture of the United States.

When the accord was finally signed, President Reagan stated: "We can only hope that this history-making agreement will not be an end in itself, but the beginning of a working relationship that will enable us to tackle the other urgent issues before us."

Gorbachev responded: "We can be proud of planting this sapling, which may one day grow into a mighty tree of peace ... May December 8, 1987, become a date that will be inscribed in the history books."

Ronald Reagan had succeeded, albeit with the coincidental help of the Soviet system itself in their selecting a leader who recognized the fait accompli of the rapidly degrading situation. This coupled with the unwavering dedication by a U.S. president who sensed the environment and seized the opportunity to peacefully begin the process of dismantling the Evil Empire. The underpinning of the Lenin inspired "tried and worn-out" contrivances began to simply unravel. And, the Soviet machine, after seventy years was finally running out of gas. Their combined struggles between the revolution of 1917 and World War II, and the subsequent Cold War years, brought on solely by themselves, began to take its final toll. They had historically suffered economically as a result of inept bureaucratic processes. Their chosen measures had consistently fostered an inability to sustain any semblance of a quality of life for their people while attempting to maintain an over-abundant military force and arsenal. Likewise, the Soviet system had literally sucked their satellite states dry. The larders, both within mother Russia and its post-war 'captives,' were empty. Mikhail Gorbachev had become the first formally educated Soviet leader who had actually graduated from a university. To his credit, he had no choice but to attempt to initially try the traditional Soviet "party line" approach in solving their growing problems; after all, he was a communist also.

Stalin's theory of predicted collapse of the western nations, the United States in particular, was based on the false perception that capitalism would destroy itself through post-war economic depression following demobilization and a loss of impetus by a weaker people. Conversely, the surge of post-war Soviet Union intentions only served to give 'impetus' to the United States and its Allies to confront the threat. The Truman containment policy coupled with the Marshall Plan proved to be the enduring under-pinning for U.S. and western strategy throughout the Cold War.

If there were a major criticism of the strategy of the United States along the way, it would lie in the all too often inclination of Americans to tilt toward the tendency to believe we could 'make others [the Soviets] think as we think'. The Cold War did not end abruptly or in a peace treaty; the principle perpetrator could simply not engage further.

Chris Adams

At the beginning of the end, two astute leaders came to closure: "Why not set a goal...privately, just between the two of us...to find a practical way to solve critical issues." Ronald Reagan, letter to M. Gorbachev, November 28, 1985.

"I also have the feeling now that we can set aside our differences and get down to the heart of the matter...we can set a specific agenda for discussing... how to straighten-out Soviet-American relations." Mikhail Gorbachev, Response to Ronald Reagan December 24, 1985.

GEORGE H.W. BUSH

George Herbert Walker Bush had been selected by Ronald Reagan to be his running mate in the 1980 presidential election. While Bush's political persuasions were more to the center than those of the ultra-conservative Reagan, he appeared to be the ideal balance to the Republican ticket. There were, however, numerous Reagan insiders who did not agree and would have preferred someone else on the ticket. Bush came to Administration as the most experienced of any vice president or president in the history of the United States. He had served as a Member of the House of Representatives, Ambassador to the United Nations, Ambassador to China and Director of the CIA. George Bush served President Reagan loyally through his two terms in the White House.

During Mikhail Gorbachev's first visit to the United States in December 1987, Vice President Bush had an opportunity to visit privately with the Soviet leader. George Bush had previously established a reputation as a conciliator and problem solver both at the UN and at the CIA, and he was eager to ply his skills with the peace-seeking Gorbachev. The Soviet leader had come to Washington to sign the intermediate-range ballistic missile treaty with the President during which time Bush went to the Soviet embassy to have breakfast with Gorbachev. In typical Soviet manner, Bush was kept waiting for two hours before he was brought in to breakfast with the Secretary. Later, Bush escorted Gorbachev to Andrews Air Force Base for his departure and during the ride he reportedly told the Soviet leader that he was going to campaign hard for the presidency which he expected to win. And, if he won, he wanted to begin in earnest to end the Cold War situation between the two governments. He also told Gorbachev that during the forthcoming campaign there would be tough anti-Soviet rhetoric by all those involved in the political event, including himself. Therefore, the Soviet leader should not take seriously what he might have to say publicly in order to make the case for his election.

George Bush campaigned strongly with anti-Soviet rhetoric aimed at continuing the Reagan pressure on to bring the Soviet Union down and the Cold War to an end. And dutifully it was said; Gorbachev assured his Soviet advisors that Bush could be trusted, that his rhetoric was the "American way" of politics. After the election, Gorbachev again visited the United States for meetings with President Reagan. At a final luncheon on Governors Island, after he had addressed the United Nations, Gorbachev publicly admonished

George Bush: "I know what people are telling you now...that you've won the election, you've got to go slow, you've got to be careful, you've got to review, that you can't trust us, that we're doing all this for show. You'll see soon enough that I'm not doing this for show and I'm not doing this to undermine you or surprise you or take advantage of you. I'm engaged in real politics. I'm doing this because I need to. I'm doing this because there's a revolution taking place in my country. I started it. And they all applauded me when I started it in 1986, and now they don't like it so much. But it's going to be a revolution nonetheless....Don't misread me, Mr. Vice President."

Bush listened intently but was not persuaded to fully embrace the Soviet leader's backhanded invitation to move into a quick and trusting relationship with the former enemy. He took strong council from James Baker, his trusted friend, Chief of Staff to President Reagan and his intended Secretary of State, along with retired Air Force Lt. General Brent Scowcroft, who was to become his National Security Advisor. Both cautioned that former new presidents, namely Kennedy and Carter, had been lulled into quick acceptance of Soviet overtures only to be taken-in. Scowcroft, who had served in the White House under both Nixon and Ford, knew the Soviets well and referred to Gorbachev as a "clever bear", requiring special skill in evaluating his apparent "un-frightening and reassuring" demeanor.

"The Soviet should always be judged by his capabilities rather than his intentions," Scowcroft cautioned. Henry Kissinger reentered the political scene. He met secretly with the president-elect along with Baker and Scowcroft, offering his opinion that Bush was the first president who really had it within his reach to end the Cold War if he went about it carefully. Kissinger mapped-out a plan suggesting that Bush offer a secret proposal to Gorbachev promising that if the Soviets would not forcibly interfere with the ongoing reforms and departures of Eastern European countries from the Soviet Bloc, the United States in turn would not exploit the situation politically or economically. Kissinger characterized the Soviet Union as being in a state of economic and political chaos with even the senior military leadership in a questionable status. Scowcroft had maintained a close relationship with Kissinger since their earlier days on the National Security Staff and respected his judgment greatly. Kissinger volunteered to act as Bush's emissary and to deliver a personal letter from the President-elect to Gorbachev——which he did. Bush's message included most of Kissinger's major points in addressing the rapidly deteriorating union of communist bloc countries, and it also emphasized that "a balance of power" would be maintained between the superpowers no matter the outcome of the loss of Soviet interests in Eastern Europe.

Gorbachev met with Kissinger, even though the messenger had no formal portfolio; his reputation was well-founded with the Soviet leader. According to reports that were later revealed, Gorbachev was pleased with George Bush's initiative. He subsequently appointed Anatoli Dobrynin, who had served as Soviet ambassador to the United States for 23 years, as his personal agent to interact with Kissinger. He also requested that for security purposes all correspondence between the two leaders should be back channel and private. In the U.S., the new president urged caution and secrecy within his own staff for fear that ultra conservatives might react unfavorably toward his moving too hastily forward with initiatives to close the differences between the United States and its forty-five year enemy.

Outwardly, the Bush Administration's party line remained one of tough anti-totalitarian rhetoric. In his inaugural address, the President made the significant point that, "The day of the dictator is over. The totalitarian era is passing, its old ideas blown away like leaves from an ancient, lifeless tree."

Meanwhile, Bush's closest staff members continued to warn that the Soviets still required watching; Gorbachev was still a communist as were his predecessors, and they had duped the West more than once with peaceful overtures. Shortly after his inauguration, and on the occasion of the deadly earthquake in Armenia, the President made a phone call to Gorbachev to express his sympathy for the dead and injured. He reassured him that the intent in the Kissinger delivered letter was valid and that now he was ready to move out swiftly to solidify relations with the Soviet Union. The plight of the Soviet regime was becoming increasingly unmanageable. Their social and economic problems continued to plague every corner of the government and the republics. The old-line communists still had a grip on the most basic of governing and issues, and it appeared that they intended to hold on until the very end. But it was evident that the final days of the Cold War were numbered.

In summary, a common thread unique among each of the nine Cold War presidents was their prior military service. President Truman served as an Army infantry officer in World War I. General of the Army Dwight Eisenhower, of course, completed an exemplary career known to all. President Kennedy was a U.S. Navy hero during World War II. Lyndon Johnson also served in the Navy in World War II, as did Richard Nixon and Gerald Ford. President Carter was a graduate of the U.S. Naval Academy and served on active duty. President Ronald Reagan served in the Army Air Corps and his successor, George H.W. Bush, a naval aviator, was shot down in the Pacific during World War II.

U.S. leaders from Truman to George H. W. Bush, although not always apparent, sustained an exceptional and unusual degree of continuity in addressing the Soviet threat. Containment remained a central objective. The United States and the Allies varied little from practicing restraint in Korea and drawing a line at the 38th Parallel, finally settling on a truce. In Vietnam, they held forth below the North Vietnamese demarcation line, but then in a move questioned to this day, conceded the whole country when victory might have been in hand. The same restraint persisted in Desert Storm; George Bush held back from pursuing Saddam Hussein's forces into Iraq. To a similar degree, the same restraint philosophy persists among many today in the ongoing war against terrorism in Iraq and Afghanistan. As opposed to earlier U.S. engagements, invading entities since World War II, by and large, remain intact today. This, in spite of the fact that they have been soundly driven back to the brink of defeat and unconditional surrender, could undoubtedly have been secured. Defeated enemies have been allowed to retain their sovereignty, even though different presidents and political persuasions were at the helm.

Cold War weapons development policy also remained reasonably consistent throughout each administration in spite of election year rhetoric; each succeeding president exerted personal influence over defense budgets and deterrent weapons development strategy. Jimmy Carter canceled the B-1 strategic bomber program and alternatively initiated the development of the cruise missile to be employed with the B-52 as a standoff weapon to saturate Soviet defenses. Four years later, Ronald Reagan, as a first act of his presidency, revived the B-1 program but at the same time retained the cruise missile concept. The cruise missile strategy proved to be one of the major breaking points for the Soviet Union; they simply could not spend enough on defenses to deny the potential massive numbers of penetrating air, sea and ground-launched missiles.   Differing challenges and circumstances influenced by political persuasions always tend to color interpretations by critics and historians alike. Even in the most celebrated responses from Korea, Vietnam and Cuba, the policy objectives toward communism and the Soviet Union remained relatively consistent: cease encroachment and preserve the status quo. Only two U.S. presidents took unmistakable measures to significantly alter the balance of power and stabilization with the Soviet Union.

Richard Nixon's China policy literally removed a chess piece from the Soviet side of the board and repositioned it on the U.S. side, or at least neutrally. The recognition of China cracked the image of a monolithic communist family and exacerbated Soviet paranoia over its Southern border with China. Ronald Reagan brokered the thirty-five year containment policy and the more moderate détente strategy by pursuing strong intimidating warnings to the Soviets. He backed up the warnings with committed defense spending programs, the B-1 bomber and cruise missiles which the Soviets could not possibly economically match. Reagan further challenged them by directing the development of the SDI concept, which even though considerably perceptional, dealt a serious blow to their ICBM attack strategy.

The real issues of the Cold War did not only concern the number, accuracy or destructive power of each side's nuclear weapons, but equally with the character, demeanor and attitudes of the principal political and military leaders. It was not just the strategic nuclear capabilities that determined the course and ultimate end to the Cold War, but the serious intentions and actions of the leaders who controlled the weapons. The national culture of the Soviet Union worked heavily to the advantage of the United States in the Cold War. The oligarchic system of the Soviet Union sought to take advantage of weak and indefensible people, but they feared U.S. strength and were always reluctant to take risks where they might lose possessions or pride. There was a post-World War II view that the Soviets had a master plan not unlike Hitler for world conquest, and every move they made was according to a timetable. Communist ideology, although altered and modified continuously, followed a steady course of domination through evolution. They always demonstrated a willingness to restrain their actions if dangers or obstacles were detected, consistently maintaining a pathological preoccupation with their security: they were always willing to take "two steps forward, and one back".

In the end, I would argue that relatively consistent articulated policies by the United States to stem communism and the Soviet tide, backed by a demonstrated commitment to execute every force necessary in retaliation to aggression, stalemated the Soviet political and military visions of world conquest.

FIVE

THE COMMANDERS

"It is the spirit of the men who follow and of the man who leads that gains the victory."

General George S. Patton

Every war produces commanders whose reputation and influence is long felt by succeeding military generations. General George Patton was such a leader. There were many other exemplary military commanders, including several out of World War II, who stepped forward during the Cold War. None were more committed than those who led the strategic nuclear forces during the period. Any such discussion, however, would necessarily begin with a special tribute to two particular Cold War commanders whose long shadows stretched far behind them and projected their military strategies equally into the future during that critical period of our history battling against conventional thought, they overcame almost insurmountable obstacles, constraints and political challenges to plan and build the greatest capabilities in history to both deter and fight a war. The extraordinary visions, perceptions and achievements of General Curtis E. LeMay of SAC and Admiral Hyman G. Rickover, the father of naval nuclear submarine warfare, set the example for strategic military leaders who followed.

Herein, we are principally discussing Strategic Air Command's role in the Cold War, but also acknowledging and honoring the critically important presence and contributions of the third leg of the TRIAD, the strategic nuclear submarine forces of the United States Navy; created in the main and developed by Admiral Hyman Rickover.

Space precludes recognizing all of the truly great commanders during the Cold War—from those who led the squadrons, wings, air divisions and numbered air forces to the thousands of skilled staff specialists. In this segment we will briefly profile the Commanders-in-Chief of Strategic Air Command: the thirteen truly outstanding men who were specially chosen to step forward to command the largest, most capable and disciplined military force in history. Notably, many of those who began their careers in SAC as aircraft and missile combat crew members later became the commanders of squadrons, wings, air divisions, numbered air forces, general officers within the Command and CINCSAC themselves. These brief sketches of the extraordinary men who led SAC during the critical Cold War years are not complete biographical stories but rather brief composites of those few who rose to stand tall among all the rest.

GENERAL GEORGE C. KENNEY COMMANDING GENERAL, STRATEGIC AIR COMMAND 1946-1948

Strategic Air Command (SAC) was established on March 21, 1946, with the remnants of the U.S. Army Strategic Air Forces of World War II. General George C. Kenney was named as the first commander. The following year the Air Force became a separate Military Service.

General Kenney was born in Yarmouth, Nova Scotia, Canada, grew up in Brookline, Massachusetts, and graduated from the Massachusetts Institute of Technology. In June 1917, he enlisted as a cadet in the U.S. Army Signal Corps Aviation Section and was instructed to fly by the noted aviator, Bert Acosta. As a lieutenant assigned to the 91st Aero Squadron during World War I, Kenney flew 75 combat missions and shot down two German aircraft. Stories persist that one of the two German pilots he shot down was Hermann Göring, later the head of the Luftwaffe in World War II. After World War I, he remained for a time with the Allied occupation forces in Germany, promoted to Captain and appointed commander of the 91st Aero Squadron.

In his words as he took on the awesome task of building a truly world-wide strategic air arm:

"The business of building SAC up to where it could be termed a striking force was a tough one. Money was short and Congress was in one of its economy moods. As more B-29s came out of mothballs, it was impossible to get personnel assigned to the new groups I was activating, so we robbed all USAF headquarters, including our own to get the bodies to fly and maintain the aircraft."

General Kenney attended Command and General Staff College and the Army War College and later participated in surveying airfield sites in Puerto Rico and the U.S. Virgin Islands; Ramey Air Force Base, Puerto Rico, was among the SAC bases he helped create. Active in aeronautical research and development, he pioneered the use of machine guns mounted in the wings of Army Air Corps pursuit planes.

In 1939, Lieutenant Colonel Kenney was appointed commander of the Air Corps Experimental Division and Engineering School at Wright Field, Ohio. A year later he went to France as U.S. Assistant Military Attaché for Air to observe Allied air operations during the early stages of World War II. He was promoted to brigadier general in 1941 and appointed commander of the Fourth Air Force, the early air defense command based in California.

Promoted to major general in August 1942, he took command of both the Allied Air Forces in the South West Pacific Area and the newly-formed Fifth Air Force, becoming the senior Allied Air Force officer under General Douglas MacArthur. Before departing for his new assignment, the naturally intellectual Kenney gathered as much data as he could about the Pacific air war. He also got Air Force Chief of Staff, General "Hap" Arnold, to assign 50 P-38s with 50 pilots from Fourth Air Force to his new command in the Pacific. General Kenney made sure that one of his former protégé's, Richard Ira Bong, the aggressive young lieutenant who had once looped the Golden Gate, would be assigned to him. Bong later became the leading U.S. fighter ace of World War II.

With headquarters in Brisbane, Australia, Kenney jointly commanded American, Royal Australian Air Force, British Royal Air Force and Dutch air units. Arriving in the Pacific, he found himself in a virtually forgotten theater of war. Europe had priority for most of the new aircraft and personnel. MacArthur's forces were expected to fight a holding action to protect Australia from the advancing Japanese. General MacArthur authorized Kenney to employ every available aerial asset that could be put to good use. He went through his command with a fine-tooth comb, weeding out officers who were not "operators" and sending them home to be replaced by men who were. He reassigned his aide, Major William "Bill" Benn, to command B-17 Flying Fortress squadron, where Benn began teaching his pilots the new skip-bombing techniques he and General Kenney had worked out during the trip over from the States. One of the most successful air operations under Kenney's direction was the destruction of a major Japanese reinforcement fleet during the Battle of the Bismarck Sea in 1943. The loss of this huge armada, loaded with supplies and troops, ended Japanese control of New Guinea.

Promoted to Lieutenant General in 1944, Kenney was appointed commander of the Far East Air Force, which included the Fifth, Thirteenth and Seventh Air Forces. Very popular among his men, General Kenney recalled in one of his books written after he retired: "Bill Benn came over for a chat. He said the men down in the 43rd Group of the Fifth Air Force wanted to call themselves the 'Kens Men' and did I have any objection. I told him that I had none and to tell the gang that I felt highly honored. The next time I inspected the group they had painted out the cute, scantily clothed girls and substituted the words "Ken's Men" in block letters a foot high. I was flattered, of course, but I sort of missed the pretty gals."

A year later following his successes in the Pacific air war, he was promoted to the grade of general on March 9, 1945. In April 1946 he was appointed the first commander of the newly formed Strategic Air Command where he began pulling together the remnants of bombers and fighter escort aircraft to build up the new command.

In spite of his extraordinary successes in the Pacific during the war, General Kenney was found perhaps not to be as aggressive as desired to create a national military air strategy to address a growing militant Soviet threat, or maybe there was a strong desire in the Pentagon to make room for the up and coming and strong-minded General Curtis LeMay. In any event, the affable General Kenney served as commander of SAC for only two years. Thereafter, he moved on to command the Air University until his retirement in 1951. Following retirement he lived in Bar Harbor, Florida, where he wrote three books about the air campaigns of World War II. His masterpiece was General Kenney Reports, a personal history of the Pacific air war from 1942 to 1945. He also wrote The Saga of Pappy Gunn and Dick Bong: Ace of Aces, about the careers of two of the most prominent pilots under his command. Living out a full life, he died peacefully on March 9, 1977.

GENERAL CURTIS E. LEMAY
COMMANDING GENERAL, SAC
1948-1953
COMMANDER, SAC
1953-1955
COMMANDER IN CHIEF, SAC
1955-1957

Lieutenant General Curtis LeMay succeeded General Kenney as Commanding General of Strategic Air Command on October 19, 1948. While not its first commander, General LeMay became SAC's "father" by all other distinctions. As the story is told, LeMay roared into his headquarters at Andrews Air Force Base like a hurricane. "Let's see your war plan," he demanded. There was no war plan.

Thereafter, General LeMay initiated the "era of SAC" and the creator of U.S. strategic deterrence. He recalled in his memoirs, "There wasn't a single realistic mission being flown. Practically nothing in the way of training...My immediate job was teaching them that they were 'sorry'." He immediately called his senior staff together and announced who was staying and who was going. His first move was to appoint Brigadier Thomas Power as his deputy commander.

Of the commanding generals, commanders and later the Commanders-in-Chief, Strategic Air Command, the titles which evolved until April 1955, General LeMay would go on to serve the longest—nine years. He was responsible for SAC's dramatic growth—not only in size, but also in war-fighting capability through technological advances in aircraft and missiles. Much like Kenney, he had designed and implemented creative and effective systematic strategic bombing campaigns in the Pacific Theatre during World War II. After the war, he was appointed to head up the extraordinary and successful Berlin airlift.

Born in Columbus, Ohio, on November 15, 1906, LeMay was infatuated with flying from his earliest remembrance. He wanted very much to attend West Point, but his family had neither influence nor acquaintance with Ohio's representatives and senators. Failing to receive any responses to his letters expressing interest in an appointment, he entered Ohio State University.

He was commissioned as a second lieutenant in June 1928, having been an honor graduate of the Army Reserve Officer Training Corp (ROTC) program. Following graduation, he attended basic training with a field artillery brigade at Fort Knox, Kentucky. Determining that the field artillery was not for him, he resigned his commission at midpoint of basic training. He then applied for appointment as an officer in the Ohio National Guard, hoping to work his way into the Army Air Corps. He received the National Guard appointment, only to find that he had to resign that commission in order to enter pilot training as an aviation cadet.

Ever determined, LeMay earned his pilot wings and was commissioned for the third time in October 1929. During the next ten years, he flew fighters and bombers in various Army Air Corps units in the United States and Hawaii. In 1937, four years before the United States entered World War II; he was assigned to a B-17 bomb group and became one of the most proficient pilots and navigators in the unit. Excelling at every assignment, he received rapid promotions. In September 1942, he took the 305th Bombardment Group to England as its commander; a year later he was promoted to brigadier general. In March 1944, at age 38, he was promoted to major general and given command of an air division consisting of 266 B-17 and B-24 bombers. He personally flew with virtually every bomber crew, leading his units in all of the major bombing attacks over Germany.

In 1944, he was reassigned to the Pacific Theater as commander of the XX (20th)Bomber Command—in effect, the first "strategic air command." Equipped with the new B-29 bombers, General LeMay developed long-range bombing tactics to strike Japanese targets directly—first from airfields in China, later from the Mariana Islands. Despite the 20th's devastating heavy bombing attacks and firebomb raids, the Japanese refused to surrender. Finally, his Bomber Command was given responsibility for planning and eventually dropping the atomic bombs on Hiroshima and Nagasaki. He gained "hero" status in news articles around the country and was featured in the New York Times, Collier's, and The New Yorker. He was also featured on the August 13, 1945, cover of Time magazine. His name and reputation became synonymous with strategic bombing tactics and professional aircrews. The story was often told that when his wife, Helen, asked him why he had decided to stay in bombers, LeMay replied, "Fighters are fun, but bombers are important."

He turned 39 years old at the end of the war and was assigned to the Pentagon as Deputy Chief of Staff for Research and Development in the Army Air Corps. While postwar downsizing and ever-decreasing budgets were a constant battle, he fought successfully for development of new bomber and fighter systems. These included completion of the four-year-old B-36 project, work on the all-jet B-47 and B-52 and development of the F-80, F-84, and F-86 jet fighters. In October 1947, he was promoted to lieutenant general and assigned to command US Air Forces, Europe (USAFE). Eight months later, the Soviets blockaded Berlin and General LeMay gained renewed fame. Under his direction, C-54 cargo planes, each carrying 10 tons of cargo began supplying the city on July 1, 1948. By the fall, the airlift was bringing in an average of 5,000 tons of supplies a day. The airlift continued for 11 months with 213,000 flights delivering 1.7 million tons of food and fuel to Berlin. Faced with the failure of their blockade, the Soviet Union relented and re-opened land corridors to the West.

The Army Air Corps became a separate service on September 18, 1947. A few months later, General LeMay became commander of SAC at age 42. Being the junior among commanders of major commands did not deter independent-minded and driven LeMay. He set out to develop SAC into the most powerful military force in the history of the world. Having successfully commanded the bomber units which were greatly responsible for the defeat of Japan and the architect of the successful Berlin Airlift operation, he easily assumed the role of commanding Strategic Air Command.

Biographers attribute his toughness and hard-work ethic to his early childhood and college days. The oldest of six children in an Ohio iron worker's family, he supplemented the family income with odd jobs such as shoveling snow, delivering telegrams, tending furnaces, and managing a newspaper route. While in college, he worked in a local foundry eight to nine hours every night, six days a week. He often displayed a stony, expressionless glare which was attributed to a sinus-caused slight paralysis in his lower right jaw and lip. In his younger days he disguised the paralysis by smoking a pipe; later, his huge "trademark" cigars played that role. Someone said he wore the cigar like a cocked pistol.

Although SAC was already in being when LeMay took command, little had been accomplished to make it a combat-ready force. He found morale reasonably high but professionalism and crew proficiency low. He did not openly criticize his predecessor; rather, he praised General Kenney for keeping the command intact during a difficult military downsizing period. During Kenney's watch and SAC's first two years of operation, bomber crews had participated in atomic bomb tests in the Pacific and had begun deployment exercises to overseas bases.

LeMay's immediate concerns were for combat crew professionalism and proficiency. He had a knack for poking into every nook and cranny of an organization and an eye for "uncovering" the slightest deviations from the expected norm. This "poking" extended from the general appearance of an Air

Force Base to the quality and service of food in the mess hall, to the cleanliness of vehicles and airplanes, to the living conditions of enlisted personnel and in particular the competence and proficiency of the combat crew force. He went to the extreme in every directional sense to impress upon his staff and unit commanders that he would not tolerate anything but the best in everything—from shoe shines and trouser creases to navigation and bombing accuracy. He established goals in every facet of SAC life and personally inspected their accomplishment. When LeMay took command of SAC, its headquarters was in the process of moving from Andrews Air Force Base, Maryland, to Offutt Air Force Base, Nebraska, and into an array of 75-year-old brick buildings left over from the cavalry days of old Fort Crook. There were also a few mostly wooden structures remaining from the Martin and Boeing aircraft plant that had turned out B-26s and B-29s during the war. It was perhaps an ironic coincidence that both the Enola Gay and Bock's Car, the two B-29s that dropped the atomic weapons on Japan, had come off the assembly line at the future home of SAC. It would be over eight years before SAC Headquarters moved into the newly constructed facility, Building 500 at Offutt Air Force Base; when the move did occur, General LeMay would enjoy his new headquarters building for only a few months before he was reassigned to the Pentagon.

SAC had seen the first delivery of the B-50A and the B-36 bombers in the months before LeMay took command. He had worked hard to get both bombers developed during his Pentagon Air Staff tour. He began to make SAC an elite institution in his first year, establishing the toughest proficiency training and evaluations ever known in flying operations. He used a number of creative techniques to instill competitiveness within the combat crew force:

- Bombing and navigation competition events.
- "Spot" promotions for combat crew members who excelled and maintained the highest levels of proficiency.
- Long-range demonstration flights by SAC bombers.
- A war planning process that included aerial reconnaissance, intelligence collection and processing, Soviet target development, and nuclear weapons employment.

During LeMay's early years, SAC participated in the Korean War with its B-29's and received the first all-jet bomber, the B-47. Long-range demonstration flights were made by B-36s to the United Kingdom and North Africa. B-29 and B-50 units conducted rotational deployments to England, Japan, Guam and North Africa. Combat-ready bomber units with their supporting tankers were capable of launching strike missions against any targets anywhere. In 1954, B-36 bomb wings began to rotate to Guam for 90-day ground alert tours; their nuclear weapons loaded on board for execution if called upon. The first B-52 was delivered to SAC on June 29, 1955. In November of that year, SAC began to integrate ICBMs into its strategic war plans.

General LeMay departed SAC on June 30, 1957, to become Vice Chief of Staff and later, Chief of Staff, U.S. Air Force. As Chief of Staff, he clashed repeatedly with Secretary of Defense Robert McNamara, Air Force Secretary Eugene Zuckert and Joint Chiefs Chairman General Maxwell Taylor. At the time, budget constraints and successive nuclear war fighting strategies had left the armed forces in a state of flux. Each of the armed forces had gradually jettisoned realistic appraisals of future conflicts in favor of developing its own separate nuclear and non-nuclear capabilities. At the height of this struggle, the U.S. Army had reorganized its combat divisions to fight land wars on irradiated nuclear battlefields, developing short-range atomic cannon and mortars in order to win appropriations. The U.S. Navy in turn proposed delivering strategic nuclear weapons from super-carriers intended to sail into range of the Soviet Air Defense Forces. Of all these various schemes, only LeMay's command structure of the SAC survived complete reorganization in the changing reality of postwar conflicts. Though he lost significant appropriation battles, Skybolt ALBM and the XB-70, B-52 replacement, he was largely successful in preserving Air Force budgets. He expanded the service into satellite technology and pushed for the development of the latest electronic warfare techniques. By contrast, the U.S. Army and Navy frequently suffered budgetary cutbacks and program cancellations by Congress and Secretary McNamara.

During the Cuban Missile Crisis in 1962, LeMay, then Chief of Staff, U.S. Air Force, clashed again with President John Kennedy and Defense Secretary McNamara, arguing that the Air Force should be allowed to bomb nuclear sites in Cuba. He opposed the naval blockade and after the end of the crisis, suggested that Cuba be invaded anyway after the Russians withdrew.

A revered, but controversial leader, General LeMay retired from active duty in 1964. Many will attest that he was truly the man for the time. After his death, and in the wave of "Cold War historical revisionism," many critics have maligned General LeMay. His character, intentions, motivation, policies— even his personal appearance came under fire from several prominent writers and journalists. Their characterizations and often wholly false accounts of events were fabricated without any of them ever having met LeMay. Nor did any of these critics fully comprehend the necessity for his call to arms and his leadership in a perilous time. According to one of the most bizarre accusations, LeMay was to have made a "secret deal with another general in

New Mexico," under which the "other general would turn over control of nuclear weapons" to LeMay "if and when he called for them." Anyone ever associated with or knowledgeable of the national accountability and safeguard rules for controlling and managing nuclear weapons will quickly recognize the fraudulence of such a claim. Another myth had General LeMay secretly ordering clandestine spy plane missions over the Soviet Union early in the Cold War without White House knowledge.

There are also uncounted anecdotal stories about General LeMay and as an old "LeMay hand" once told this author with a smile, "They're all true!" The accepted fact throughout SAC was that you could believe most any story involving General LeMay, no matter how outrageous. The truth of the matter was that General LeMay is likely remembered more for things that he allegedly said and did rather than what he actually said or did. In closing with a touch of respectful humor, we will repeat just a few such stories:

Walter Boyne, in his book, Boeing B-52, relates a story about General LeMay told by George Schairer, Boeing's Chief Aerodynamicist, during the early development days of the B-52 while Boeing was also attempting to "sell" improvements to extend the life of the B-47.

Putting his arm around Schairer at a meeting at Boeing, General LeMay said, "George, whatever you are doing to improve the B-47, stop it." But that wasn't sufficient for the eager Boeing engineers; Guy Townsend, test pilot for the B-47 and B-52, traveled to Omaha to brief LeMay on an improved B-47 powered by the J-57 engine. LeMay stopped the briefing before it got started by asking: "Just how deep does a program have to be buried before you dumb sons-a-bitches at Wright Field will stop digging it up?" The selling of the enhanced B-47 stopped and the B-52 got built.

[Author's note: I witnessed a similar event in November 1980. Growing up in SAC in the "wake" of LeMay's great leadership, I didn't find myself in his presence except for a few times in his later years. On one such occasion, long after his retirement, the General was visiting SAC headquarters at the invitation of the late General Richard Ellis, who was CINCSAC at the time. Having served as his executive assistant years before, General Ellis was always very comfortable with his former boss. General Ellis invited four of us on the senior staff to meet with General LeMay in the Command Conference Room to discuss current issues. General Ellis had intended to "try out" a new bomber program initiative on General LeMay within this small group, hoping to get his nod of approval, but before we had all settled in our chairs, General Ellis was called out of the room to take an important phone call. In departing, he asked the Vice CINC, Lt. General Dick Leavitt, to give General LeMay a brief overview of a SAC proposal to radically modify the FB-111 bomber, making its capability similar to that of the B-1, which had been canceled by President Carter. When the first slide popped up on the screen, revealing an FB-111 in flight, the "fuse was lighted!" General LeMay slapped the conference table with the palm of his hand, stood up and said, "Listen, you guys, Lyndon Johnson shoved that Texas-built F-111 up my a-- once, and I'll be damned if I'll be a party to it a second time! What else do you want to talk about?" It seemed an eternity before any conversation resumed.]

General Ellis related another LeMay account not untypical of events that seemed to occur around him. He told about once while serving as General LeMay's executive officer and attending a meeting of the Joint Chiefs of Staff to review a revision of the SAC War Plan, and recalling General LeMay's reputation for "petrifying" briefing officers; Ellis said a young captain was scheduled to brief the legendary general. The captain was standing at the lectern when the "Boss" came into the room and took his seat. Several minutes elapsed while LeMay discussed various subjects with the staff around him. Meanwhile, the young briefing officer at the lectern had apparently become "locked" in fear and "frozen" in his standing position, gripping the lectern for support. When General LeMay turned suddenly to the captain and said, "Well what are **YOU** going to tell me?" The young briefer just "keeled forward," lectern and all, as he fell face-down on the carpet. The young briefer wasn't injured, but his boss had to give the briefing.

General LeMay lamented in his memoirs that commanders would almost always defend their pilots if one was involved in an accident by saying, "He was one of my best pilots." LeMay would then respond, "Don't tell me it was your best pilot that cracked up the airplane."

The late Lt. General Warren D. Johnson, former Chief of Staff, SAC, tells about an encounter he had with General LeMay at a time when Johnson was a young officer assigned to the SAC headquarters training division. SAC policy required that only officers with engineering or equivalent degrees be assigned to operate the intelligence collection hardware onboard RB-50 reconnaissance aircraft and to analyze the data collected.

"After I flew several missions on the RB-50s to observe what they were doing," he said, "I became convinced that the six 'recon' officers onboard were 'over-kill' and that well-trained enlisted personnel could accomplish the duties even better and far less expensively, and that they would enjoy much better job satisfaction. I visited the Training Command people at Keesler and they assured me that they could train a bright young enlisted man to do the job in six months. (Officers had been required to complete a one-year SAC-programmed course.) So, I went to my boss and in turn to the SAC Director of Operations, both of whom were not only reluctant to take the idea to the CINC, General LeMay, but were downright fearful of 'rocking the boat.' Finally, after a lengthy period of badgering, they both agreed to allow me to brief the general on my initiative—which they would attend, but not endorse the notion. I gave my briefing to General LeMay, who sat puffing his cigar, devoid of expression. When I finished, he said, 'Who the hell's idea was this?' Both of my bosses looked blankly at each other as I finally gulped, "General, it was my idea." General LeMay paused for a very scary moment, then growled, "Best damned idea I've heard in five years. Do it!"

Lt. General Edgar S. Harris, Jr., former Vice CINCSAC and Commander, Eighth Air Force, believed that General LeMay foresaw the impending nuclear era and the need for SAC to implement unit-level possession of nuclear weapons. The old ways, LeMay believed, would have to change dramatically. He therefore set out to bring about those changes: to convince Congress that SAC should have its own assigned nuclear weapons in an airplane, ready to go by order of the president and not before. He also knew that with the responsibility of the "care feeding of nuclear weapons", SAC would have to adhere to an impeccable standard; in other words, absolute professional accountability. In the doing of it, a number of people reputed to be LeMay's former associates, if not his friends, thought he was putting SAC under a constraint that was unreal—that it couldn't be done. Some didn't fully subscribe to LeMay's demanding regimen. The proof of the general's grit lies in the fact that he held his position regardless of friend or foe, laying the groundwork for a "no nonsense" approach to responsibility. SAC achieved extraordinary professional standards that became accepted as such and although seldom admitted, the envy of the rest of the Air Force. General Harris vividly recalls, "From that willy-nilly, harum-scarum, carefree, drink heavy, party, be-an-all around-good-guy out of the 'flyboy' World War II days, SAC became to the most professional and responsible fighting force ever assembled."

Latter day critics often traveled the last mile in their irreverent attempts to denigrate General LeMay. But even his harshest critics could not deny his greatest achievement in developing for his nation the strongest and most enduring defense posture ever known. He did not win the Cold War single-handedly, but he was one of the principal architects of the U.S. deterrence that eventually brought it to an end.

General LeMay died on October 1, 1990, and was buried in the United States Air Force Academy Cemetery at Colorado Springs, Colorado. In his memory, the former home of SAC Headquarters, Building 500, at Offutt Air Force Base where he spent but just a few months after its completion now fittingly bears the name, "General Curtis E. LeMay Building."

ADMIRAL HYMAN G. RICKOVER

An equally committed and driven Cold War commander as those of Strategic Air Command was Admiral Hyman Rickover. Admiral Rickover, every bit the controversial and as frequently impudent as General LeMay, can take his place in history as an equally bold pathfinder.

Biographers have attempted to reach into Rickover's early life and the lives of his parents, but have had little success. The admiral would seldom sit still for interviews or provide enlightenment about his background. Two different dates reflect his birth: His Naval Academy biography states that he was born on January 27, 1900; other records reflect that he was born eighteen months earlier, on August 24, 1898. By some accounts, his father immigrated to the United States in 1899; others suggest 1904. It has been concluded that Hyman Rickover was born of Jewish parents in the small village of Makow, 50 miles north of Warsaw, Poland. His father, Abraham, a tailor, found work in New York and saved enough money to bring his family to the United States. There is no clear record of exactly when Rickover, his mother and his older sister arrived in New York. It is known that the family relocated to Chicago around 1908.

Admiral Rickover attended John Marshall High School in Chicago, graduating with honors in February 1918. While attending high school, he worked as a Western Union messenger; a job that put him in frequent contact with the Chicago office of U.S. Congressman Adolph Sabath, also a Jewish immigrant. Impressed with young Hyman, Congressman Sabath awarded him an appointment to the US Naval Academy.

Never one to make many friends, Rickover remained a loner at the Academy and studied hard; earning a reputation as a "grind." Shunning extracurricular activities, he finished 106th in a class of 539. At graduation he received his diploma from Assistant Secretary of the Navy, Theodore Roosevelt. In his first assignment, Rickover served as a watch officer aboard the destroyer USS La Vallette; a year later, he was appointed engineering officer. There he found his element; running the ship's engine room. He was a "spit and polish" supervisor and a tough taskmaster. On one cruise, his engine room crew completely overhauled the ship's engines—a job that would normally be accomplished by contractors while the ship was in dry dock.

Rickover, who loved being at sea, spent 11 of his first 17 years aboard ships. Following the La Vallette, he was assigned to the battleship Nevada for two years as electrical officer. In 1927, Rickover attended postgraduate school at Annapolis. Two years later he earned a master's degree in electrical engineering from Columbia University. Thereafter he was accepted for submarine school and assigned to the submarine school.

In May 1946, following a series of assignments as engineering officer, commanding officer of a minesweeper, commander of a ship repair facility, and inspector general of the nineteenth fleet, he was assigned to the Bureau of Ships (BuShips) as liaison officer to the Manhattan Project at Oak Ridge, Tennessee.

By then a captain, Rickover had already begun to drift away from the structure of the uniformed Navy. He had also become even more of a workaholic—a tough and frugal taskmaster who forced his staff to travel on Sundays to save duty days. To save money for his departments, he would sponge from contractors or friends wherever he traveled. He and his traveling staff always stayed in the cheapest hotels available. He never wore his uniform on travel, much to the displeasure of his superiors. He was rapidly becoming a legend for both his eccentric habits and for his driving genius to get the job done. Errors and sloppy work were unacceptable. He was referred by subordinates and colleagues alike as ruthless, tyrant and worse. A "TOBR Club" developed—"tossed out by Rickover."

At Oak Ridge, Rickover immediately caught the eye of Edward Teller; an association that would greatly assist Rickover in his quest to create nuclear propulsion for ships. Although his first tutorials on nuclear power did not generate immediate enthusiasm, he eventually convinced Teller and others in the atomic community that nuclear energy for ship and submarine propulsion was the future of the US Navy. An assembly of atomic weapons scientists agreed that nuclear propulsion might be feasible, told him it would take 20 years to develop a demonstration model.

As Rickover argued for nuclear propulsion, the Air Force was winning the budget battles for developing strategic systems—the B-36 and atomic weapons delivery capability in particular. Missions to hit potential strategic targets within the Soviet Union were being given to the newly created Strategic Air Command, in large part because the Navy had no long-range delivery vehicles. Neither did the Atomic Energy Commission (AEC) believe that priority development of nuclear reactors for ship propulsion was the proper way to proceed. During the brief period between World War II and the Cold War, the AEC was busy developing atomic weapons for aircraft delivery.

Rickover was fighting everyone who questioned his nuclear propulsion concept. His efforts found a friend in Dr. Lawrence R. Hafstad, whom he had known during his earlier assignment in the Pentagon. When Hafstad was appointed head of the AEC's atomic reactor program, Rickover wasted no time in prevailing upon him to consider organizing a Naval Reactor Program.

Admiral Earle Mills, who had been impressed with Rickover while working in BuShips and who supported the nuclear propulsion concept, agreed that a naval branch should be created within AEC's Division of Reactor Development. Hafstad was convinced, and Rickover was named director of the new branch.

Rickover's assignment went largely unnoticed until seniors within the Navy and the Washington community realized that Captain Rickover had taken command of both the Navy's and AEC's nuclear propulsion activities. He could send priority requests to himself from either office, obtain instant "sign-off," and proceed on his merry way. He was never accused of abusing his positions, but he did drastically cut red tape to move the program along. He was also a genius at selling ideas to the AEC and industry while saving money for the Navy. He convinced Westinghouse that building smaller nuclear power plants for ship propulsion would be an ideal way to pursue the goal of building industrial nuclear power plants. Westinghouse also got on board Rickover's drive to divert fissionable materials from bombs to power reactors. The AEC and a number of influential members of Congress were delighted with a US industry sharing the new technology and creating revolutionary business potential.

Meanwhile, Captain Rickover continued to build his small empire. He took over Tempo-3, a group of prefabricated buildings set up on Constitution Avenue during the War to prevent overcrowding. He ripped out all carpeting and other items that reflected a cushy Washington environment and established work schedules of 14 to 16 hours a day. Money was still scarce, but Rickover managed to leach enough from the Navy and other sources to continue developing a nuclear reactor and a suitable submarine. He selected the Nautilus to receive the new propulsion engine.

Rickover consistently created serious problems for himself and his programs. He was a nonconformist, fought convention and bureaucracy at every turn, developed complete contempt for the conventional Navy and saw the military only as a source for getting his work done. He shunned the Navy uniform, finally giving it up altogether. Stories out of his office had it that he owned two suits—a gray baggy tweed that he wore to work every day and a blue one that he wore on trips and special meetings. He grew more and more frustrated with the people he had to advise on the complexities of managing military nuclear reactors and nuclear-powered propulsion systems. His reputation as a notorious taskmaster and brutal interviewer of job applicants continued to grow. Interviews were "cat and mouse" games. He threw temper tantrums, cursed at what he considered wrong answers to questions and generally intimidated officers and civilians alike. Not surprising, candidates kept coming; those who were finally selected to work on the program became Rickover disciples.

His philosophical battles were equally challenging. The atomic physicists tended to "rule" over his engineers, baffling them with the magic of the atom and the complexities of their work. Rickover could see his programs grinding to a halt with the "twenty-year" program approach preached to him earlier. He finally got the theoretical physicists together and told them, "The atomic-powered submarine is 95 percent engineering and only five percent physics." He issued the same challenge to the engineers. Program delays, bickering and "turf battles" all but disappeared.

As a Naval officer, Rickover had not endeared himself to the Navy's senior officers. He came up for promotion to rear admiral in 1951 and wasn't selected. When his records came before the promotion board in 1952, he had garnered the support of Navy Secretary Dan Kimball, AEC Chairman Henry Jackson, Congressman Mel Price and numerous others in Congress, had few supporters in the Navy.

When he was passed over for promotion the second time, which meant mandatory retirement by mid-1953, the Navy's promotion system came into question influential members in the Congress. The Senate Armed Services Committee, goaded by House members, called for inquiries. In the end, the Navy Secretary prevailed. The following year, the promotion board was presented a set of criteria for considering specially qualified engineering officers who had excelled in their duties. Rickover was selected for promotion to rear admiral in July 1953. He had also earned a label identifying him with "Congressional influence;" a designation shunned by military officers and one that would both haunt and sustain him for another 40 years.

Rickover's hard work and perseverance paid off on December 30, 1954, when the specially designed Nautilus, outfitted with the first shipboard-installed nuclear propulsion power plant, was brought up to running power. And, on January 17, 1955, the Nautilus cast off under nuclear power with Rear Admiral Rickover standing next to his handpicked commanding officer, Eugene Wilkinson. The Nautilus' power plant was considered "crude" by many in the atomic energy community, but it launched the Navy and the United States into a new era of war-fighting capability.

Two of Rickover's staunch supporters, Congressman Mel Price and AEC Chairman Clinton Anderson, immediately called on the Navy to design nuclear-powered submarines to carry missiles with nuclear warheads. Hyman Rickover successes are legend and led to the Polaris submarine and SLBM programs; followed by the largest submarine building program in history——all powered by nuclear energy. Rickover was promoted to vice admiral in 1958 and became only the third naval officer in history to be awarded the

Congressional Gold Medal. Admirals Richard Byrd and Ernest King were the other two.

In 1961, the Navy was again preparing to retire Admiral Rickover from active duty. Senior leaders arranged a ceremony on board the Nautilus to present him the nation's highest peacetime decoration, the Distinguished Service Medal. The Navy released a story to the press that Admiral Rickover would be mandatory retired on July 1, 1962. But the Navy was foiled again; Navy Secretary John Connally announced that Admiral Rickover had been asked to stay on to complete the work he had started. President Lyndon B. Johnson then initiated a series of two-year appointments to retain him on active duty. Presidents Nixon, Ford, and Carter continued the two-year appointments. The Chiefs of Naval Operations were apparently never consulted.

In 1973, a Congressional Resolution recommended to the Navy that an engineering building at the Naval Academy be named after Rickover; reluctantly, the Navy complied with the recommendation. That same year, in a joint Senate and House Resolution, Rickover was promoted to full admiral. So, the "twice passed over" captain whom the Navy wanted to retire and "move out of the way" became a four-star admiral. Admiral Rickover saw his promotions only as a means to facilitate his work. A nonconformist throughout his service, he appeared at times to go out of his way to demonstrate the same. He openly criticized the Navy's senior military leadership, including Admiral James L. Holloway, whom he had selected as a nuclear-Navy candidate early in his career and whose father had helped Rickover's own career.

When Holloway was selected as Chief of Naval Operations, Rickover pressured him to make the Navy "all nuclear." But Holloway recognized the budgetary implications and did not support Rickover's effort. When Rickover went over Holloway's head to Congress, the CNO promptly sent a signed statement to Capital Hill: "The issue is which advice should the Congress follow: the advice of the CNO, the senior uniformed official responsible for the readiness of naval forces now and in the future, or the advice of Admiral Rickover." Holloway made his point regarding "chain of command," but several congressmen made speeches chiding the Navy for conspiring to get rid of Admiral Rickover.

Holloway's predecessor, Admiral Elmo Zumwalt, had applied for the nuclear Navy as a lieutenant commander and had endured Rickover's legendary interviews. He later decided to take a different route in his career. As CNO, he had a continuous battle with the "Little Admiral." Rickover challenged Zumwalt—almost always indirectly, through his Congressional contacts—on personnel issues, shipyards, ship-building techniques and any other fault he could find. He was particularly fond of criticizing the Naval

Academy, saying he much preferred university ROTC graduates over those from Annapolis. Academy graduates were "coddled", he would comment, through their training and couldn't handle the academic challenges of the nuclear Navy.

Norman Polmar and Thomas Allen, in their biography of the admiral, cite Rickover as "The Unaccountable Man." There is ample evidence that indeed he was "unaccountable."

Operating on a near-parallel course, and with the same zeal and crude unconventionality, General Curtis LeMay was also "unaccountable." Yet, these two Cold War commanders, who made enemies quicker than friends, were the geniuses who literally forced the creation and development of the most powerful war-fighting forces in the history of the world. Admiral Rickover died in 1986 before the Cold War ended, but his legacy to deterrence will endure through the ages to come.

GENERAL THOMAS POWER
CINCSAC 1957-1964

General Thomas Sarsfield Power succeeded General LeMay as Commander-in-Chief, Strategic Air Command. Known by his colleagues as a pro-active aviator, he maintained flying proficiency in the military aircraft he flew for more than 30 years. Perhaps no one else at the time was more qualified or suited to step into the shoes left by General LeMay than Thomas Power. Tough, hard-minded and committed to the mission of SAC, he moved into the command position with ease.

General Power was born in New York City in 1905, attended Barnard Preparatory School and entered the Army Air Corps on February 17, 1928. He earned his pilot wings and was commissioned as a second lieutenant a year later. His early assignments included Chanute Field, Illinois; Langley Field, Virginia, as commanding officer of the 2d Wing Headquarters Detachment; Bolling Field, Washington, D.C., as an Army air mail pilot; Randolph Field, Texas, as a flying instructor; Maxwell Field, Alabama, to attend the Air Tactical School and as an engineering and armament officer at Nichols Field, Philippines.

During World War II, General Power first saw combat flying B-24's with the 304th Bomb Wing in North Africa and Italy. He was appointed commander of the 314th Bomb Wing in August 1944 and moved his B-29 unit to Guam as part of the 21st Bomber Command. From Guam, Colonel Power led some of the first large-scale fire bomb raids on Tokyo, Japan, on March 9, 1945.

He earned recognition as a bright aviation operations strategist by General Carl Spaatz, commanding general of the U.S. Strategic Air Forces in the Pacific, and brought him over to his staff as deputy chief of operations on August 1, 1945. He served in this position during the atomic bomb attacks on Hiroshima and Nagasaki.

After the war, he participated in Operation Crossroads, the atomic bomb tests at Bikini Atoll in 1946, as assistant deputy task force commander for air on Admiral William H. P. Blandy's staff. Thereafter, he served as deputy assistant chief of air staff for operations in Washington and air attaché in London, prior to his transfer to the Strategic Air Command as Vice Commander in Chief to General LeMay in 1948. During the next six years he assisted LeMay in building up SAC.

In 1954 he departed SAC to command the Air Research and Development Command, a position he held for three years. When General LeMay was named Vice Chief of Staff of the Air Force in 1957, General Power was the obvious choice to became Commander-in-Chief, SAC. And during the Cuban missile crisis in 1962, General Power supported his out-spoken predecessor and now Air Force Chief of Staff, General LeMay, by strongly advocating an all-out response, including nuclear weapons. General Power presided over the integration of intercontinental ballistic missiles into SAC. The first system began with Atlas, then Titan I, Titan II and three versions of Minuteman. The innovative General Power also directed the development of operations plans for "Reflex Action", the SAC program plan to deploy alert B-47 bombers to bases in Spain, the United Kingdom and Morocco. Operation Reflex brought response capability to potential Soviet moves in Europe, and that such as they had that created the Cuban Crisis.

General Power was known by his colleagues and subordinates, including SAC combat crew members, as a no-nonsense, hard-nosed often unforgiving commander and task master, much like that of his mentor, General LeMay. General Power was known to have brought an imperialistic swagger to the office of CINCSAC. Everyone knew who *He was* and where *They stood* with him. He delighted in having the SAC Elite Guard posted at the doors of the Officers Club when he attended a function there. Quite different than General LeMay, in time he generated his own legacy of stories and anecdotes that followed him during his illustrious career and thereafter. He was also a near equal in quips cutting to the core of a subject as that of his predecessor, General LeMay.

Ground alert became an enduring requirement for the SAC combat crew force under General Power on October 1, 1957. "Sputnik" provided the impetus to place at least one-third of the bomber and tanker crew force on alert, residing in facilities within seconds of running to their aircraft, the bombers fully loaded with nuclear weapons. The crews conducted training and target study while they spent up to seven days at a time away from their families. He also implemented "Operation Reflex Action": the rotation of B-47 bombers and their accompanying tankers to overseas bases where they also stood ground alert in the event the Soviets initiated an attack. When ground alert and Reflex operations began, General Power wrote a personal memo addressed to the SAC combat crew force; it read in part:

"As a member of SAC's alert force, you are contributing to an operation which is of the utmost importance to the security and welfare of this nation and its allies in the free world...As long as the Soviets know that (you are loaded with weapons and ready to take off with a moments notice) no matter what means they may employ to stop it, a sizeable percentage of SAC's strike force will be in the air for the counterattack within minutes after they have initiated aggression...It is my considered opinion that a combat ready Alert Force of adequate size is the very backbone of our deterrent posture."

In November 1957, Power announced that the latest SAC initiative would be bombers airborne around the clock. "Day and night, I have a certain percentage of my command in the air." He titillated the media by saying: "These planes are bombed up and they don't carry bows and arrows." SAC crews began testing and training "airborne alert" missions with B-52's. The nominal 25-hour missions from take off to landing included two aerial refuelings. By the time the Soviets provoked the Cuban Crisis, SAC was fully trained in airborne alert and President Kennedy promptly ordered SAC to implement the procedure. Upwards to fifty-five B-52's loaded with nuclear weapons, the combat crews with target plans took off and remained airborne until Khrushchev capitulated.

In later years, the Soviet Premier would lament in his memoirs his reaction and response to his critics for giving into the American military force: "They looked at me as though I was out of my mind or, what was worse, a traitor. The biggest tragedy, as they saw it, was not that our country might be devastated and everything lost, but that the Chinese or Albanians would accuse us of appeasement or weakness...at least the national honor of the Soviet Union was intact."

The aggressive General Power, never one to stand back, stated to a Senate committee during the time of the Cuban Crisis, "Restraint? Why are you so concerned with saving their lives? The whole idea is to kill the bastards. At the end of the war if there are two Americans and one Russian left alive, we win." And, "Putting aside all the fancy words and academic doubletalk, the basic reason for having a military is to do two jobs—to kill people and to destroy."

President Kennedy ordered the Joint Chiefs of Staff to implement DEFCON 2 on October 24, 1962 for all military forces. SAC immediately generated its entire bomber, tanker, reconnaissance, and ICBM units to full readiness condition. General Power broadcast a voice message through the world-wide unit command posts, which in part he stated:

"This is General Power speaking. I am addressing you for the purpose of reemphasizing the seriousness of the situation the nation faces. We are in an advanced state of readiness to meet any emergencies, and I feel that we are well prepared. I expect each of you to maintain strict security and use calm judgment during this tense period. Our plans are well prepared and being executed smoothly...Review your plans for further action to insure that there will be no mistakes or confusion. I expect you to cut out all nonessentials and put yourself in a maximum readiness condition. If you are not sure what you should do in any situation, and if time permits, get in touch with us here."

For those of us, including this author, working in the 72nd Bomb Wing Command Post at Ramey Air Force Base, Puerto Rico, at the time, you could hear a pin drop. It highly unusual, like virtually 'never', to hear the voice of the Commander in Chief of SAC pipe-in on the Primary Alert System. We were on the verge of world crisis and we all felt it.

I recall another particular event with General Power shortly after the Cuban Crisis when he visited those of us who had been flying B-52 airborne alert sorties out of Ramey. After giving the combat crews a *pep talk*, he asked if any of us had any questions or complaints about our mission. After a minute or so of stone silence from any of us sitting there...not daring to utter a "dumb" question or to make a complaint with our own commanders in the room, General Power boomed out, "What do we have here...a bunch of ninnies...cat got your tongues? Hard to believe everybody is so damned happy working your asses off that you can't find something wrong with this chicken outfit. Speak up!"

Finally after another several silent seconds, a good friend of mine and fellow B-52 co-pilot, Chuck Tolsma, slowly raised his six foot four-inch frame out of his chair and said, "Sir, with due respect, there's a bunch of us here flying the BUFF that came out of the B-36 with a lot of flying hours and we are still co-pilots after a couple more years. Do you think we will get our chance pretty soon?"

"What's your name, Captain?" General Power blurted and looked to his chief master sergeant who jotted down Chuck's name when he responded. "Thanks, Captain; anybody else?" he asked. No one else asked a question and the meeting was soon over. A week later Chuck received orders to Castle Air Force Base and aircraft commander upgrade school. The rest of us "chickens" patiently waited out our time.

General Power retired from the Air Force on November 30, 1964, and a year later published Design For Survival: A Crucial Message to the American People Concerning Our Nuclear Strength and Its Role in Preserving Peace. A rated command pilot and aircraft observer, during his distinguished career he was awarded the Distinguished Service Medal, Silver Star, Legion of Merit with oak leaf cluster, Distinguished Flying Cross, Bronze Star Medal, Air Medal with oak leaf cluster, Commendation Medal with oak leaf cluster and the French Croix de Guerre with Palm. He died December 6, 197

GENERAL JOHN D. RYAN
CINCSAC
1964-1967

General John "Jack" Ryan was born in Cherokee, Iowa, in 1915. Following graduation from Cherokee Junior College in 1934, he entered the United States Military Academy, graduating in 1938. He attended flying school at Randolph and Kelly fields, Texas, and received his pilot wings in 1939 and remained at Kelly Field as a flight instructor for the next two years. From January 1942 until August 1943, he was director of training at Midland Army Air Field, Texas and was instrumental in establishing an advanced bombardier training school. Next he was assigned to Second Air Force at Colorado Springs, Colorado, as operations officer. In February 1944, he was transferred to Italy and commander of the 2d Bombardment Group. During one bombing mission he lost a finger to enemy antiaircraft fire. This battle wound eventually earned him the nickname, "Three fingered Jack."

He returned to the United States in April 1945 becoming deputy air base commander, Midland Army Air Field, Texas. In September 1945, he moved on to Air Training Command at Randolph Field, Texas, where he remained until April 1946 until he assumed duties with the 58th Bombardment Wing and participated in the Bikini Atoll atomic weapons tests. From September 1946 to July 1948, he was assistant chief of staff, 58th Bombardment Wing and then Eighth Air Force director of operations. For the next three years, he commanded the 509th Bombardment Group at Walker Air Force Base, New Mexico.

Between July 1951 and June 1956, General Ryan commanded the 97th Bombardment Wing and, in turn, the 810th Air Division, both at Biggs Air Force Base, Texas. Thereafter, he became commander of the l9th Air Division at Carswell Air Force Base, Texas.

General Ryan became Director of Materiel for the Strategic Air Command in June 1956 and four years later assumed command of SAC's Sixteenth Air Force in Spain. In July 1961, he was named commander of the Second Air Force at Barksdale Air Force Base, Louisiana. In August 1963, he was assigned to the Pentagon as inspector general for the U.S. Air Force. One year later he was named Vice Commander-in-Chief, Strategic Air Command and in December 1964, became Commander-in-Chief. The opposite in demeanor of General Power, General Ryan was characterized by all who knew and served him, as humble and unassuming.

"Opposite of courtly ways of General Power, General Ryan frequently entered the Officers Club unannounced in civilian attire," someone said. "He would enjoy dinner with his wife and friends...and, even waited in line to pay the cashier or cash a check."

During his command of SAC, the Air Force decided to phase out the B-58 bomber and most of the early model B-52's. In replacement, Secretary McNamara approved the purchase of 210 FB-111's. They were hardly a replacement for either the B-58 or the early model B-52's, but SAC took them. General LeMay's expressed opinion of the FB-111 and any "creative version" thereof is mentioned earlier. General Ryan's tenure also included the retirement of the last B-47 bomber in 1966 as the Minuteman ICBM fleet began to expand to the planned 1050 missiles relieving the bomber force of many of its targets and providing prompt response and kill with its 35 minute flight time from launch to impact.

SAC entered the Vietnam War with B-52 strike missions on June 18, 1965, flying out of Anderson Air Force Base, Guam, and began dropping conventional 750 and 1000 pound bombs on Viet Cong bases. General Westmoreland was convinced that SAC B-52's could be effectively employed in the war and called for more and more sorties. By the end of 1965, SAC had flown over 100 bombing missions over South Vietnam using the B-52F. Meanwhile B-52D models were being retrofitted to expand their bomb load capacity from 27 to 184 500-pound bombs. Combat crews rotated back and forth to Guam on a six months basis. Once they returned, they again assumed their nuclear war plan ground alert responsibilities. Bomber and tanker crews became the real Cold War heroes during the period with much more expected of them than anyone outside could imagine. We will discuss that in more detail later.

In February 1967, General Ryan departed SAC to become Commander in Chief, Pacific Air Forces. He became Vice Chief, U.S. Air Force in August 1968 and finally, Chief of Staff, United States Air Force.

The much decorated General Ryan earned numerous military recognitions and awards which included: the Air Force Distinguished Service Medal with three oak leaf clusters, Army Distinguished Service Medal, Silver Star with oak leaf cluster, Legion of Merit, Distinguished Flying Cross with oak leaf cluster, Air Medal with five oak leaf clusters, Purple Heart, French Croix de Guerre with Palm, Chinese Order of the Cloud and Banner, 1st Class with Grand Cordon, and 2d Class, Republic of Korea National Security Merit First Class, the Vietnamese National Order of Vietnam/Commander and

Gallantry Cross with Palm, Grand Cross, Royal Order of Phoenix (Greece) and Grand Cross of Aeronautical Merit (Spain).

General Ryan died an untimely of a heart attack at age 67 in San Antonio, Texas, on October 27, 1983. In later years General Ryan's son, Michael E. Ryan, also rose to the grade of general and Chief of Staff of the United States Air Force.

GENERAL JOSEPH J. NAZZARO
CINCSAC
1967-1968

General Nazzaro was born in New York City in 1913. He attended high school in New York, Millard Preparatory School in Washington, D.C., and graduated from the United States Military Academy in 1936 with a commission as second lieutenant in the Infantry. After graduation from advanced flying school at Kelly Field, Texas, in October 1937, he was transferred to the U.S. Army Air Corps. General Nazzaro held assignments with the 7th Bombardment Group, Salt Lake City, Utah, the 39th Bombardment Group, Geiger Field, Washington, and commanded the 302nd Bombardment Group at Tucson, Arizona. Early in 1943, he was named commander of the 381st Bombardment Group, Pyote Air Base, near Big Springs, Texas, eventually taking the unit to England where it became a part of Eighth Air Force. In January 1944, he became deputy director of operations, U.S. Strategic Air Forces in Europe. In August 1944, he returned to the United States to become deputy commander, 316th Bombardment Wing at Colorado Springs. The 316th moved to Okinawa in December 1945, at which time he assumed command of the wing.

When Strategic Air Command was formed, he became its first Chief of the Operations Division. From there he attended the Air Command and Staff School at Maxwell Field, Alabama; following graduation he stayed on as an instructor, a position he held until December 1948 when he departed to join the War Plans Division in Headquarters, U.S. Air Force.

In August 1952, General Nazzaro took command of the 68th Bombardment Wing at Lake Charles Air Force Base. A year later he was named commander of the 38th Air Division, Hunter Air Force Base, Georgia. In June 1955, he was appointed commander of Strategic Air Command's 15th Air Division in Morocco. Returning to the United States in July 1957, he was assigned to U.S. Air Force Headquarters as Director, Personnel Planning.

In July 1959, General Nazzaro was named Deputy Commander, Fifteenth Air Force, March Air Force Base, California, and in October 1962, he became Commander, Eighth Air Force at Westover Air Force Base, Massachusetts. In December 1964, he was appointed Vice Commander in Chief, Strategic Air Command and on February 1, 1967, he became CINCSAC. As the war in Vietnam wore on, the demand grew for more and more B-52s and KC-135s. In spite of the increased deployments, Nazzaro insisted that the primary mission of nuclear deterrence would not change. He directed creative rotation of combat crews and aircraft. The job of the combat crew member was never more demanding or stressful...rotation to Guam or U-Tapao, Thailand, for three or four months then return to pull nuclear ground alert. During the chaotic period, the Command continued to maintain an amazing 40 percent of its bombers and 100 percent of its ICBMs on alert. The KC-135 crews shuffled all over the world, supporting B-52 ground alert, aerial refueling training, deployment of TAC and Navy fighters to Southeast Asia and the subsequent combat operations support.

A year and a half after taking command of SAC, General Nazzaro departed to become Commander in Chief, Pacific Air Forces at Hickam Air Force Base, Hawaii. General Nazzaro was a command pilot with numerous military decorations including the Air Force Distinguished Service Medal with oak leaf cluster, Silver Star, Legion of Merit with three oak leaf clusters, Distinguished Flying Cross and the Air Medal with oak leaf cluster. He retired from active duty on August 1, 1971 and died of cancer at age 76 on February 7, 1990, at the Tucson Medical Center.

GENERAL BRUCE K. HOLLOWAY
CINCSAC
1968-1972

General Bruce K. Holloway grew up in Knoxville, Tennessee. He studied engineering for two years at the University of Tennessee before entering the U.S. Military Academy, where he graduated in 1937. After receiving his pilot wings in 1938 at Kelly Field, Texas, he served for two years with the Sixth Pursuit Squadron and 18th Pursuit Group in Hawaii before taking a postgraduate course in aeronautical engineering at the California Institute of Technology.

Shortly after the United States entered World War II, General Holloway went to Chungking, China, to begin his combat experience as a fighter pilot with the Flying Tigers of the American Volunteer Group. Remaining with that group after it was activated as the Army Air Force's 23d Fighter Group, he became its commander before returning to the United States in 1944. During his tour in China, General Holloway became a fighter ace, shooting down 13 Japanese planes. As commander of the Air Force's first F-80 jet-equipped fighter group in 1946, the general performed pioneer service in this new field of tactical jet air operations.

After graduation from the National War College in 1951, he progressed through key staff assignments in both operations and development fields at Headquarters U.S. Air Force. Later, as director of operational requirements, he played a key role in preparing and evaluating proposals for many aircraft and missiles.

General Holloway spent four years in Tactical Air Command as deputy commander of both the 9th and 12th Air Forces, and in 1961 he was named deputy commander in chief of the U.S. Strike Command at MacDill Air Force Base, Florida. Later in that assignment, he also fulfilled additional responsibilities as deputy commander in chief of the Middle East/Southern Asia and Africa South of the Sahara Command. General Holloway assumed command of the U.S. Air Forces in Europe (USAFE) in July 1965, serving in that capacity until his appointment as Vice Chief of Staff, U.S. Air Force August 1, 1966. He was appointed Commander in Chief, Strategic Air Command on August 1, 1968. A shy and humble Tennessean, his manner belied the fact that he had been a fighter pilot and warrior who had shot down 13 Japanese aircraft with the *Flying Tigers* in World War II.

Under General Holloway, SAC's involvement in the Vietnam War escalated with more and more B-52 requirements in addition to the already heavy load on the KC-135 crew force. In addition to flying bomber missions out of Guam, U-Tapao, Thailand became both a bomber and tanker operating base with the introduction of the later model, B-52G.

General Holloway's decorations include the Army Distinguished Service Medal, Air Force Distinguished Service Medal, Silver Star, Legion of Merit, Distinguished Flying Cross, Air Medal, and foreign decorations which include the Order of the Sacred Tripod (China), Chinese Order of the Cloud, Chinese Air Force Pilot Wings, The Grand Cross of the Order of Merit of the Federal Republic of Germany with Star and Sash, German Air Force Command Pilot Wings, The Most Noble Order of the Crown of Thailand-First Class--Knight Grand Cross, Honorary Royal Thai Air Force Wings, the Order of Aeronautical Merit (Brazil), and French Legion of Honor - Order of Commander.

General Holloway retired April 30, 1972, and died September 30, 1999.

GENERAL JOHN C. MEYER
CINCSAC
1972-1974

With the retirement of General Holloway, General John Charles Meyer, a World War II flying ace, became the second fighter pilot after General Holloway to become Commander-in- Chief, Strategic Air Command and Director, Joint Strategic Target Planning Staff on May 1, 1972.

General Meyer was born in Brooklyn, New York, where he attended school. He left Dartmouth to become an Aviation Cadet in 1939. After the war he returned to graduate from Dartmouth College with a Bachelor of Arts degree in political geography. Following his commissioning in July 1940 and receiving his pilot wings, 2nd Lieutenant Meyer was assigned to flight instructor duty at Randolph Field, Texas, and Gunter Field, Florida. He was then transferred to the 33rd Pursuit Squadron of the 8th Pursuit Group at Mitchell Field, New York, to fly the P-40 fighter. During the tense days before the United States entered World War II, the Group was sent to Iceland, to fly convoy patrol missions. In September 1942, he reported to the newly formed 352nd Fighter Group at Westover, Connecticut, where he, as a 1st Lieutenant, assumed command of the 34th Pursuit Squadron that had recently returned from fighting in the Philippines in *name only* and was in need of new equipment and personnel. By the end of December that year, Meyer had acquired most of the ground personnel and had twenty six pilots assigned, but no aircraft. In January, the unit moved to New Haven, Connecticut, and began receiving the first P-47 Thunderbolt fighters which it would eventually take into combat. The 34th was re-designated as the 487th Fighter Squadron in May 1943 prior and deployed to the United Kingdom.

Captain Meyer took the 487th to its new base at Bodney in East Angelica and on into combat, scoring his first shoot-down in November while flying the P-47. By then he had been promoted to major and began leading the group in aerial victories. He continued to score against German fighters and remain the leading ace after the 352nd transitioned to the P-51 Mustang and adopted their famous "Blue Noses". By November 1944, he was deputy commander of the 352nd Fighter Group and the fourth highest scoring American ace in Europe with 24 confirmed air-to-air victories and 13 destroyed on the ground.

In December Lt. Colonel Meyer, deployed with the 352nd to a forward base in Belgium, designated "Y-29". His foresight in having the 487th squadron aircraft pre-flighted and ready to takeoff averted a major disaster on January 1, 1945, when the field was attacked by the massive German aerial assault known as Operation Bodenplatte. Meyer led his squadron on takeoff under fire and scored a kill against a strafing FW-190 even before he had retracted his landing gear earning a Distinguished Service Cross. Later, he would suffer a vehicle accident which left him with a severe leg injury and ended his combat flying at 200 missions, 462 flying hours, 24 aerial victories and an additional 13 credited to him for ground strafing.

In 1948, General Meyer was selected by the Secretary of the Air Force as the principal point of contact with the U.S. House of Representatives where he served for two years. He returned to a tactical flying unit in August 1950, assuming command of the 4th Fighter Wing at New Castle, Delaware, equipped with the F-86 Sabrejet. He took the wing to Korea where the unit flew in the First United Nations Counteroffensive and Chinese Communist Forces Spring Offensive campaigns. He shot down two MiG-15s, bringing his total of enemy aircraft destroyed in two wars (air and ground) to 39½.

Following a tour of duty as Director of Operations, Air Defense Command General Meyer attended the Air War College, graduating in June 1956 and remained as an instructor at the college. As a fighter pilot and "fish out of water", he was assigned to Strategic Air Command where he commanded two different air divisions. In July 1962, he moved to the Headquarters SAC as the deputy director of plans and SAC representative to the Joint Strategic Target Planning Staff.

In November 1963, General Meyer moved back to his fighter world as commander of Tactical Air Command's Twelfth Air Force headquartered near Waco, Texas. Twelfth Air Force provided tactical air units for joint logistic and close air support training with Army ground units stationed in the western half of the United States.

He was assigned to the Pentagon and the Joint Chiefs of Staff in February 1966 where he served first as deputy director and then vice director of the Joint Staff. In May 1967, he became the director of operations on the Joint Staff.

General Meyer was appointed Vice Chief of Staff, United States Air Force in August 1969 where he served until April 1972. On May 1, 1972, he became the seventh Commander-in-Chief of Strategic Air Command and Director of the Joint Strategic Target Planning Staff. The dual responsibility of supporting the SIOP with combat crews on nuclear alert and the continued rotation of bombers and tankers to Southeast Asia continued virtually throughout his tenure as CINCSAC. General Meyer was a tough-minded and demanding commander of the LeMay-Power *ilk*. As they say, he "took no prisoners" when it came to demanding the best from his staff, commanders and combat crews in the field.

Fighter pilot or not, he fit the SAC mold for toughness and the demand for hard work, performance and results...some may have thought to the extreme.

General Meyer's military career included a broad variety of Air Force and joint assignments. He held operational jobs in air defense interceptors, tactical fighters and strategic bombers. He had also been a key member of the Joint Staff, the Headquarters U.S. Air Force staff, and the Strategic Air Command staff. He had been called upon to command major tactical and strategic units and retired on July 1, 1974.

His military decorations included the Distinguished Service Cross with two oak leaf clusters, Distinguished Service Medal with oak leaf cluster, Silver Star with oak leaf cluster, Legion of Merit, Distinguished Flying Cross with six oak leaf clusters, Air Medal with 14 oak leaf clusters and the Croix de Guerre with palm from both France and Belgium. In March 1973 be received the Frank Hawks Memorial Award for his many contributions to aviation. He retired July 1, 1974.

General Meyer died of a heart attack on December 2, 1975.

GENERAL RUSSELL E. DOUGHERTY
CINCSAC
1974-1977

General Dougherty was born in Glasgow, Kentucky, in 1920 and passed away in 2007. He was a graduate of Western Kentucky University, the Law School of the University of Louisville and the National War College. In addition, General Dougherty held an honorary doctor of laws degree from the University of Akron, an honorary doctor of science degree from Westminster College and is an "Old Master" of Purdue University.

Following service with the Federal Bureau of Investigation, he entered active military service as an aviation cadet at the outbreak of World War II. He had previously served with the 123rd Cavalry, Kentucky National Guard. He received a commission and pilot wings in March 1943.

During World War II, General Dougherty served as an instructor pilot with the Air Force Air Training Command and later with the Third Air Force as an instructor pilot in the B-17 Flying Fortress and the B-29. Post World War II, his duties encompassed a variety of postings in air operations, maintenance, administration, policy and command duties within the Air Force, joint service and international assignments.

In 1947, he was assigned as a unit instructor with the Air Force Reserve at Standiford Field, Louisville, Kentucky, and in 1948 was transferred to the Far East Air Forces and the 19th Bombardment Wing where he served as staff judge advocate and later as assistant staff judge advocate for the 20th Air Force. In April 1950, he became the assistant staff judge advocate for Far East Air Force (FEAF) Headquarters in Japan. At the outbreak of the Korean War, he was assigned to temporary duty in intelligence with FEAF.

General Dougherty returned to the United States in 1951 and was assigned to Air Materiel Command at Wright-Patterson Air Force Base, Ohio, as Chief, Appeals and Litigation Division and assistant U.S. Air Force trial attorney for litigation arising out of Air Force procurement and contractual activities.

In December 1952, he elected to leave the Judge Advocate General's Department for assignment to the Strategic Air Command where he attended B-29 refresher training and KC-97 transition. In June 1953, he began a series of assignments in SAC as operations officer for the 303rd Air Refueling Squadron: Commander, 303d Armament and Electronics Squadron; Deputy

Chief, Operations, 303d Bombardment Wing; and Commander, 358th Bombardment Squadron, Davis-Monthan Air Force Base, Arizona. In 1957, he was assigned to Headquarters, 15th Air Force as Chief, Operations Division, where he planned the B-52 round-the-world flight, Operation Power Flite. Later he became the Deputy Director of Operations with 15th Air Force.

General Dougherty attended the National War College during 1959-60 and following graduation he was assigned duty in Headquarters, U.S. Air Force with the Office of the Deputy Director for War Plans. In April 1961, he was appointed Deputy Assistant Director of Plans for joint matters and in February 1963, became the Assistant Director for Plans for Joint and National Security Council matters.

General Dougherty served four assignments in joint and international duties. During 1964-65, he was the Deputy Director, Plans and Operations (J-3), Headquarters U.S. European Command, in Paris, France. During this assignment in November 1964, he was the United States' planner for the successful U.S./Belgian rescue operation at Stanleyville in the Congo. In August 1965 he returned to Washington as Director, European Region, Office of the Secretary of Defense (International Security Affairs). In July 1967 he returned to Europe and served until August 1969 as Director, J-5 (Plans and Policy) at Headquarters U.S. European Command, Stuttgart, Germany.

In September 1969, he was again assigned to Headquarters, U.S. Air Force where he served as Assistant Deputy Chief of Staff, Plans and Operations; in February 1970, he became Deputy Chief of Staff, Plans and Operations. In April 1971 he was appointed commander, 2d Air Force, SAC, with headquarters at Barksdale Air Force Base, Louisiana, which was the U.S. Air Force's largest numbered Air Force, consisting of the majority of SAC's B-52 bombers and KC-135 tankers. Promoted to the grade of general on May 1, 1972, he became the Chief of Staff, Supreme Headquarters Allied Powers Europe (SHAPE). On August 1, 1974, he moved to Omaha, becoming the eighth Commander in Chief, Strategic Air Command.

The Vietnam War came to a close in 1975; SAC B-52's completed eight years of operations in Vietnam, Cambodia and Laos. The B-52's along with all other air operations dropped over six megatons of conventional ordinance, or three times that dropped during all of World War II. SAC KC-135 tanker crews had flown 194,687 sorties, completing 813,878 refuelings off-loading 1.4 billion gallons of fuel.

Shortly after his inauguration, President Jimmy Carter in a much touted television appearance surprised the Air Force and SAC with his announcement of the cancellation of the much needed B-1 bomber program. The B-52's, heavily exercised in Vietnam, were growing old nearing the end of their useful lifetime. Carter reasoned that the development of cruise missiles employed with the later model B-52H were the way of the future for deterrence and more "cost effective" than developing a new bomber.

An exceptional and personal addendum to the profile of General Russell Dougherty's command leadership of SAC is provided in the following interview conducted on August 31, 1996, by *The National Security Archive,* a non-governmental, non-profit organization founded in 1985 at George Washington University by a group of journalists and scholars who sought a centralized home for formerly classified government documentation obtained under the Freedom of Information Act. The interview was intended to make a substantial contribution to the U.S. Cold War archives. The essential text of the interview follows:

Interviewer: "Sir, would you tell us who you are."

General Dougherty: "Well, I'm a retired officer now and my name is Russell Dougherty; Russell Eliot Dougherty retired General, United States Air Force. Been retired eighteen years and I'm now an attorney and I'm out here in Tyson's Corner in the suburbs of Washington practicing law."

Interviewer: "That's fine, thank you sir. Can I ask you...the first question is: As the Eisenhower presidency came to an end and Kennedy...and McNamara came in, what was the...nuclear strategy of the early Sixties, particularly as far as SAC's concerned?"

General Dougherty: "Well, to the extent that that I can properly reflect the nuclear strategy of the transition period between the Eisenhower and the Kennedy years we were transitioning from a very precise basic national security policy written, understood interdepartmental in its context into what I call a more pragmatic policy, one that had the advantage of being timely and being applied to the circumstances but had the disadvantage of not being widely understood and sometimes not even widely accepted within the Administration. So we went from a period of set pieces to a period of turbulence. Now turbulence is not necessarily bad and the strategy that the nuclear forces employed during that period of time was driven in great measure by the technology of the times and by the weapon systems available. Often times we had desires that could not be fulfilled because technology was not competent and capable. But technology was really on a roll in the period of 1961, '62. Things were beginning to happen. Things in the propulsion area, things in the guidance area, things in the range and access area because jet engines were now good and reliable and air re-fuelling was becoming a matter of course for manned bombers. It was a very dynamic changing time in the strategic sense. The submarines were coming in and all of the advantages of submarines were becoming apparent to people in the strategic world."

Interviewer: "Am I right in saying that when the Eisenhower Administration had pursued a policy that was known as 'massive retaliation' and what would that have involved?"

General Dougherty: "Well, as I understood massive retaliation during the period of the Eisenhower Administration it was to take that very small force that we had of almost inestimable strength and to use it in a coercive way to prevent something worse from happening. Whether we actually would have responded massively to minor attacks is problematical and we didn't. But we could've and it could well have been the thing that prevented something worse from happening. But massive retaliation was inconceivable to a lot of people and then of course brought about the later discussions of flexible response but massive retaliation was an attempt to do with very little something that had very big effect. And I think it worked.

Interviewer: "Excellent answer. Could you tell me, in the early 1960s, how much of the American nuclear arsenal did the Air Force control?"

General Dougherty: "It varied. The early period of 1960s, the nuclear arsenal was, I would say, 90 percent controlled by Air Force delivery units. That changed considerably as the Polaris submarine came on the scene and the Polaris missile began to use nuclear warheads. There was a shift, but there was a counteracting shift because many of the carriers that had nuclear weapons on board were getting rid of them. They were getting nuclear weapons off of the carriers and into the submarines. So I would say that the balance early on in the 1960s was probably ninety ten. Later in the Sixties it was probably seventy thirty. And, I don't know what it is today."

Interviewer: "Is that what became known as the Triad as it started to split up?"

General Dougherty: "That's right. The Triad was to try to in short, keep from putting all of our eggs in one basket; because if you had one failure in a single system, you were out of business. And if there was one thing that my seniors and I were determined not to have happen, is that our weapon systems would go down and be impotent. Because we always operated under the concept that if they really were incapable, that the Soviets would really know it. We liked to think that the strength of our deterrent force during those years was because it was real and it was never down, and the Triad gave us three cuts at it. The old phrase 'don't put all your eggs in one basket' applied. Never so vividly as you look around where we planted it American elm trees all over the United States and then had the Dutch elm disease that wiped us out. We now plant different kinds of trees."

Interviewer: "Interesting answer. How important was the B-MEWS, the early warning radar systems and I'm thinking specifically here, going back even to Pearl Harbor, was there a mentality in the Sixties that America was never going to let Pearl Harbor happen again?"

General Dougherty: "I think that's...may have been a widespread mentality. The Pearl Harbor, we must have notice, we must learn to react more rapidly. But it's always been there in the military. It's just a function of the technology of the times to make it capable. But the Ballistic Missile Early Warning System was very important to me as the combat commander for our particularly for our airborne force. I did not want to be caught on the ground. And if I could be caught on the ground and destroyed on...and I could be destroyed on the ground, then I lacked capability and I lacked credibility. And so the warning system that we had in effect was vital to the bomber force. Less important but still important to the missile force because a large-scale attack could conceivably disenable all your missiles. And very important to any force that had to get off the ground, get out of port, get to sea, get into the air. We considered it crucial, and when it was incapable, I was uncomfortable. Not that that ever happened, but I saw it...could have happened once or twice through enemy action."

Interviewer: "How important were the bombers to the (inaudible) policy? I'm curious here because Khrushchev by that time had decided that bombers were too vulnerable and they could be shot down too easily and concentrated on missiles. But America maintained quite a strong policy, particularly with B-52s. Why was that?"

General Dougherty: "We did. The bomber was an essential part of the TRIAD—still is. Its capability transcends many of the other things... its flexibility transcends. The bomber is vulnerable, but can be made less vulnerable through protective measures which we constantly upgraded through electronic shielding which we constantly...and through dispersal and through mechanisms that enabled us to detect the possibility of an attack or the effect of an attack and get the bombers airborne. Once airborne, they were fairly protected once they could get out of a blast environment. We never felt that our bomber force was incapable. We never felt that it was probably more effective than any other force when it came to delivery and it was controllable. And we used some very exotic techniques to keep it strong. I felt confident and comfortable with the bomber force. Also it was an instrumentality that was flexible that I could do something with to an extent that I couldn't with missiles. Missiles got better as the guidance system became more flexible, as computers and electronics made it possible to change targets, made it possible to rapidly shift from one weight of effort to another weight of effort. So technology was helping all the time, making bombers more credible and capable; making missiles more flexible and accurate."

Interviewer: "Excellent answer. General, can I ask you then, as the new Administrations came in the Sixties, McNamara started to change a lot of the plans that had been (inaudible). What was the Air Force's feeling of McNamara and his whiz kids?"

General Dougherty: "Well, it was a hate-love relationship I suppose. McNamara is a creature of the Air Force. Now his first assignment in the military came when he worked as an analyst for General LeMay and for other senior Air Force generals and analyzing effect of bombardment. He was very brilliant. We didn't like the way in which he rejected contrary opinions to those that he had formed. So, you know, Mr. McNamara did some very wonderful things but one of the things that we were concerned about was his inability to listen or his almost rejection of military advice in many instances. I thought General LeMay was a brilliant man with magnificent military acumen. He was rejected out of hand often times. He's not an easy man to take. He's not personable and he's not a jokester. Neither was Mr. McNamara. So they had a very tough relationship. On the other hand Mr. McNamara came in with some ideas of how he was gonna change a lot of things, many of which he abandoned early on when he came face to face with the cost. The cost of flexible response, as it was articulated by Maxwell Taylor and had been picked up by the Kennedy Administration, you know, became astronomical. And like all other Secretaries of Defense and Ministers of Defense, you must deal with the realities of fiscal policy and a lot of the things he wanted to do he couldn't do and it cost too much. It cost too much in manpower, it cost too much in money and the economy of nuclear forces, you know, really gets to a decision-maker. It got to NATO when they found the cost of trying to mount conventional defense against the huge hordes of the Soviet Army and they grasped nuclear deterrents as an economic measure, and it was economical, awesome in its potential, but economic in its impact on fiscal things. So McNamara really began to recognize that and he began to put attention and money into the vitality of the nuclear force. He did a lot of good insofar as bringing along missiles, bringing along the Polaris submarine, bringing along improvements in accuracy. He was surrounded by an analyst who pooh-poohed many of the things that were done, and he listened to him too much in my judgment. Some of my friends in the systems analysis would say 'we looked at that, it was not economical, we cancelled it. We looked at this, it was not viable, we cancelled it.' And they did that with almost knee-jerk uh wisdom. That irritated the military. But on the other hand that was the way that the world was going. Things were gravitating to the Secretary of Defense to an amazing degree and the military resented that because there was a fierce battle constantly going on and he was constantly resolving the turf battle adverse to what had been the conventional military wisdom. So it was a difficult time and the history of the times is still misunderstood from the perspective of many of us. Mr. McNamara wrote a book the other day that it was widespread but to me there is a thing in that book that indicates the problem is still there. You know, he said in that book several different times that he and the President sought the advice of the military but that advice came every time with a caveat, that this posed problems and it could conceivably cause the Soviets or the Chinese to intervene, and that he and the President had already decided that's a risk they were not going to take. They made that decision insofar as the United States is concerned, but then the United States turned around and sent fifty five thousand men over there, many involuntarily, that risked everything and lost it. And a nation that is unwilling to take risks cannot long require its young men and now its young women to take total risks. Therein is the fallacy. You can't play in that game without taking some risk and you must take some risk as a nation if you're asking your people to take some risk. And that's what we did for too long. You might get away with that for a while, but you can't get away with it forever."

Interviewer: "Thank you, General Dougherty, for this exceptional opportunity to speak with one of the truly great leaders of our time."

For those who were privileged to know and serve under this great leader will no doubt agree that the interview responses were vintage Russell Dougherty. Always looking after his troops, he was once quoted in an interview with the George Washington University newspaper: "If you're asking your military people to take risks, then the nation has to be willing to take risks, as well." He said it was a fallacy to expect young men and women to risk everything while the nation risks nothing.

The largest part of his legacy is the impact he had on people. He wasn't a fire-breathing commander, but he got the job done in a strong, quiet manner. He once gave a plaque to each member of his staff at SAC Headquarters that read: "There is nothing in your job description that requires you to be an S.O.B." General Dougherty had time for everyone...janitors, chock pullers, secretaries and especially his cherished bomber, tanker, recce and missile combat crew members. He had a very special knack for knowing and greeting officer and enlisted Airman alike by their first name. He considered every man and women assigned to SAC as his special family.

General Dougherty retired from the United States Air Force on October 1, 1977 and passed away on September 7, 2007. He was a command pilot, and during his illustrious career earned numerous military awards and decorations including, the Defense Distinguished Service Medal, Air Force Distinguished Service Medal with two oak leaf clusters, Legion of Merit with two oak leaf clusters, Bronze Star Medal and the Joint Service Commendation Medal. He is a member of the Kentucky State Bar Association and the Bar Association of the U.S. Supreme Court.

GENERAL RICHARD H. ELLIS
CINCSAC
1977-1981

General Richard H. Ellis became the ninth Commander in Chief, Strategic Air Command and Director, Joint Strategic Target Planning Staff on July 1, 1977. He would be the third CINCSAC that did not "grow up" in the Command, although he had served as Executive Officer to General LeMay after World War II. During his tenure as CINCSAC, the JCS created the Joint Strategic Connectivity Staff (JSCS) making him also director of that activity which became responsible for the analysis of strategic connectivity systems and procedures to ensure compatibility and commonality of strategic command, control and communications systems. A Navy rear Admiral was assigned as deputy director to General Ellis for the new JSCS.

General Ellis was born and grew up in Laurel, Delaware. He received his Bachelor of Arts degree in history from Dickinson College, Carlisle, Pennsylvania in 1941. He entered active military duty in September 1941 as an aviation cadet at Maxwell Field, Alabama. He received his commission and pilot wings at Turner Field, Georgia in April 1942.

During World War II, General Ellis served with the 3rd Bombardment Group in Australia, New Guinea and the Philippines, and flew more than 200 combat missions in the Western Pacific. In April 1945, he was appointed Deputy Chief of Staff, Far East Air Forces covering the Philippine Islands and Japan.

After the war he left active duty, entered the Air Force Reserves and attended Dickinson School of Law. He graduated in 1949 and was admitted to the Delaware Bar. Thereafter, he practiced law in Wilmington, Delaware. He was voluntarily recalled to active duty in October 1950 and assigned to Headquarters, Tactical Air Command, Langley Air Force Base, Virginia. From there, he moved on to deputy for operations, 49th Air Division near Sculthorpe, England, and later to Chief, Air Plans and Operations Section, Supreme Headquarters Allied Powers Europe.

From January 1956 to May 1958, General Ellis served as Deputy Chief of Staff, Operations, Headquarters, 19th Air Force, Tactical Air Command (TAC), Foster Air Force Base, Texas. From there he was assigned to the Directorate of Plans, Headquarters U.S. Air Force in the Pentagon, first as Chief, Weapons Plans Branch, then Assistant Director, Plans and later Assistant Director, of Joint Matters.

In July 1961 General Ellis became Executive to the Chief of Staff, U.S. Air Force. From there he moved to Japan in August 1963 where he commanded the 315th Air Division at Tachikawa Air Base until June 1965. Returning to Washington, D.C., he became the Deputy Director, J-5 (Plans and Policy), with the Joint Chiefs of Staff. Promoted to Lt. General in 1969, he assumed command of 9th Air Force, TAC, headquartered at Shaw Air Force Base, South Carolina.

General Ellis was appointed Vice Commander in Chief, U.S. Air Forces in Europe (USAFE) in September 1970. In April 1971, he became Commander, 6th Allied Tactical Air Force, at Izmir, Turkey. In June 1972, he became Commander of Allied Air Forces, Southern Europe with headquarters in Naples, Italy, with additional duty as Commander, 16th Air Force, Torrejon Air Base, Spain.

Ellis served as Vice Chief of Staff, U.S. Air Force from November 1973 to August 1975, later appointed Commander, Allied Air Forces Central Europe and Commander in Chief, USAFE. He assumed command of SAC in August 1977.

Quietly brilliant and focused, General Ellis took command of SAC with a broad background in international operations and an awareness of the requirement to keep SAC on the edge of preparedness and maintaining deterrence. He directed numerous exercises of the entire force and challenged the SAC and JSTPS staffs to remain creative and vigilant. During the Iranian Crisis resulting from takeover of the U.S. Embassy in Tehran, he directed SAC B-52's to deploy to Diego Garcia in the Indian Ocean as a show of force and capability. Two B-52H crews were directed to fly a mission out and back over the Middle East as a show of presence; when they arrived over Central Europe, General Ellis decided to send the two bombers on around the world, which they did, arriving back at their home base at K.I. Sawyer, Michigan, 19,300 miles later. The two SAC combat crews were later honored with medals presented by Air Force Chief of Staff, General Lew Allen.

The election of Ronald Reagan in 1980 re-energized the Military Services and SAC, in particular. The previous four years of malaise in addressing the Soviet threat had taken its toll on capability, resources and morale in maintaining deterrence. The Iranian Crisis had weakened the perception of U.S. resolve and reputation to address threats. After four years of under funding military requirements, the Reagan Administration increased spending forty percent during his first term. His military budgets focused on pay, spares, training, family housing and medical services. He announced a provocative initiative to develop a Strategic Defense Initiative (SDI) or "Star Wars" which amounted to an anti-missile defense shield to protect the U.S. from incoming ballistic missiles. SDI caught the Soviets by surprise. President Reagan had reasoned that while the United States could well afford a renewed arms race challenged; the Soviets could not. They would either quit the Cold War or go bankrupt.

General Ellis was a command pilot and wore the Master Missile and Parachutist badges. His numerous awards included the Distinguished Service Cross, Distinguished Service Medal with three oak leaf clusters, Silver Star, Legion of Merit with two oak leaf clusters, Distinguished Flying Cross, Air Medal with four oak leaf clusters, Purple Heart and Grand Officer of the Italian Republic. He was awarded the State of Delaware Distinguished Service Medal by Governor Bacon in 1946. In September 1980 he was presented the Air Force Association's highest honor, the H.H. Arnold Award for significant contributions to national defense. As the recipient of this award he was also named as the association's National Aerospace Man of the Year. General Ellis received the Korean Order of National Security Merit First Class (Tong II Jang) on May 13, 1981 from the Korean Minister of National Defense in Seoul. The highest honor given by the Republic of Korea to a foreign military leader, it was presented to the general for his important contributions to national defense of the Republic of Korea. He was awarded an honorary doctor of science degree from Dickinson College in 1961, honorary doctor of laws degrees from Dickinson School of Law in 1974, from the University of Akron (Ohio) in 1979 and from the University of Nebraska, Omaha, in May 1981.

General Ellis retired July 31, 1981, and died on March 28, 1989 in Washington, D.C.

GENERAL BENNIE L. DAVIS
CINCSAC
1981-1985

General Davis was born in McAlester, Oklahoma, in 1928. He graduated from the U.S. Military Academy in 1950 with a commission as a second lieutenant and a Bachelor of Science degree. He later earned a Master of Science degree from The George Washington University in 1967. He is a graduate of the Armed Forces Staff College and the National War College.

Following graduation from West Point, he entered the U.S. Air Force, attended pilot training at Vance Air Force Base, Oklahoma, earning his pilot wings in August 1951. Thereafter, he was assigned as a multi-engine pilot at James Connally Air Force Base, Texas.   General Davis completed B-29 combat crew training in October 1953 and reported to Okinawa as a B-29 aircraft commander with the 19th Bombardment Wing. He returned to the United States with the 19th Bomb Wing in June 1954 and transitioned into the B-47. Thereafter he became an aircraft commander and instructor pilot at Pinecastle Air Force Base, Florida.

Completing B-52 combat crew training in September 1961, he became a B-52H instructor pilot with the 93rd Bombardment Squadron at Kincheloe Air Force Base, Michigan. In February 1964, he entered the Armed Forces Staff College, graduating in June 1964 and assigned to SAC headquarters at Offutt Air Force Base in the Plans Requirements Division.

General Davis entered the National War College in August 1966 and while attending the college he earned a Master of Science degree. Following graduation he was assigned to Clark Air Base, Philippines, in October 1967 as a B-57 tactical bomber pilot with the 13th Bombardment Squadron. He flew more than 350 combat hours on 142 missions over Vietnam.

In August 1968, he was assigned to the Joint Chiefs of Staff where he served in the Directorate of Operations as an operations officer and later as Chief, Current Operations Branch, Strategic Division. He became the Air Force member of the Chairman's Staff Group, Joint Chiefs of Staff in August 1970. In 1969 he attended the advanced management program at the Harvard School of Business.

General Davis transferred to Randolph Air Force Base, Texas, in June 1972, to serve as Vice Commander, U.S. Air Force Military Personnel Center and Deputy Assistant Chief of Staff, Military Personnel for Headquarters U.S.

Air Force. In June 1974 he became Commander, U.S. Air Force Recruiting Service and Deputy Chief of Staff, Recruiting, Air Training Command.

In July 1975, General Davis became Director, Personnel Plans, Headquarters U.S. Air Force until June 1977 when he was named deputy Chief of Staff, Personnel. He became Commander, Air Training Command at Randolph Air Force Base in April 1979 until his appointment as the tenth Commander in Chief, Strategic Air Command on August 1, 1981.

On October 2, 1981, President Reagan announced reinstatement of the B-1 bomber program previously cancelled by Carter. The decision called for the production of 100 B-1's. The President also retained the Carter air launched cruise missile (ALCM) program with additional emphasis on stealth technology for aircraft and missiles. He also approved the continued development of the MX ICBM, 36 in number and deployed in retro-fitted Minuteman silos. The first B-1 bomber was delivered to the 96th Bomb Wing at Dyess Air Force Base, Texas, on July 7, 1985.

The Reagan initiatives to retake the Cold War lead moved in dramatic fashion in the early 1980's; SAC garnered the most prompt results. The resurrected B-1 bomber, the projected developments of the MX ICBM and the B-2 stealth bomber provided renewed energy and enhanced budget considerations for U.S. strategic systems.

A significant milestone took place in February 1985 with the announcement by General Davis that all female Minuteman launch control combat crews would become the norm in SAC. Heretofore, Minuteman crews consisted of only male crew members while Titan II combat crews were integrated.

General Davis retired as a command pilot with more than 9,000 flying hours. His military decorations and awards include the Distinguished Service Medal, Silver Star, Legion of Merit, Distinguished Flying Cross with two oak leaf clusters, Bronze Star Medal, Air Medal with seven oak leaf clusters, Joint Service Commendation Medal, Air Force Commendation Medal, Presidential Unit Citation Emblem and Air Force Outstanding Unit Award Ribbon. He currently resides in Texas.

GENERAL LARRY D. WELCH
CINCSAC
1985-1986

General Welch was born in Guymon, Oklahoma, and graduated from Liberal, Kansas High School in 1952. He received a Bachelor of Arts degree in Business Administration from the University of Maryland and a Master of Science degree in International Relations from The George Washington University. He is a graduate of the Armed Forces Staff College and the National War College. General Welch is also an Eagle Scout and recipient of the distinguished Eagle Scout Award.

He enlisted in the Kansas National Guard in October 1951, serving with the 161st Armored Field Artillery until he enlisted in the United States Air Force in November 1953 and entered the aviation cadet program where he received his pilot wings and commission as a Second Lieutenant. General Welch served initially as a flight instructor before being assigned to tactical fighters in Europe and the U.S. before transferring to Vietnam where he flew combat in F-4C's.

After completing the Armed Forces Staff College in 1967, he was assigned to Headquarters U.S. Air Force for the next four years. Upon graduation from the National War College in 1972, he was assigned to Tactical Air Command where he served in succession as Deputy Commander for Operations, Vice Commander and Wing Commander.

General Welch moved to Headquarters, Tactical Air Command in August 1977, where he served as the Inspector General, Deputy Chief of Staff, Plans and Deputy Chief of Staff, Operations. In June 1981 he became Commander, Ninth Air Force and Air Force component commander for the Rapid Deployment Joint Task Force. In November 1982, he became Deputy Chief of Staff, Programs and Resources, Headquarters, U.S. Air Force and on to Vice Chief of Staff, U.S. Air Force in July 1984. He was appointed Commander in Chief, Strategic Air Command and Director, Joint Strategic Target Planning Staff on August 1, 1985.

The SAC Airborne Command Post, known as Looking Glass, which began round the clock operations in 1961 with an EC-135 aircraft manned by a command and control operations crew including a general officer on board, celebrated its 25th Anniversary on February 3, 1986. General Welch flew the morning eight-hour shift on the day of the anniversary.

Known for his brief, cryptic conversations, the deeply driven and studious General Welch's tenure as CINCSAC was the shortest—10 months. He departed SAC on June 22, 1986, becoming the 12th Chief of Staff of the United States Air Force. As chief, he served as the senior uniformed Air Force officer responsible for the organization, training and equipage of a combined active duty, Guard, Reserve and Civilian forces serving throughout the world.

Welch retired from the Air Force as a command pilot with more than 6,500 flying hours and military decorations and awards which included the Defense Distinguished Service Medal with oak leaf cluster, Air Force Distinguished Service Medal with oak leaf cluster, Legion of Merit with oak leaf cluster, Distinguished Flying Cross, Meritorious Service Medal, Air Medal with six oak leaf clusters, Air Force Commendation Medal with two oak leaf clusters, Joint Meritorious Unit Award and Air Force Outstanding Unit Award with "V" device and two oak leaf clusters.

GENERAL JOHN T. CHAIN
CINCSAC
1986-1991

General "Jack" Chain was born in Wilmington, Delaware and attended high school at Fork Union Military Academy. He earned a Bachelor of Arts degree in history in 1956 and was awarded an honorary doctorate in humane letters in 1990, both from Denison University. In 1971, he graduated from the National War College and concurrently earned a master's degree in international affairs from George Washington University.

General Chain enjoyed a wide and varied military career, serving in a number of important positions. He accrued over 5,000 flying hours, including 400 combat hours in Vietnam. He is a master parachutist with 66 jumps, and has been awarded the Defense Distinguished Service Medal, the Legion of Merit, the Distinguished Flying Cross, and the Bronze Star.

He was commissioned as a Second Lieutenant through the Air Force Reserve Officer Training Corps (ROTC) program, received his pilot wings in 1957 and entered fighter pilot training. From 1958 to 1959 the general was an F-100 Super Sabre pilot at Toul-Rosieres Air Base in France and from 1959 to 1962 at Ramstein Air Base in West Germany. General Chain then served as a flight examiner at Cannon Air Force Base, New Mexico. In 1964 he was assigned as a forward air controller in Fort Campbell, Kentucky. While there he became a master parachutist and flew Army O-1s and Air National Guard F-84 Thunderjets.

In 1966 Chain flew combat in Vietnam out of Tan Son Nhut Air Base. From 1969 to 1970, he served as an exchange officer with the U.S. Department of State. He entered the National War College in 1970 and upon graduation was assigned to Davis-Monthan Air Force Base, Arizona, as wing Deputy Commander, Operations.

During 1972-73, General Chain returned to Southeast Asia and flew combat in F-4 Phantoms from Korat Royal Thai Air Force Base in Thailand. Upon his return, he served as Deputy Commander, Operations at George Air Force Base, California. In 1974, he was assigned as wing vice commander at Nellis Air Force Base, Nevada. He moved on to Headquarters, Tactical Air Command at Langley Air Force Base in 1975 as Director, Fighter and Reconnaissance Operations.

General Chain became Military Assistant to the Secretary of the Air Force in 1978. He then served as Deputy Director of Plans at Headquarters, U.S. Air Force until 1980, when he became Director of Operations. He served as Assistant Deputy Chief of Staff, Plans and Operations in 1981, becoming Deputy Chief, Staff, Plans and Operations in 1982. He served as Director of the Bureau of Politico Military Affairs for the Department of State from 1984 until 1985, when he was promoted to general and became Chief of Staff for Supreme Headquarters Allied Powers Europe in Belgium.

On June 22, 1986, General Chain was appointed Commander in Chief, Strategic Air Command. He took over SAC at the height of President Reagan's strategic modernization initiatives and currently brought back to the Command a reminder and reverence for their heritage and General Curtis LeMay. The B-1 bombers went on full ground alert on October 1, 1986, and the MX Peacekeeper, ten-warhead ICBM assumed alert on October 10th. The B-1 was SAC's first new bomber in seventeen years and first new ICBM in sixteen years.

SAC combat crews began ground alert on October 1, 1957, and went mostly unnoticed and unheralded by the rest of the Air Force, the Military Services and the nation at large. General Chain initiated recognition of the thirty years that SAC combat crews had been performing alert duties with "The Year of the SAC Alert Force." President Reagan joined in the commemoration with a letter to Strategic Air Command. It read in part:

"In October 1957, aircrews of the Strategic Air Command went on alert for the first time. From that historic day forward, SAC's demonstrated readiness has been a cornerstone of peace and security for the free world. Today, strategic deterrence is still the foundation on which rest the peace of the world and the protection of freedom."

Operation Desert Storm was launched on January 17, 1991, in response to the invasion of Kuwait by Iraqi forces just two weeks before General Chain was due to retire. He was in command, however, when the JCS approved a B-52 attack on Iraqi forces and captured territory in Northern Saudi Arabia. Seven B-52G models departed Barksdale Air Force Base, Louisiana, with each carrying five conventional ALCM weapons. The record-breaking 35-hour mission delivered 35 ALCM's on their designated targets. Thereafter, SAC B-52's continued to participate and contributed greatly to the finish of the war against Iraq.

General Chain relinquished command of SAC and retired from the Air Force on January 31, 1991. A command pilot with 5,000 flying hours, including 400 combat hours, in more than 45 different military aircraft, he was also a master parachutist with 66 jumps. His military decorations and awards include the Defense Distinguished Service Medal, Distinguished

Service Medal with oak leaf cluster, Legion of Merit, Distinguished Flying Cross with oak leaf cluster, Bronze Star Medal, Meritorious Service Medal with two oak leaf clusters, Air Medal with 10 oak leaf clusters, Air Force Commendation Medal, Army Commendation Medal, Air Force Outstanding Unit Award with oak leaf cluster, Air Force Organizational Excellence Award, Combat Readiness Medal, National Defense Service Medal, Armed Forces Expeditionary Medal with service star, Vietnam Service Medal with four service stars, Air Force Overseas Ribbon-Short with oak leaf cluster, Air Force Overseas Ribbon-Long with oak leaf cluster, Air Force Longevity Service Award Ribbon with six oak leaf clusters, Small Arms Expert Marksmanship Ribbon, Republic of Vietnam Armed Forces Honor Medal, Republic of Vietnam Distinguished Medal, Republic of Vietnam Special Service Medal, Republic of Vietnam Gallantry Cross with Palm and Republic of Vietnam Campaign Ribbon.

GENERAL GEORGE L. BUTLER
CINCSAC
1991-1992

General Butler received undergraduate pilot training at Williams Air Force Base, Arizona, followed by basic instructor school at Randolph Air Force Base, Texas. He served as an instructor pilot in T-33s and academic instructor at Craig Air Force Base, Alabama from March 1963 to December 1964. General Butler was selected for study in France as an Olmsted scholar. He received French language training at the State Department's Foreign Services Institute prior to attending the University of Paris. Following graduation, he attended F-4 combat crew training school and was assigned in March 1968 to the 12th Tactical Fighter Wing, Cam Ranh Bay Air Base, South Vietnam. From August 1968 to March 1969 he was aide to the Commander, 7th Air Force, Tan Son Nhut Air Base, South Vietnam. Returning to the United States and the U.S. Air Force Academy, he served as an instructor in the political science department, an executive officer and air officer commanding in the academy's military training department.

In July 1971, General Butler was assigned as special assistant to the Director, Office of Emergency Preparedness, Executive Office of the President. He returned to the Air Force Academy in January 1972 as an assistant professor in the political science department.

Following completion of combat crew training in October 1972, he was assigned as chief pilot of the 53rd Military Airlift Squadron, 63rd Military Airlift Wing, Norton Air Force Base, California. He entered the Armed Forces Staff College in July 1973 and following graduation was assigned as an air operations officer, International Relations Branch, Directorate of Plans, Strategic Arms Limitation Talks, Headquarters, U.S. Air Force. Remaining at the Pentagon, he served from October 1974 to September 1975 as executive officer for the special assistant for strategic initiatives, Office of the Deputy Chief of Staff, Plans and Operations, Air Force headquarters.

Other Pentagon assignments in the following years included plans and programs officer, Strategy Development and Analysis, Directorate of Plans; Executive Director, Air Force Budget Issues Team; Executive Director, Airborne Warning and Control System task force; and Chief, Congressional and Joint Matters Division, Directorate of Concepts.

Following B-52 combat crew training in May 1977, General Butler was assigned to the 416th Bombardment Wing, Griffiss Air Force Base, New York, as wing Assistant Deputy Commander, Operations and later, as Deputy Commander, Operations. In June 1979, he returned to Air Force headquarters. From March 1981, to June 1983 General Butler was assigned as Vice Commander, 320th Bombardment Wing, Mather Air Force Base, California and later wing commander. He subsequently took command of the 96th Bombardment Wing, Dyess Air Force Base, Texas, in June 1983. Promoted to brigadier general in July 1984, he was assigned to Headquarters, Strategic Air Command as the Inspector General. He returned to Air Force headquarters in August 1986 as Deputy Director, Operations and late Director of Operations.

In May 1987 General Butler became Vice Director for Strategic Plans and Policy, J-5, Office of the Joint Chiefs of Staff; in July 1989 he was appointed Director. He assumed command of SAC on January 25, 1991. By August, 1991, for intents and purpose the Soviet Union had collapsed. Eastern Europe had been lost; a coup ensued with the overthrow of Mikhail Gorbachev. President George Bush moved almost as quickly to declare victory in the Cold War and on September 27, 1991 directed that all strategic bombers, ICBM's and SLBM's stand down from their alert posture.

General George L. Butler, broadcast a message to the SAC Alert Forces the following day on September 28th which in part, he announced:

"It is clearly one of the singular events of our time that I sit here in my command center I see all of SAC's bomber forces off alert. Today we especially salute the men and women of the Minuteman II force. Their contribution to this mission has now been achieved and they can stand down from alert with enormous pride and the gratitude of the entire nation, indeed of the entire world. This is a great day for SAC. It's sweeping tribute to 45 years of unparalleled devotion along with our brothers in the SLBM force. We can sit quietly and reflect on the wondrous news that we've begun to climb back down the ladder of nuclear confrontation."

The era of Strategic Air Command was at a close.

General Butler became the first Commander-in-Chief, United States Strategic Command when it was activated at Offutt Air Force Base in June 1992. He retired from active duty on February 28, 1994, as a command pilot with more than 3,000 flying hours. He also held navigator and parachutist ratings. His military awards and decorations included the Defense Distinguished Service Medal, Air Force Distinguished Service Medal, Legion of Merit with oak leaf cluster, Distinguished Flying Cross, Bronze Star Medal, Meritorious Service Medal with two oak leaf clusters, Air Medal with two oak leaf clusters and the Air Force Commendation Medal.

The brief profiles of these thirteen valiant Cold War commanders, men who stood tall among all the others, hardly scratch the surface of the depth and substance of the courage and commitment of these who led Strategic Air Command during the stressful years of the Cold War. Legends within their own time...LeMay, Power, Ryan, Dougherty, Ellis, among all the others...the names are etched in history and the hearts and minds of those who served them. Within each CINCSAC, the responsibility for being prepared to execute the largest and most powerful war plan ever created was steadfast. Under each of these commanders, exacting discipline, unyielding performance and morale of the SAC forces remained paramount. Each SAC commander-in-chief brought his own personality, experience and manner of leadership to the Command, and each carried out his authority and mission responsibilities with the consistency required to lead.

HEROES

"Put none but Americans on guard tonight."

General George Washington

SIX

THE COLD WARRIORS

"I charge you to be the vigilant, ready enemy of those who would abort individual liberty and individual freedom, whoever and wherever they may be. You must morally and intellectually oppose any ideology that holds mankind in perpetual bondage."

General Curtis E. LeMay
Commander in Chief
Strategic Air Command

Few could have affirmed the mission of the American Cold War combat crew member more succinctly or compelling than did General LeMay. Someone once said that "war is faceless" and perhaps there was no other conflict in history where two avowed enemies created unprecedented arsenals of weapons, developed war plans, trained their forces and remained poised to attack or be attacked by the opposing "faceless" warrior for such a sustained period as did the United States and the Soviet Union during the forty-five year impasse which became known as the Cold War.

The Cold War remained the primary mission of the SAC warriors and their Navy counter-part nuclear submarine sea launched ballistic missile (SLBM) force. This is not to overlook or diminish the participation and commitment of the many other military components that were involved in the protracted stalemate: men and women in tactical ground and air, airlift, Navy and Marine units of all categories amongst millions of others. Most Americans had little knowledge about the lives of these young warriors

171

much less the stress and the intensity that pervaded the depths of their daily lives. Stress was caused by the physical, mental and continuous pressure of maintaining constant unwavering and unfailing perfection in their daily job performance and the ever-present awareness that they could be called upon to risk their lives at any given time.

Few fully comprehended the life of the Cold War airman or sailor; flight crew members, missileers and submariners operated, trained and prepared to go the limit to fight and defend their country. While airborne, crew members hunkered around within their confined cockpit spaces, flew training missions ranging from 10 upwards to 25 hours, grew weary in their seats, frequently omitted their flight lunches and brief leg stretch or trip to the latrine relief tube were made only when absolutely necessary. The ever-persistent drone of the aircraft engines penetrated their ears. Nevertheless, their keen minds remained sharp and tuned to the tasks at hand often aided by deep draws of 100% oxygen from the masks attached to their flight helmet. Once the mission was completed and the aircraft safely back on the ground, the machine's vibration continued to transmit through the fatigued bodies of the crew members while their minds burned with the blur of activities now completed.

Concurrently, somewhere in the American Midwest, a missile combat crew sits below ground in a snug hardened, nuclear-proof, deadly quiet capsule maintaining their own vigilant watch over the ICBM's assigned to their flight. The crew occupies themselves by reading or chatting about family, upcoming vacation leave, sports or their jobs. The boredom and silence is only broken by the sounding of the PAS calling a practice alert and simulated missile countdown or the Facility Manager topside with an intercom announcement that meal time has arrived and food is on the way. While the operating environments of the respective flight crews and missileers are totally different, their missions are the same—preparation and vigilance. Meanwhile, the outside world moved on routinely, none the wiser that dedicated patriots remained silently vigilant over the security of the nation.

[Author's note: If I may indulge, the Cold War air crewman, missileer or casual reader who may quarrel with my assertion that SAC aviators and missile crew duties were challenged with equal stress challenges, I wish to do so. Having served as a B-36 and B-52 combat crew member for ten years before becoming a missile combat crew member, I spent three years manning a Minuteman ICBM Launch Control Center capsule. Through those incredible experiences, I learned firsthand that the duty assignments were relative; each had its own special and extraordinary challenges. The observations herein concluded that during the long drawn-out years of the Cold War few Americans ever really grasped the gravity of the precarious era unless they were in some way personally touched by it. Doubtless many were even aware of the persistent dangers posed by our Cold War enemies. There were occasional wakeup calls; the Cuban Crisis was perhaps the loudest. There were hundreds of others that did not make the headlines, but the wives and families of these heroes knew and understood.]

This chapter attempts to recount the unflinching commitment and bravery of the men and women who served voluntarily and selflessly in the uniform of their country against an avowed enemy. They are the stories about their missions, their confrontations and their sacrifices as aviators, missileers, ground support and numerous others. As you follow them through their extraordinary experiences, you will also find that, indeed, they were not "faceless."

It became General LeMay's steadfast objective that SAC combat crews discipline themselves by flying training missions as realistically as possible, just as if they were actually going to war. Accordingly, it became common practice to train with "shapes", as they were referred to—unarmed atomic bombs—loaded into the bombers in order for the aircrews to get used to the "feel" of the bomber fully loaded with fuel and weapons. The training devices were in fact, fully functional atomic weapons containing the designed high explosives but with an inert lead "core", or atomic component. The lead cores were carried aboard the bombers instead of the actual plutonium insertion device so that crews could practice configuring the weapons as they would on an actual combat mission. The impact of this highly specialized, responsible and disciplined training was just one of the many factors that made Strategic Air Command the elite combat ready military force during the Cold War. As we will see, these training methods were also the essential components that conditioned SAC combat crews to deal with adversity on virtually any level.

THE AVIATORS

NOTABLE MISHAP.

With SAC's complex training operations came the inevitable unforeseen and unexpected. An example of just such a mission that went terribly awry occurred on February 13, 1950, when a B-36B bomber departed Eielson Air Force Base, Alaska on a routine training mission with a crew of seventeen men. The weather was brutally cold—40 degrees below zero with snow and wind. De-icing was virtually impossible; the engines were started early and kept running continuously long before take-off. The flight plan was scheduled to include navigation practice and electronic countermeasures training en route back to the Continental, a simulated bomb run on San Francisco and return to their home base at Carswell Air Force Base, Texas. Shortly after reaching cruising altitude, the bomber encountered the first of three engine fires attributed to carburetor icing which couldn't be extinguished and resulted in shutting down all three engines. The bomber was carrying a Mark IV atomic training weapon or "shape." As the aircraft accumulated more ice and losing altitude due to lack of power, the pilot maneuvered the bomber out over the Pacific Ocean and dropped the Mark IV training device from an altitude of 8,000 feet. The crew witnessed the flash of the bomb exploding at the programmed altitude of approximately 4,000 feet. Still unable to maintain safe flight, the aircraft commander, Captain Harold Barry, flew the aircraft back to the coast of British Columbia and ordered the crew to bail out just inland. Once he felt assured that the crew had safely departed the bomber, he turned the aircraft back out to sea and bailed-out himself. Thereafter, for some unknown reason, the bomber turned itself back inland after the crew bailed out and crashed some 200 miles into the snow-packed mountains of British Columbia. The wreckage was not discovered until four years later in 1953. An Air Force team visited the site, removed a small amount of sensitive parts and destroyed the wreckage with explosives. Speculation in Canada remains within some quarters to this day that the aircraft was carrying an actual atomic bomb and that it crashed with the aircraft. A Canadian research team visited the crash site in 1997, found numerous pieces of crew member personal effects, jackets, scattered pieces of wreckage, etc., but no evidence of a bomb or any indication of measured radiation from an atomic device. This incident did not deter SAC from continuing the practice of training with simulated atomic weapons.

OPERATION "BIG STICK"

In August 1953, following the truce in Korea, President Eisenhower directed General LeMay to fly a "training" mission to the Far East as a demonstration of U.S. capability and resolve as the Korean Conflict drew to a close. Colonel (later, Lt. General) James W. Edmundson, Commander of the 92nd Bomb Wing, was initially scheduled to lead a flight of twenty B-36 bombers from Fairchild Air Force Base, Washington, to Okinawa to standby on ground alert in the event "they were needed." It wasn't clear what they might be "needed for." In General Edmundson's own words: "I took off with 17 airplanes for Eielson Air Force Base in Alaska. We were loaded with complete atomic weapons, but only the outside shell, or the 'shape'. Nuclear inserts if necessary could be added later. There were not the correct shapes available at Fairchild for the three additional aircraft, and the plan was for them to join us en route.

We took off from Eielson with seventeen B-36's late the next afternoon and headed for Attu Island at the end of the Aleutian chain, where we were to rendezvous with the three planes taking off from Fairchild Air Force Base, near Spokane, Washington. When we made radio contact with them I found that there were six aircraft instead of three, so we had some airborne spares. We were all milling around over Attu at staggered altitudes in the middle of a black night, and I had to decide which 20 bombers were going on to Okinawa and which 3 had to go back to Fairchild.

"I called on the radio, 'This is Big Stick One. Check in by the numbers with your fuel and mechanical status, and don't give me any of that six churning and four burning B.S. I know your jets are shut down, and I want to know how many fans you have feathered and why.'

"It was like pulling teeth to get what I wanted to know, but eventually we decided on the three losers and pointed them toward home. The remaining twenty of us quit circling and headed for Okinawa.

"I was flying with Lt. Colonel Granville (Granny) Wright and his crew, and we were the first to land at Kadena Air Base on Okinawa. General Walter Sweeney, BIG STICK Task Force Commander, was there to meet us. We watched together as the rest of my twenty-ship flight arrived, one at a time, made a low pass over the field and circled into the landing pattern. Nearly everyone buzzed in with at least one engine feathered, which concerned General Sweeney, and when one came in with three feathered, the General became quite upset.

"I said, 'General, I've been in radio contact with all of them ever since we left Attu. Nobody has any serious problems. Most of the engines are shut down because of low oil. That last guy was just showing off. You noticed his jets were at idle just in case he needed them. When he pulls up and comes in to land, he'll have six churning and four burning.'"

Edmundson continues, "General Sweeney looked at me kind of funny for a minute. Then he broke into a smile and said, Eddie, you B-36 guys are all a little bit crazy—but, I love you anyway.

"We sat on alert on Okinawa for about 10 days in all of our atomic splendor. The Korean peace treaty got successfully signed. Operation Big Stick was declared concluded and we took off for Fairchild like a flight of ten-engined geese. It was a one-of-a-kind operation!

"The presence of the huge bombers in the Far East was the beginning of an awesome, indelible and enduring sight in that part of the world. The Big Stick exercise began a policy of maintaining a sustained alert force of B-36's at Anderson Air Force Base, Guam throughout the 1950's. Flight crews from each B-36 base took turns rotating along with their aircraft to Guam every 90 days. During their period of duty on the island, SAC maintained a nominal force of thirty B-36's with one-third of the bombers on alert at all times. The aircraft on alert were fully loaded with fuel and nuclear weapons; and the crews housed in a nearby facility were ready to take-off on their assigned mission if the U.S. war plan against the Soviet Union was executed. The combat crews rotated on and off alert with those not assigned to an alert aircraft, flying routine training missions throughout the South Pacific."

SNEAKY ATTACK

In his memoirs, General Jim Edmundson provides another B-36 bomber story that highlights the serious nature of the perceived threat and the intense training imposed on SAC combat crews:

"To appreciate this particular mission," Edmundson said, "One needs to remember the utter realism which General LeMay evaluated the units under his command. I launched from Fairchild Air Force Base, Washington in the lead B-36 in a 15-ship effort at 4:00 a.m., climbed to altitude and headed for Davis-Monthan Air Force Base near Tucson, Arizona. I picked up a block clearance from FAA and we established a bomber stream, using radar station keeping with each B-36 tracking the bomber ahead of him, staying about 100 feet above him and about a half mile behind. When we arrived in the Tucson area, I checked n with approach control and the tower for landing permission for the flight at Davis-Monthan and closed out our flight plan with FAA. We set up a pattern to bring the flight into land at 3-minute intervals. As each B-36 came in on final approach and reached 500 feet, they retracted the flaps, sucked up the landing gear, poured on some power and headed for Mexico at 500 feet altitude. We were on radio silence for the rest of the mission. As far as FAA knew, we were on the ground at Davis-Monthan. SAC had placed a trusted agent in the tower at Davis-Monthan who knew what was going on. Sneaky bunch that we were, we were on our way!

"We flew about 300 miles into Mexico and then headed north, flying at 1000 feet. We headed northerly all day long and about 10:00 that night we were off the coast of Vancouver Island. At that point, we lit up the jet engines, turned southeast toward the United States and began a max climb to 40,000 feet. We assembled a spread formation, with our radars on station keeping so that they would not be detected on the ground, remained under radio silence and turned off our aircraft running lights. When we began showing up on Air Defense Command radar screens, they were sure the Russians were coming! SAC had also placed a trusted agent in the Air Defense Command operations command post, who then announced: 'They aren't Russians; they are B-36's. Go see what you can do about it.

"When we hit our pre-IP, each B-36 went after his assigned target. We conducted simulated bomb runs on Seattle, Bremerton, Renton, Tacoma, Portland and a lot of other places. Our lead crew 'bombed' the Hanford nuclear facility and after bombs away, I went on the radio, told everyone to turn on their running lights and contacted FAA for descent clearance for the flight back to Fairchild. It was a pretty good mission. We hit all of our targets and nobody laid a glove on us. Air Defense Command was mad as hell, but I am sure General LeMay was chuckling. He had found out what he wanted to know about one of his SAC units!"

A DODGED BULLET

During the early and primitive bomber operations with atomic weapons, entering the bomb bay of a B-36 bomber in flight was never routine. Adding the requirement to conduct tedious procedures while working in that precarious environment often tested both the skill and nerves of the combat crew members. During the period of retiring the B-36 bombers in 1958, the aircraft units were required to ferry their nuclear weapons from local base storage facilities to the main weapons depot at Manzano Base near Albuquerque. The logical way to haul them back was in the bomb bays of the bomber in the manner which they were designed to be carried. This negated the requirement to bring in special transports to ferry them. One hot summer July day a combat crew assigned to the 95th Bomb Wing near El Paso, Texas, was tasked to ferry a MK-17 nuclear weapon to Manzano. The Mark-17 was the largest in physical size of any thermo-nuclear bomb ever built for air delivery, weighing some 40,000 lbs. The flight was a brief 40-minute or so from El Paso to Albuquerque and on a hot summer day over the desert could be very turbulent. The normal operating procedure in the B-36 with a weapon on board was to have manual safety pins inserted in the bomb release mechanism in the bomb bay on the ground before take-off and then removed by the radar-navigator after take-off. The safety pins were then re-inserted just prior to landing. The purpose of the safety pins was to preclude the weapon from inadvertently releasing during take-off or during landing. On this fateful day everything was working well. It was, as predicted, a hot and extremely bumpy flight up the valley to Kirtland Air Force Base which was the off-load point for the weapons. As the pilot prepared to enter the traffic pattern to set-up his landing approach, he directed the radar-navigator to go into the bomb bay and insert the safety pins. The B-36 bomb bay was a virtual jungle of cables wires, fuel and hydraulic lines. All of the cables having to do with the bomb release mechanism were enclosed in metal tubes and clearly marked: "NO HAND HOLD". As the radar-navigator was maneuvering his way along the narrow passage in the bomb bay to a position to insert the pins, the aircraft now flying at 2000 feet in the traffic pattern, was bouncing around as it encountered numerous abrupt ground thermal bumps. One severe bounce threw him off balance and forced him to grab anything in sight to keep from falling onto the bomb bay doors. Unfortunately, he grabbed a "NO HAND HOLD" cable tube which controlled the manual bomb release mechanism; just as suddenly, the 42,500 lb nuclear bomb released through the bomb bay doors and plowed into desert sand below. One can only imagine the thoughts that reeled through the minds and hearts of the air crew and especially the panicked radar-navigator hanging onto the cable tube and looking down at the shattered bomb bay doors and the ground below. But, the critically important epilogue to this event and story is, the bomb worked perfectly! It "failed safe" just as it was so designed. The impact resulted only in a small high explosive detonation, because it had not been armed by the bomber crew. The incident proved to be testimony and considerable tribute to the scientific ingenuity and skill that designed, engineered and developed the technology and the attendant built-in safety features of U.S. nuclear weapons—otherwise, it could have been the tragic incident that created a new Grand Canyon in New Mexico!

SIBERIAN OVERFLIGHT

Airborne reconnaissance became an important and integral part of the U.S. strategy to determine what the Soviet Union military forces were up to, their type of war fighting aircraft, equipment and forward basing locations.

In the spring of 1952, President Truman was briefed on the Soviet increased deployments to Siberia and the Intelligence Community concern. Troubled by the questionable motives, he agreed with the JCS to order a series of reconnaissance flights over the region to confirm the reported activity. Earlier in December, he had approved flights over the Soviet Union when warranted to access Soviet capabilities. But at that time, the designated RB-47 was destroyed by fire in a ground refueling accident and the missions were postponed.

By early 1952, the seesaw war in Korea had not slacked off and the Soviet activity at Siberian air bases was increasing. Tu-4 bombers had been detected at two other bases, Mys Schmidta Air Base on the Chukchi Sea coast and at Provideniya Air Base on the Chukotskiy Peninsula. Each of these airfields was just across the Bering Strait from Alaska. Upon the recommendation of his Secretary of Defense, Robert Lovett, the President approved one of two proposed reconnaissance flights over Siberia. Colonel Don Hillman, Deputy Commander of the 306th Bombardment Wing at MacDill Air Force Base near Tampa, Florida, was selected by SAC to conduct the mission. His co-pilot was Major Lester E. Gunter and his navigator was Major Edward A. Timmins. A back-up crew was commanded by Colonel Patrick D. Fleming. The B-47's were to be supported by two KC-97 tankers from the 306th Air Refueling Squadron also stationed at MacDill.

The crew in strict secrecy at MacDill planned the sensitive mission. The two bombers and tankers were pre-positioned to Rapid City Air Force Base, South Dakota, for six days of additional planning and training flights.

This author met with Colonel Don Hillman, then long since retired, over dinner at Offutt Air Force Base, Nebraska, in May 1996. He was healthy, viable and full of enthusiasm. He told me about a near disaster during one of their training flights out of Rapid City. He said the local SAC wing commander at Rapid City, Brigadier General Richard E. Ellsworth, asked if he could accompany Hillman on one of his training flights during their stay.

Colonel Hillman agreed, of course, and on the next planned training flight, General Ellsworth occupied the co-pilot's seat with Major Gunter, the crew co-pilot, in the aisle way along side the General. During the take-off roll, Hillman said the aircraft began to accelerate normally down the runway, but did not exhibit any indication of becoming airborne. He said that he promptly glanced down at the wing flaps indicator and to his horror discovered they were in the "Full-Up Position." He said that in a split second he knew that his ground speed was too fast to abort the take-off without crashing off the end of the runway. With the flaps not extended, he knew that he couldn't get the B-47 safely airborne, so he quickly "swatted" the flap handle to the Down Position and waited. He said grinning, that the longest seconds of his life seemed like hours as the flaps slowly crept down against the forward pressure of the aircraft rapidly propelling down the runway. Finally, the bomber began to lift slowly into the air just as it reached the end of the runway.

Colonel Hillman further lamented their great escape and the lesson for trained and disciplined aircrews; "when a non-checked-out person is occupying a crewmember's position in the aircraft, the remainder of the crew cannot double-check their procedures too many times!" A close call he confesses he never forgot, nor repeated.

Hillman and the other reconnaissance crews along with their supporting tankers continued on to Eielson Air Force Base, Alaska, where he and his crew finally launched the over-flight sortie on October 15, 1952, almost two years after the decision by the President to conduct the missions. The flight was accomplished like clock-work according to Hillman, with the crew flying over the heart of Siberia along the Chutkotskiy Peninsula photographing an 800-mile strip of Soviet airfields and installations. Several MiG-15's scrambled to intercept his RB-47, but never made it to their altitude. The important message received by the Soviets was that the United States was aware of their presence in the forward area of Siberia and knowledgeable of their activities. Later, intercepted messages revealed that the Soviet regional commander in Siberia had been removed and additional MiG-15 air defense units were being moved into the coastal areas to beef-up the vulnerable flank. The Cold War further evolved while the openly contested hot war raged on in Korea.

ENSUING TRAGEDY

On March 18, 1953, Captain Jacob Pruett Jr., Aircraft Commander, and Captain Orion Clark, 1st Pilot, along with Brigadier General Richard Ellsworth, Commander, 28th Strategic Reconnaissance Wing, Major Frank Wright, Co-pilot, and a crew of nineteen others took off in an RB-36H from Lajes Airdrome in the Azores at 11:00 PM local time. Their destination was their home base of Rapid City Air Force Base, South Dakota. The planned flight path would take them across the Atlantic Ocean and over Newfoundland into the United States. The flight was expected to take approximately 25 hours.

The pre-flight weather briefing indicated that their flight path would take them to the south of a low pressure weather system in the Western Atlantic. The counter-clockwise rotation of the low was predicted to produce headwinds that were forecast to average 17 knots out of the northwest.

General Ellsworth and Major Wright were not current in take-offs and landings, so Captain Jacob Pruett Jr. and Captain Orion Clark were undoubtedly at the controls during the take-off. Sometime after take-off, it is presumed that Major Wright then moved into the Aircraft Commander's left seat and General Ellsworth got into the right seat.

Major Wright and General Ellsworth likely flew the over water portion of the flight and at about 1,000 feet above the water for best range performance. They monitored their altitude above the water with the radar altimeter as they flew through the darkness. The navigator would be expected to turn on the mapping radar an hour before the time that he expected the aircraft to reach landfall. The pilots would then climb to an altitude that would carry the aircraft safely over the coastal mountains of Newfoundland when they were approximately 20 miles from the shore.

Most of the flight was flown in overcast conditions that prevented the navigator from using the sextant for a celestial observation to determine the true position of the airplane. The low pressure system moved south of its predicted position before the RB reached its vicinity. The aircraft passed to the north of the low. Instead of the anticipated headwinds, the airplane encountered tailwinds that averaged 12 knots from the south southwest.

Ocean Station Delta received a position update from the RB-36H at 3:45 AM. The navigator reported that the ground speed of the aircraft was 130 knots. The position was in error by 138 nautical miles and the true ground speed was closer to 185 knots.

The RB-36 reached the Newfoundland coast approximately an hour and a half earlier than the crew planned and they made no attempt to contact air defense as required when they were fifty miles off shore. The navigator apparently did not turn on his radar. The pilots continued to fly at low altitude. In the last twenty minutes of the flight, the ground speed was estimated to be approximately 200 knots. The visibility was less than one eighth of a mile as the airplane flew straight and level through sleet, freezing drizzle and fog.

At approximately 4:10 AM Newfoundland time and thirty miles after crossing the coastline the RB-36H struck an 896-foot tall ridge at an elevation of 800 feet near Burgoynes Cove. The six propellers chopped the tops off numerous pine trees before the left wing struck the ground ripping it off and igniting the spilled fuel into a huge fireball. The fuselage and right wing impacted 1,000 feet beyond the left wing.

Coincidentally, Air Force First Lieutenant Dick Richardson heard the engines of the giant aircraft as it approached his cabin at Nut Cove. The sound of the engines stopped suddenly followed by a loud explosion. He woke up the other men stationed with him, organized a search party and proceeded up the mountain through deep snow to the crash site. They found no survivors. Rapid City Air Force Base was later named Ellsworth Air Force Base in honor of its fallen commander.

MIGS OVER MURMANSK

As the Cold War intensified, SAC took on the significantly important role of airborne intelligence gathering, particularly regarding Soviet air, missile and space operations. It was felt that SAC had the necessary "global reach" experience and disciplined aircrews necessary to survey Soviet military operations. Previous specially configured reconnaissance RB-29 and RB-36 aircraft were replaced with RB-47 photographic and electronic surveillance aircraft. These reconfigured bombers could fly higher and faster in order to penetrate Soviet airspace, if required, to conduct their intelligence gathering and hopefully escape unscathed. The collected information about Soviet military capabilities, installations and operations was invaluable in developing U.S. Cold War strategies.

Among those early heroic reconnaissance achievements was a mission flown on May 8, 1954, by Captain (later, Colonel) Harold (Hal) Austin and his RB-47 crew which included Captains Carl Holt, co-pilot, and Vance

Heavlin, navigator. The mission launched out of Fairford Air Base, United Kingdom, to make a daring photographic over-flight of Soviet air bases near Murmansk. The purpose of the mission was to confirm the reported existence of MiG-17 fighters at three Northern USSR bases. Prior to the actual over-flight of Soviet territory, numerous other RB-47 'feint' sorties had been flown around the periphery of the Soviet border to get the ground radar controllers 'used to' foreign traffic in the region. On the day of the mission, three RB-47's launched and skirted around Norway toward a "turn-in point" to Murmansk. At a pre-determined point along the route, two of the RB-47's turned around and headed back to their home base, leaving the single reconnaissance aircraft flown by Captain Austin and his crew to proceed in over the Soviet airfields. The lone RB-47 "coasted-in" at 40,000 feet, considered a safe altitude from the known MiG-15's in the area. As the crew completed photographing the first two of six targeted airfields, they were joined by a flight of three MiG-15's who stayed out off the wing of the RB-47 and flew formation with the aircraft, ostensibly attempting to make visual identification of this errant bomber. As the crew proceeded, six additional MiGs joined in to 'look over' at the RB-47. They were also identified as MiG-15's and took no provocative actions or attempts to make large maneuvers at such a critical high altitude. By this time Austin and his crew had completed taking pictures of the next two airfields near Arkhangelsk while the Soviets had also likely confirmed the identification of the RB-47. They had also apparently completed their complicated ground command and control checks and had launched six more fighters. This time they sent up MiG-17's which had more than enough capability to out-maneuver and shoot down the RB-47. The new MiG arrivals immediately began firing at the reconnaissance aircraft, but without hitting it. Meanwhile, Carl Holt, the co-pilot began trying to get his thoroughly 'cold soaked' and malfunctioning 20mm cannon tail guns to fire. At first they didn't. He finally coaxed the guns to fire-off a couple of bursts which caused the MiG pilots to back-off. And then, one of the more daring of the Soviet pilots made an extremely close firing pass and hit the RB-47 in the left wing, knocking-out the intercom radio system. Captain Austin, un-phased by the attack, continued on his mission, taking photos of the last of his six airfield targets. The MiG-17's continued to make firing passes at the RB until it was well out of Soviet territory, but failed to make any further hits. The RB-47 crew, low on fuel, managed to get back over the United Kingdom and "hook-up" with a KC-97 airborne tanker, take on fuel and land back at Fairford Air Base. According to the crew, who were invited to Omaha to personally debrief General LeMay, "The intelligence people were ecstatic with the quality of the Soviet airfield photographs, as well as one close-up photo of a MiG-17 making a close pass under our aircraft."

General LeMay commented, "There are probably several openings today in [Soviet] command positions over there, since you were not shot down."

Carl Holt, the co-pilot, commented with considerable innocence to General LeMay, "Sir, they were trying to shoot us down!"

LeMay in a typical response, soberly responded, "What did you think they would do, give you an ice cream cone?"

After the debriefing, General LeMay, without the traditional pomp accorded such ceremonies, awarded two Distinguished Flying Crosses each to the three crewmembers, commenting that he would like to have awarded them the more deserving Silver Star, but that he would have to go to Washington for approval and that would take "too much" explaining.

EXTRAORDINARY AIRMANSHIP

SAC training, discipline and adherence to the mission became legend and envied throughout the Air Force and the other Military Services. The Soviet Union knew all to well that SAC combat crews were cut from the best the United States had to offer and sustained U.S. deterrent policy against nuclear war.

A perfect example of a SAC crew member's unselfish courage and valor occurred on April 28, 1958, when during a routine B-47 bomber training mission flying out of Dyess Air Force Base, near Abilene, Texas, one of the aircraft's engines exploded and caught fire. When it was determined that the fire couldn't be extinguished, the pilot ordered the crew to bail out and blew the canopy. The copilot, 1Lt James E. Obenauf, could not get his ejection seat to fire, so he proceeded to climb down to the navigator's escape hatch where he could bail out manually. There he found the instructor navigator, Major Joseph Maxwell, unconscious. Obenauf tried to revive him so they could both escape the aircraft, but was unable to do so. Obenauf then climbed back into his copilot seat and brought the B-47 under control (the fire had extinguished itself). He then proceeded to descend and head back to Dyess Air Force Base. Sitting in the rear copilot seat, the aircraft canopy gone, the incredible wind lashing his face from the open cockpit, Lieutenant Obenauf landed the aircraft safely and saved Major Maxwell's life. The incredible feat almost cost Obenauf his eyesight in the process and yet provided another great example of professionalism, discipline, bravery and airmanship not untypical of young aviators.

The reader will even more enjoy this extraordinary event as described in Jim Obenauf's own words:

"Twenty minutes past Amarillo there was a huge explosion...you could definitely hear it. The aircraft shuddered and rocked and the right wing appeared to be engulfed in flames. It was shooting flames and sparks 30 to 40 feet in every direction. The Aircraft commander gave the "bail out" order twice over the interphone. The first man I know of that left the aircraft was the observer...I tried to eject. My ejection seat failed. I went all the way through the seat sequence. The control column stowed, the seat bottomed, the canopy left, and I just couldn't trigger it off. Approximately the time the observer, Lieutenant Cobb, bailed out. Major Maxwell was already in the navigator's position in the fourth man slot up near he observer. He was blown back head first and hit somewhere near my position. Immediately after this he seemed to shake his head and went forward. I assumed he was all right.

"Since I could not eject, I immediately tried to get out of my seat. I had an awful lot of trouble because my survival kit kept catching on everything. I got down to the escape hatch, pulled the master lever but the pressure door did not operate...helmet bags, flight lunches, and other things were caught in there. I was then going up to the observer's hatch to bail out when I noticed that Major Maxwell was still lying in the aisle. I assumed he was hypoxic, so I immediately climbed back up in the seat and checked on the fire. If it was too bad, I was going over the side. But I thought if there was half a chance of going on I would stay with the aircraft.

"The fire seemed under control. It was confined to No. 6 engine, so I actuated the throttle to cut off and it did turn the fire down to a bright glow all over the engine. I immediately started a descent...to get to lower altitude so that Major Maxwell would wake up and bail out and I could get out.

"At approximately 11,000 feet my oxygen cut out and I was unable to read the liters in the converters because of dust in my eyes and wind blast. I could not see my instruments accurately. I was mostly flying by feel. I leveled off about 10,000 feet. Major Maxwell started shaking his head and I started hitting him on the head and convincing him to bail out. Apparently he could not find his parachute.

"For at least 20 minutes I tried to talk him into bailing out. Finally I checked the engine and there was no more red glare. I had been giving maydays over the radio but I realized that my interphone cord had been disconnected, so apparently I was a little hypoxic myself. I connected my interphone cord and immediately gave a mayday, the position, and that the other crew-members bailed out. Altus Air Force Base Direction Finder picked up my mayday call. Also, Eyelash 32 was in the air and he was telling people on the ground exactly what I could do from the back seat. Ground was asking me to squawk mayday, etc., and he convinced them that I couldn't do it from the back seat.   "I kept descending until I got down to 5500 feet and Altus gave me a heading for, Dyess. I tried to maintain that heading but couldn't see the directional indicator. I. had no idea what my heading was and so I realized more or less this was a gyro out steer which worked out fairly well until Fat Chance GCI picked me up; but he was coming in so garbled I was unable to read most of his transmissions. Finally Dyess DF and Reese DF got me into the station.

"Major Maxwell was now half-conscious and I convinced him to try to turn on the landing lights. He made eight or ten attempts before he finally turned them on. Coming into the GCA pattern they ran me into some moderate-to-severe turbulence and made it very difficult to fly the airplane. A couple of times I caught myself in 40 and 50-degree banks, with the airplane practically out of control. Coming around the GCA pattern I had no idea what my airspeed was but I was flying a constant 88 percent power setting. I could not see my airspeed indicator but I think it was a little bit slow because I encountered slight buffeting and stalls so I moved it up to about 94 percent.

"Then GCA lined me up on final but I couldn't hold any heading since I just couldn't make out the directional indicator. GCA advised me I was too far to the left. I knew I just couldn't go around because I couldn't see much any more and I couldn't see the airspeed indicator. I was flying final approach by just feel, so I made up my mind the only thing to do was to go on in. The round-out was...I just stepped it down until I hit the ground and I immediately pulled the brake chute. After that everything seemed normal. I chopped No. 1, 2 and 5 immediately after touchdown and started knocking off everything as far as electrical goes. Immediately upon stopping I cut the other engines and was very cautious about getting out of my seat because I was almost sure it was going to trigger. Exit from the aircraft was okay and I would say I was on the ground about 20 seconds when I went completely blind due to the wind blast." Lt. Obenauf recovered his eyesight and lived to fly another day demonstrating the discipline, commitment and courage of Cold Warriors.

GARY POWERS

Anticipating that Soviet air defenses would continuously improve, the Central Intelligence Agency funded the design and development of an extreme high altitude reconnaissance aircraft in the mid-1950's that was capable of global photography and electronic emissions collection far exceeding anything that reconfigured bomber aircraft offered. The Air Force was given the mission to train their own as well as Air Force pilots specially selected by the CIA to become their own pilots in the new U-2. The extraordinary high flying and virtual "around the world" range of the U-2 added a whole new dimension to SAC's reconnaissance mission and U.S. intelligence information collection capabilities. It was also believed that the U-2 could over-fly and evade any Soviet anti-aircraft defensive system.

On May 1, 1960, a pilot recruited from the Air Force by the CIA, Gary Powers was scheduled to fly a U-2 mission from his duty station in Peshawar, Pakistan. His mission was to be a circuitous route (to avoid known surface to air missile (SAM) sites) to Stalingrad, the Tyuratam missile test facilities, nuclear power plants in the Ural Mountains, suspected ICBM site construction at Yurya, a known ICBM site at Plesetsk, submarine pens at Severodvinsk and the naval base at Murmansk. He was to land at Bodo, Norway. Powers was well along into his flight, 1,300 miles into Soviet territory, when he was hit by an SA-2 Fan Song antiaircraft missile. His altitude was never revealed, but he was more than likely flying between 70,000 and 80,000 feet. Soviet Premier Khrushchev was participating in the annual May Day celebration in Moscow when he received notification of the shoot-down. President Eisenhower was informed when Powers was overdue at Bodo, but US authorities were unaware that he had been shot down. A brief game of "poker" ensued. The Soviets set a trap by revealing only photographs of the wreckage and no mention of the pilot. The US position was that there had been an..."unfortunate incident involving an errant navigation flight which strayed off course."

Authorities in Washington believed Powers had been killed and the U-2 completely destroyed. They were "sure" that the timing explosives would have been armed when Powers ejected and the aircraft would have been virtually destroyed. If true, the Soviets would be unable to disprove the US position. As it turned out, Powers could not eject and the timing device did not destroy the classified equipment due to the damage to the aircraft when it was hit. Powers bailed out manually, fell freely until his pre-set timer opened his parachute at 15,000 feet and he was quickly captured upon landing. The Soviets now had "everything"—the U-2 spy plane and its pilot—but Khrushchev allowed Washington to continue creating its "story." When the Soviets did finally announce that they not only had the plane, but also the pilot, Eisenhower promptly stepped forward and admitted the whole event.

Taken off-guard by Eisenhower's admission, Khrushchev "played it back" as U.S. arrogance and contempt. The U-2 incident generated a few interesting sidebars, one of which was that Powers, while getting out of his parachute harness on the ground, saw another parachute descending not far away. He thought at first that it might be a missile booster stage; later, he guessed it was probably a hapless Soviet pilot who had been "in the chase" and had gotten caught in the barrage of SAMs that had been fired at the U-2.

Another story, which was not revealed until 1996, concerned Igor Mentyukov, a Soviet pilot. Mentyukov reported to the Russian newspaper, Trud that he had been sent aloft in an "unarmed" Sukoi Su-9 (Fishpot B) interceptor to locate and "ram" the U-2. He said he overtook the U-2 and "... it got into (my) slipstream and its (the U-2's) wings fell off." He also said his story had been "covered up" by the Kremlin to avoid "weakening the faith" in the Soviets' air defense capabilities. The questions remain regarding the Soviet pilot's claims.

INCIDENT OVER THE BARENTS

SAC introduced "ferret" missions in the late 1950's. These tedious reconnaissance flights were designed to literally flush-out radio communications and other electronic emissions from Soviet military installations. The crew of these sorties was increased to six members with the three additional "Ravens," or electronic specialists, housed within a capsule inserted into the bomb bay of the RB-47. The ferret missions were generally planned to not fly directly over Soviet territory, thereby not violating international borders and offering better protection for the aircraft and crew, rather skirt the coastline to stimulate their search radars and collect and record the resultant communications and electronic emissions with the aircraft's sophisticated equipment. While ferret missions greatly enhanced U.S. intelligence collection capabilities, they also confused and harassed Soviet forces with not unexpected reactions.

A ferret mission flown on July 1, 1960, over the Barents Sea did not fare as well as did Captain Hal Austin's earlier mission over the Soviet Union. Ferret missions were designed to fly along Soviet borders and collect electronic emissions from radars and communications transmitters. On this particular flight, commanded by Major Willard G. Palm, the crew included Captain Bruce Olmstead (copilot), Captain John McKone (navigator) and three Ravens: Major Eugene E. Posa, Captain Dean B. Phillips, and Captain Oscar L. Goforth.

The RB-47 crew took off from the United Kingdom and headed toward their surveillance area, skirting around Norway to the Barents Sea and 50 miles off the northern coast of the Soviet Union. Just before 3:00 p.m., McKone verified the aircraft's position at greater than 50 miles north of Cape Svatoj Nos, a prominent navigation landmark on the coast. At that point, copilot Olmstead sighted an unspecified MiG fighter off the right wing, but the MiG disappeared and the crew continued on their flight plan. Soon thereafter, Major Palm was surprised to see a MiG-17 flying about 50 feet off his right wing. As Palm maneuvered his aircraft to provide some distance between himself and the MiG, the Soviet fighter pulled in behind the RB-47 and began firing his guns. The first burst from the MiG's cannons hit the two engine pod on the left wing, causing the RB-47 to go into an uncontrollable flat spin. Unable to get the aircraft under control, Palm ordered the crew to bail out. Only Olmstead and McKone were able to successfully eject from the aircraft. It isn't clear whether Major Palm bailed out or stayed with the aircraft in an attempt to give his crew time to safely escape and attempted to ditch the RB-47 at sea. Allied radars tracking the aircraft reported that it crashed two hundred miles off the Soviet coast. The Soviets recovered Major Palm's body and turned it over to United States authorities; he was later buried with honors in Arlington National Cemetery. The bodies of the three Ravens were never found. McKone and Olmstead were rescued by Soviet naval vessels, taken to Moscow and charged with espionage.

In a memorandum from the head of the KGB, Alexandr Shelepin, to Premier Khrushchev dated October 17, 1960, Shelepin reported the discovery of parts of the RB-47 at the bottom of the Barents by a Soviet trawler. He stated that the aircraft was located about 60-70 miles off-shore, approximately where the crew said they were. The discrepancy in location of where the aircraft went down versus where the Soviets reported they located the wreckage was likely due to tracking errors or pure distortions.

The Soviet trawler also reported bringing up partial remains of "a U.S. Air Force pilot, Evgenij Ehrnest Poz, (Major Eugene Posa.)" They said they could read the nametag on his flight suit along with an ID card bearing his finger print and serial number. However, the final burial place of Major Posa's remains has never been determined or reported by the Russians. Several of the crewmember's wives petitioned the United Nations for information on the disposition of their missing husbands, with Major Posa's wife, Patricia, finally receiving a letter from Henry Cabot Lodge expressing his regrets. McKone and Olmstead were released on January 24, 1961, on orders from Premier Khrushchev after seven months in prison. Their release was called a goodwill gesture to the newly inaugurated President Kennedy.

Meanwhile, Gary Powers remained in a Soviet prison for more than a year after the return of McKone and Olmstead. He was finally released in exchange for Colonel Rudolph Abel, a convicted espionage agent being held by the United States.

Following is an insightful interview with Colonel John McKone conducted by The National Security Archive on August 30, 1996, as a part of their substantial contribution to the Cold War history series:

Interviewer: "First of all would you tell me your name and your title?"

John McKone: "I'm John McKone, I'm a retired Air Force colonel and that's my name and my rank is a full colonel in the United States Air Force and I'm retired."

Interviewer: "Thank you. Colonel McKone, can I ask, first of all just could you take us back to 1959-1960, what were you doing at that period?"

John McKone: "At the time of my life back in nineteen hundred and fifty nine, nineteen hundred and sixty, I was flying with the Strategic Air Command as a bomb person on a RB-47 and I was flying with the 55th Strategic Reconnaissance Wing, 343rd Squadron out of Forbes Air Force Base, Topeka, Kansas."

Interviewer: "And what was their role?"

John McKone: "The role at that particular wing at that time was to fly electronic warfare missions against different places in the world, throughout the entire world, to pick up information for the United States."

Interviewer: "When you say information, what sort of information were you out there looking for?"

John McKone: "Just about anything that you might want to think electronically, whether it was voice communications or radar sites, information, radio transmissions, telemetering type of information, anything in that particular area that was transmitted through the air, we were out to try to pick up."

Interviewer: "Just in general terms, can you tell me how you went about that? What would a mission involve?"

John McKone: "Well, to explain those missions would be rather complex, because some of them were rather complex in nature. But very simply put, the missions were... we would take off from a forward locating base, whether it was in England or Japan or Alaska, wherever it would be, and we would fly around the periphery of the Soviet Union and do what we could to pick up this airborne radiological type of information."

Interviewer: "How many of these sort of flights were taking place?"

John McKone: "Well, for me as an individual crewmember, it'd be hard to estimate. But I can remember that I would fly in a particular month, anywhere from six to ten to fifteen missions, maybe a month when I was overseas. So it was fairly often for me, I did not have at that particular time the information of how many total missions our particular unit was flying, so it would be hard to estimate, but we did have, I would say, four, five airplanes on station overseas at any one particular time, so we were fairly busy."

Interviewer: "It's astonishing. Could you tell me, before we get on to specifics of the infamous day, what was it like flying these missions? Was it frightening, was it boring?"

John McKone: "Well, let me say that flying these missions, we did not ever take as routine. We knew that these missions were vitally important to the security of our country. At that particular time in the Cold War, for us, it was almost a Hot War, and in fact at times it did become a Hot War. The only armament we had on our airplanes were two twenty-millimeter canon in the tail. We test fired those canon before we'd take off on these missions overseas to make sure they'd function and if they didn't function, we would go back and land. So again, while we were not very heavily defended to protect ourselves, whatever defense we had, we ensured worked; the same way with the radios. We did have radios that had long-range capability and we could talk to our different bases with our radios and we made sure those worked and if they didn't work, then again we'd turn around and land. We knew that other people - and in fact I had been on flights where we had airplanes that would come up and visit us as we call them, that had the red stars on 'em and painted green and we knew that they were there and sometimes were very friendly. They would wave at us and we would wave at them and then they'd leave. There'd be other times when they would be...airplanes that would come up like that, we'd have one on either side of our wings, flying in formation with us, and then we'd call a junior coming up the tail, about two thousand feet below us and firing his canon and you could see the shells exploding in front of our airplane. So again there were times that things got very, very tight and there would be times when they would actually shoot at us. So, again, it was anything but routine as far as we were concerned, but at the same time, we knew that we had a very important and vital mission to fulfill, because we knew that if we didn't do our job, the bomber streams that would come in behind us would not know where to go on to avoid or to jam their ground to air radar systems and radio systems and so forth."

Interviewer: "How did you and your colleagues at the time view the Russians?"

John McKone: "Well, let's just say that we did not believe that they were 'friendlies'. the Russians at that particular time were in a very antagonistic, aggressive posture, this was the time if you remember in history where President Eisenhower tried the open skies program. Khrushchev at that time, who was the Premier of the Soviet Union, rejected that out of hand. He came to the UN and pounded his shoe on the table there at the UN, trying to get his way. They were very aggressive and in Western Europe a few years before that we had the Berlin Airlift, then we had Korea and the Korean War. We knew that they were supplying pilots to the Korean air force at that particular war time stance and it was a very terse time, as far as we were concerned."

Interviewer: "Could you take me through what happened on the first of July 1960?"

John McKone: "I recall that particular flight very vividly. That we took off from Brize Norton Air Base in England, that was our forward operating location on that particular day, and we were supposed to fly this quote-unquote 'milk run'. There were not supposed to be any particular problems during that particular flight and we thought that this would be a rather simple flight, although it was a twelve-hour mission. We did refuel with a brand new

KC-135 jet tanker from SAC and that was quite a thrill, because we didn't have to fly behind the old KC-97 propeller driven tanker and we did that about a hundred and fifty miles off the coast of Norway, flying in (inaudible) out to the coast of Norway and Norwegian Sea. We got up into the Barents Sea, which was north and east of Norway, in the Arctic Ocean, we started flying (inaudible) out to the Soviet coastline, which had Murmansk and the mouth of the White Sea and so forth up there, and we knew there was quite a bit of activity going on up there by the Russians at that time. So we were quite interested in that particular area. And as we were flying parallel to the coastline, a couple of fighters came out and made a beam pass on our airplane from ninety degrees to our aircraft; we could see the con trails, but that's all we saw, and then as it came closer to the turning point, after flying for about thirty minutes, we came close to the mouth of the White Sea and in order to stay in international waters, we were about fifty to sixty miles away from the nearest Soviet land mass, we had to make about a ninety degree left turn. And I'd already given the aircraft commander the new heading to take and had a radar fix of a couple of known points at that particular point, and I said, OK, Bill, it's time to make your left turn now, because I had the fix, very positive, I knew exactly where we were and at that time, just about at the same time, the co-pilot said, check, check, check right wing and the aircraft commander, Major Pond said, where the hell did that guy come from? And he started his left turn and as we started our left turn, the co-pilot watching this aircraft said that he saw him come down below and behind and without any warning, started firing his canon and the canon shells hit the number two and three engine. They caught fire, according to the co-pilot and seized and went ninety degrees to the air-stream, like this, and served as a big rudder and that was at about thirty thousand feet; that was the altitude we were flying at that time. And then we had a second burst of fire from the fighter, after we'd leveled out about twenty eight thousand feet and I see the holes opening up around where I sat in the fend of the airplane in my station, and I saw fire coming down the aisle way and then I heard the aircraft commander say, 'Bail Out! Bail Out! Bail Out!' on the intercom.

"I saw red bail out lights going off and alarm bells ringing to bail out. I heard a couple or explosions behind me and I decided that was the time to get out of that thing. So then I went ahead and pulled my ejection seats and handles and then I was shot out of the airplane on a seventy five millimeter canon shell and free fell from twenty eight thousand to fourteen thousand feet, whereupon my chute automatically opened and I looked around and I saw a bunch of papers flying in the air, saw a very intense fire on the water and a couple of chutes below me. One of them was about a thousand feet below me, another about two thousand feet and they had the same orange and white panels as mine, so I assumed they were other crew members and the first one looked like my aircraft commander. The second was closer and I could almost identify him as Captain Olmsted the co-pilot, and the first fellow was hanging limp in his chute, he never moved all the way down to the water, so I assumed he was unconscious and that was probably aircraft commander Pond. The other three crew members; we had a six-man crew member."

Interviewer: "Thank you, Colonel McKone, you are a true hero."

Captains McKone and Olmstead were personally welcomed home by President Kennedy after their repatriation. The President cautioned the two that he had agreed with Khrushchev and that their families should not make their release a large celebrated event to avoid embarrassment of the Premier. Consequently, their release and return went scarcely unnoticed and each officer continued with their Air Force careers. Forty three years later in September 2003, John McKone and Bruce Olmstead, long since retired from active duty, were finally recognized for their heroic resistance while held prisoner in the KGB Lubyanka Prison, with the award of the Silver Star by Chief of Staff of the Air Force, General John Jumper.

At least 70 SAC and Navy reconnaissance aviators were lost during the Cold War period. However, due to the sensitivity and continued classification of U.S. reconnaissance operations, the names of many of these men are still not revealed.

BMEWS "HICCUP."

On the night of November 24, 1961, all communication links between SAC Headquarters and North American Air Defense Command (NORAD) suddenly went silent, cutting SAC off from the three highly dependent Ballistic Missile Early Warning sites (BMEWS) at Thule (Greenland), Clear (Alaska) and Filingdales (England). CINCSAC, General Thomas Power at SAC Headquarters in Omaha, had to quickly consider perhaps the only two possible explanations for the abrupt communications failure; either a Soviet terrorist attack on the warning systems or the virtual unlikelihood of a coincidental failure of all the communication systems which he knew had sophisticated redundant and ostensibly independent circuitry routing, including backup commercial telephone systems. He couldn't take a chance on the latter. All SAC units were promptly alerted with B-52, B-47 and B-58 nuclear bomber crews responding to their aircraft, starting engines and standing by for further orders to launch an attack against the Soviet Union if necessary. Radio contact was finally made with a B-52 on airborne alert orbiting near Thule. The bomber crew contacted the BMEWS station at Thule by radio who reported that no attack had taken place at their location, but they had lost communications with NORAD Headquarters at Colorado Springs. Following several frantic minutes of reestablishing communications to confirm that no attack of any kind had taken place, CINCSAC called off the alert. A prompt investigation into the unusual and "coincidental" failure revealed that the redundant routes for all telecommunications between NORAD, the outlying BMEWS sites and SAC Headquarters all ran through one relay station in Colorado and a motor at the relay station had overheated, causing a world-wide interruption of all critical communications channels. The fragile Cold War relations between the United States and the Soviet Union survived a critical near-miss and a vulnerability was immediately corrected... not to mention the great relief of the SAC bomber crews.

CUBAN MISSILE CRISIS

The Cuban Missile Crisis lasted two weeks, October 14 – 28, 1962. Many dangerous events took place during the brief period—some directly related to the critical situation, others were ancillary and unrelated, but compounded the drama.

Following several days of increasing tension growing out of a conflict with the Soviet Union over their intent to place medium range Soviet bombers and medium range ballistic missiles in Cuba, President Kennedy ordered the Commander-in-Chief, Strategic Air Command (SAC) to prepare to fully implement the B-52 airborne alert operation plan, Chromedome, on October 22nd. During August and September, the United States Navy had monitored a steady influx of suspicious Soviet cargo ships crossing the Atlantic and docking in Cuban ports. The U.S. had, over a period of several months, steadily tightened an economic embargo on Cuba in an attempt to coerce Fidel Castro into curtailing his bellicose activities in the Caribbean and to cease the inhumane treatment of his people. General Maxwell Taylor, Chairman of the Joint Chiefs of Staff, sent a brief assessment to Secretary McNamara as the crisis heightened: "We have the strategic advantage in our general war capabilities; we have the tactical advantage of our moral rightness, of boldness, of strength, of initiative, and of control of this situation. This is no time to run scared."

The crisis increased in intensity when a U-2 reconnaissance aircraft flown by Major Rudolph Anderson was shot down by a Soviet built anti-aircraft missile fired from a Cuban base. Major Anderson was killed and became the first casualty of the Crisis. U.S. radar controllers had tracked Anderson's aircraft from the time it took off from McCoy Air Force Base, Florida, until the moment it was shot down. Major Anderson apparently could not eject. His body was found strapped in the wreckage of the U-2 and was held by the Cubans until a personal appeal was made by United Nations Secretary-General U Thant to Fidel Castro for return of his remains.

SAC B-52 crews and their bombers fully loaded with nuclear weapons began flying airborne alert sorties from their bases in the United States and Puerto Rico. On any given day, between 40 and 50 B-52's were in the air and standing-off in orbit not too distant from the borders of the Soviet Union where they waited for an order from the President to strike their designated targets. Each bomber refueled twice during their mission, taking on a nominal 120,000 pounds of fuel during each aerial refueling. They remained in their designated orbit pattern locations until their fuel reserve dictated that they return to their home base. In the event of landing weather problems at their home base or other emergency situations, KC-135 aerial tankers were always on standby to respond. Concurrent with each bomber's return from the tense and arduous 25-hour flights, another fully nuclear configured B-52 and its combat crew took off to replace the returning aircraft and its very fatigued crew.

This author flew two airborne alert sorties in the B-52G during the Cuban Crisis event. The 25-hour missions were indeed, grueling. Perhaps one of the telling as well as a turning point in the crisis was the procedure directed by SAC; "Transmit position reports in the clear on HF radio band." This meant that HF (high frequency) transmissions could be heard world-wide, including the Kremlin command post. We commented in the cockpit at the time that our position reports, 30 or 40 seconds in length, were being given in turn and un-encoded by fifty to sixty B-52's flying literally around the perimeter of the Soviet Union, and what the Soviet leaders must be thinking when they heard the virtual endless stream of transmissions?

During the period, SAC had also relocated the majority of its B-47 bomber force and supporting tankers to forward bases to shorten their flying time in the event they were also ordered to launch a direct attack against the Soviet Union.

The reaction to the overt attempt by the Soviet Union to place medium bombers and MRBM's (medium range ballistic missiles) capable of delivering nuclear weapons on the island of Cuba and 90 miles from the U.S. coast, without question, placed the United States and the Soviet Union at the closest point of an all-out war, nuclear exchange and Armageddon. Thereafter, Soviet policy appeared content to support conventional proxy confrontations such as Vietnam while the U.S. declaratory policy of nuclear deterrence remained firm.

ANCILLARY CUBAN CRISIS EVENTS

An anomalous event occurred at the height of the Cuban Crisis on October 24, 1962, when the Soviets unexpectedly launched a missile carrying a satellite. Shortly after entering its parking orbit, the satellite exploded. Sir Bernard Lovell, director of the Jodrell Bank observatory in the United Kingdom wrote in 1968: "The explosion of a Russian spacecraft in orbit during the Cuban Missile Crisis...led the U.S. to believe that the USSR was launching a massive ICBM attack. The NORAD Command Post logs of the dates in question remain classified, perhaps to conceal the nature of the critical concern and reaction to the event." The occurrence is recorded, however, and U.S. space tracking stations were informed a week later on October 31, 1963, of the space debris resulting from breakup of "62 BETA IOTA".

CURIOUS TRESPASSER

Neither was there a shortage of humor during the tense days of the Crisis. On October 25th, yet another event occurred around midnight when a guard at the NORAD Duluth, Minnesota Sector Direction Center saw a figure climbing the security fence. He shot at the intruder and activated the "Sabotage Alarm". This automatically set off sabotage alarms at all military installations in the area. At Volk Field, Wisconsin, the alarm triggered the Klaxon horns which automatically ordered the pilots on alert during the Cuban Crisis to launch their nuclear-armed F-106A fighter-interceptors. The pilots had been briefed that: "there would be no practice alert drills while DEFCON 3 was in force." Consequently they believed World War III had started and they would be directed toward incoming Soviet intruders. Immediate communication with the Duluth Direction Center indicated that the Sabotage Alarm had been activated in error. By this time, the interceptor aircraft were starting down the runway. A staff car raced from the Volk Field Command Center and successfully signaled the aircraft to stop their take-off roll. The intruder climbing over the fence at Duluth had been a bear.

"ROUTINE" LAUNCH

On October 26th at Vandenberg Air Force Base, California, there was a program of routine ICBM test flights. When SAC declared Defcon 3 during the Cuban Crisis, all ICBM's at the test base were fitted with nuclear warheads with the exception of one Titan II missile that had been scheduled for a test launch. Without further instructions from SAC Headquarters or the Pentagon, the Titan II was *routinely* launched at 4:00 a.m. It can be assumed that the Soviets were closely monitoring U.S. missile activities as were U.S. observers monitoring all Soviet and Cuban activities. They would have also likely known of the expected changeover to nuclear warheads when they observed the increase in the defense readiness condition (DEFCON 3). Upon receiving notice of the unexpected test launch, the Pentagon hastened by every communication means to allay the fears of the Soviets.

UNINTENDED CONSEQUENCES

Yet another coincidental and particularly significant event unrelated to the Cuban Crisis occurred on October 26th, which had the potential to seriously exacerbate the tenuous situation. A previously planned reconnaissance mission irrelevant to the events in the Caribbean scheduled SAC U-2 pilot, Captain Chuck Maultsby, to fly an experimental navigation route over the North Pole.

Captain Maultsby would be required to make geographic position checks on his flight using only the sextant as his only navigation instrument. The following narrative describes the harrowing mission in the pilot's own words edited posthumously by his widow, Jeanne Maultsby, and provided to this journal by Major General Pat Halloran, former U-2 pilot colleague of Chuck Maultsby.

"Things were beginning to heat up down in Cuba, just before I was to make the flight to the Pole. We heard some of the U-2 drivers in our squadron were over flying Cuba to ascertain whether or not the Russian missiles were being off loaded on Cuban soil. If they were, things could get dicey in a hurry. It was October 25th, 1962; the day Billie Bye, Fred Okimoto, Bob Yates and I would plan my flight the following day.

"Since my take off was scheduled for midnight the 26th, I tried to get plenty of sleep during the day, but it was next to impossible. People were tromping in and out of the BOQ in their heavy snow boots throughout the day. The harder I tried to sleep, the more awake I became. I finally gave up and went down to our operation building and sacked out on a cot. No one would show up until three hours before my take off time. I awoke around eight pm and proceeded to the Officers mess for a breakfast of steak and eggs. Bob, Billie and Fred were there wondering where I was. They didn't get much sleep either. Pre-flight preparations having been completed, I took off on time and proceeded direct to Barter Island. Duck Butt Control (an airborne control team aboard an Air Force C-54 monitoring the flight) gave me a call on a pre-briefed frequency and said we both should arrive over Barter Island about the same time. They wished me luck and said they would keep a light in the window for me.

"Over the Barter Island radio beacon, I set course for the Pole and prepared to take the first (sextant) fix. All went according to plan until I was about half way between Barter Island and the Pole. Streaks of light started dancing through the sky, making it difficult to take a fix on the star I was shooting. I had heard of the phenomena 'Aurora Borealis' or the Northern lights, but this was my first experience with them. They couldn't have occurred at a worst time. The further North I got, the more intense they became. I held my heading and just hoped the star I thought I saw was the right one.

"The last few fixes before reaching the Pole, if in fact I did reach it, were highly suspect. You can see anything if you want to bad enough. I had no reason to believe I was off course, in spite of the suspect fixes, so I decided to go ahead and do a 90-270 degree turn; left for 90 degrees then immediately turn at the pre-determined time that would put me over the Pole. This track should have headed me straight for Barter Island. I was out of radio range with Duck Butt, not that there was anything they could do, but I would like to hear a friendly voice now and then!

"I had never flown over a land mass that you couldn't see a single light from horizon to horizon. Of course there were no lights on the ice caps, but didn't the Duck Butt crew say they would leave a light in the window? The first two fixes I took after leaving the Pole were wishful hoping and I began to realize something was terribly wrong. I began calling in the clear, hoping somebody out there might hear me and steer me in the right direction. I still thought I was on the right track for Barter Island, but the ETA was still some time away. It wasn't until I was out from under the Aurora Borealis effect that I knew for sure I was off course, but which way? I didn't bother to attempt to take any more fixes...just fly time and distance and hope for the best. I was approximately three or four hundred miles north of Barter Island, or thought I was when the first radio contact with Duck Butt was accomplished.
I heard someone in our command post back at Eielson calling over the single side band radio, but they couldn't receive my call. Surely I was in range of the radio beacon at Barter Island, but I couldn't pick it up. Had it shut down, or what?

"As the ETA for Barter Island wound down to 30 or 40 minutes, Duck Butt called and said they would start firing flares every five minutes, starting immediately. They were orbiting over Barter Island and said the radio beacon was in operation and they were receiving it loud and clear. I didn't see the flare and asked them to fire another one. By this time I should have been over Barter Island and should have been able to see the flare. They fired another... nothing. It was all I could do to fight off a panic attack. I was either many miles east or west of Barter Island...but which?

"The navigator aboard the Duck Butt called and asked me if I could identify a star. I told him I had the Belt of Orion constellation about 15 degrees left of the nose of the aircraft. Several minutes later the navigator aboard

Duck Butt called and told me to steer 10 degrees left. Almost immediately I received another call from an unknown source, using my call sign, telling me to turn 30 degrees right. What the hell is going on? The navigator in the Duck Butt didn't hear the latest call, so I just knew I was miles west of Barter Island. Again I received a call from the unknown source, telling me to turn right 35 degrees. I challenged him, using a code only a legit operator would know, but did not receive any response. Duck Butt called and asked me if I could see a glow on the horizon to the east. I replied, 'Negative.'

"Transmissions from Duck Butt were getting weaker by the minute and the last one I heard was 'turn left, 15 degrees.' The transmissions from the unknown source were loud and clear, but I ignored them. I selected the emergency channel and broadcast, 'MAY DAY! MAY DAY! MAY DAY!' as loud as I could. I only had about 30 minutes of fuel left, with no prospect of landing back at Eielson or anywhere else, for that matter. The U-2 carries enough fuel for nine hours and forty minutes of flight and I had been airborne nine hours and ten minutes. Suddenly I picked up a radio station directly off the nose of the aircraft, it sounded like Russian music. It came in loud and clear. Now I knew where I was!

"The suppressed panic started to set in. I knew one thing though, I wasn't going to be another Gary Powers and spend time in a Russian prison. With what little fuel I had left, I decided to get as far away as possible from that radio station. I turned left until it was directly behind me...I kept calling 'MAY DAY!' until I became hoarse. Why bother, there's nothing anyone could do, so I may as well save my breath. Twelve minutes of fuel left now, so I made a call in the clear, to let anyone who might be listening, know that I was going off the air. A sense of despair set in as I shut the engine down. Here I was just above 75,000 feet over God knows where, encased in a pressure suit which had inflated to keep my blood from boiling and all I could think of was, 'This is a fine mess you got yourself into Charlie.'

"When the suit inflated I neglected to pull the lanyard which keeps the helmet from rising and had a hellava time seeing the instrument panel, until I finally got it back into place. The windshield fogged up immediately and the face piece followed shortly thereafter. I wanted to conserve the battery, so I could make one call before I punched out. I thought for a while that the altimeter had stuck. At least ten minutes went by before the aircraft started to descend. In order to see the instrument panel, I had to press my helmet as close to my face as possible, in order to lick the condensation off the faceplate. Now all I had to do was keep the wings level, maintain a rate of descent for maximum range and hope my guardian angel wasn't taking a nap! The silence was deafening. All I could hear was my labored breathing. Up to now Mother

Nature hadn't extended an invitation to relieve my bladder, but wouldn't you know she makes a call at the most inopportune time.

"I wasn't about to unzip the pressure suit and have my 'winky' pinched off. Besides, I didn't think I could find it under all the winter gear I was wearing. I felt like a forty-pound robin! I wandered off the heading I had established; not that it mattered that much, but I still wanted to feel I was in control of an impossible situation.

"It had been twenty minutes since flame out and damned if I didn't see a faint glow on the horizon directly in front of me. I thought, I'd hold this heading and rate of descent until I reach 20,000 feet. If I'm in an overcast I'd better punch out, because I don't want to meet up with a mountain, if one is indeed in my flight path. If there aren't any clouds, I'll descend to 15,000 feet and take it from there. As I descended through 25,000 feet there weren't any clouds and the pressure suit started deflating.   Thank God, now I could look around, because it was light enough to see the terrain, which was blanketed with snow. There were no mountains in sight, but what I did see were two F-102's, one on each wing. They were both flying at near stall speed and their angle of attack looked dangerously steep. I actuated the battery switch and gave them a call on the emergency frequency. They welcomed me home and said they had been following me for the past fifteen minutes. They also said I had just passed over a little airstrip about twenty miles back. I told the F-102 driver off my left wing that I was going to make a left turn, so he'd better move out. He said 'No sweat, come on.'

"When I turned into him, he stalled out and disappeared under my left wing. Later he said, 'While I'm down here, I'll look for that little airstrip.'

"The F-102 drivers were getting nervous when I descended below 5,000 feet. They were use to setting up a flame out pattern with a high key of 10,000 feet but they weren't flying a glider. When I reached 1,000 feet, I could not detect any crosswind, which relieved my mind somewhat. I started a left turn out to sea and the F-102 drivers came unglued!...'Bail Out! Bail Out!' they yelled.

"I continued my turn on around to low key, lowered the flaps and decided I was getting too much thrust out of the idling J-57 so I shut it down. Everything looked good so far. I was coming up on the runway now with more airspeed than I wanted. As I passed over the end at about 15 feet, I deployed the drag shoot and kicked the rudder back and forth. That took care of the excessive airspeed nicely. The U-2 didn't seem to want to stop flying, even without an engine. Call it luck or whatever; I think I made the best touchdown to date. I hardly felt a thing as both landing gear settled in one foot of snow. The landing roll was less than 200 feet, thanks to the snow piling up in front of the landing gear. When the U-2 came to a complete stop, I just sat there staring straight ahead, as if in a trance. I was completely drained both physically and emotionally. I don't remember how long I sat there, but a knock on the canopy startled me. I turned to face a bearded giant who was grinning from ear to ear. He wore a parka that I recognized as being Government Issue. He reminded me of 'Grizzly Adams.'

"Before I opened the canopy, I un-strapped the seat belt and shoulder harness, made sure all switches were off and stowed the maps that had been useless to me; off with the faceplate and a breath of real air. After I opened the canopy the bearded giant said, 'Welcome to Kotzebue.'

"I said, 'You don't know how glad I am to be here!' It was bitter cold as I tried to climb out of the cockpit with all the heavy flight gear. I didn't think my legs would support my weight...they were numb. My new found friend sensed the difficulty I was having, so he put his hands under my armpits and gently lifted me out of the cockpit and placed me on the snow as if I had been a rag doll. He wasn't standing on a ladder or box! There were several more personnel from the radar station that gathered around, plus a half dozen Eskimos who came from the shacks I saw while airborne. 'Grizzly' gave me a hand taking off the helmet and had someone place it on the vehicle they arrived in. The two F-102's buzzed us rocking their wings, and then headed east. I thought, I'll have to thank them somehow for making this landing possible. My bladder was about to burst so I excused myself and shuffled to the other side of the U-2. The Eskimos followed me, but when they saw what I was about to do they politely turned their heads. Soon more people showed up to look at the strange bird, until there were about twenty or so gathered. I never had such a large audience before to watch me tinkle.

"I was glad to be inside a warm building and couldn't wait to get out of the pressure suit. The radar site commander let me use a secure phone in his office and brought me a mug of hot coffee to sip on. Sure enough it was 'Whip' Wilson, he had been standing by the radio ever since I took off. I told him the aircraft was okay, no damage done, but the fuel tanks were dry. He said a C-47 was loading up now with drums of fuel and maintenance people and that he would be along to fly the U-2 back to Eielson. I asked if anyone had notified my wife, Jeanne that I was over due. He said no one had. Good! At least she won't know a thing until I tell her. He did say however that my little excursion over Russia sure had the White House and SAC Headquarters shook up.

"I thought, 'I'll bet!' It was several hours before the C-47 landed at Kotzebue, so I had time to unwind and get acquainted with the radar site personnel. The site commander asked if I would like to see where I had been. I nodded, yes. He took me into a room with the largest plotting screen I had ever seen. There was a map of the polar region to include Alaska and Siberia

DETERRENCE

about fifteen Feet Square, over-laid with clear plastic glass. When he flipped a switch, a battery of lights illuminated the entire screen. And there it was, my entire flight from start to finish, indicated by little tick marks made with a yellow grease pencil. The tick marks traced a path from Eielson Air Force Base direct to Barter Island and to the North Pole. A 90 degree left turn over the Pole was indicated, but instead of a 270 degree turn in the opposite direction, it looked like I turned 300 or 310 degrees before rolling out and heading for Siberia. At this point I was beginning to see. I followed the tick marks where the Duck Butt navigator told me to steer 10 degrees left and later 15 degrees left. Then the tick marks made a sharp left turn and headed for Kotzebue. I was about to turn to the radar site commander and ask him, why in hell I hadn't been given a steer when all along they knew where I was, but my attention was directed to six little tick marks on either side of my flight path as I changed course to Kotzebue.

"I asked, 'What are those little curly Q's?'

"He said, 'Those little curly Q's represent the six MiGs that were nipping up trying to shoot you down.'

"I thought, 'Shit oh dear!' I'm glad I didn't know it at the time...Whew!' I stumbled over to a chair and took the weight off, fearing my legs were about to give out. He pulled up a chair alongside mine and said, 'I know what you are thinking and I don't blame you, but there is a good reason why we couldn't help you, I can't tell you, but maybe someone higher up will.'

"I said, 'Gee thanks, I hope the reason justifies throwing away an aircraft and crew.'

"I was still digesting all that I learned when the phone rang. Someone in another room said it was for the U-2 pilot. It was one of the F-102 pilots stationed at Galena Air Base who had escorted me into Kotzebue. He said he was glad to see that I had made it down safely and apologized for yelling 'Bail Out' when I turned out to sea at 1,000 feet. He had never seen a U-2 before and couldn't believe one could glide like that. I told him to come visit us at Eielson and we would give him a cook's tour.

"The C-47 finally arrived and took me back to Eielson. When I arrived there was a KC-135 waiting to fly me to SAC Headquarters at Offutt Air Force Base in Omaha, Nebraska. There I was to brief General Power and his staff on my flight, especially the over-flight of Russia. He also told me that Major Rudolph Anderson had been shot down over Cuba today by a SA-2 surface-to-air missile. That took the wind out of my sails. Everyone that knew him would sorely miss him.

"I had hoped to get a bite to eat after arriving at Eielson, but there wasn't any time. I thought, maybe they'll have some chow on the KC-135. I don't remember how long the flight to Offutt took, but it couldn't have taken long

201

enough to suit me. I wasn't anxious to meet General Power, after all that had happened in the past twenty-four hours. I was the only passenger on board the KC-135, which gave me a feeling of anxiety about the briefing I was to give at SAC Headquarters. General Power must deem it very important to learn the circumstances surrounding my over flight. Surely he must know all the details by now, but I suppose he wanted to hear it from the 'horse's mouth.'

"The flight crew on board the KC-135 was dying of curiosity to learn why they were flying me to SAC Headquarters, but never came right out and asked. They had probably been briefed not to discuss the reason for the flight with anyone, especially me. They did provide that hot meal I was hoping for. After landing at Offutt, a staff car took me to SAC Headquarters, where a full Colonel who escorted me to the underground command post met me. The place was a beehive of activity; people actually running from place to place, as if their lives depended on it. Adjacent to the command post there was a large briefing room, with a table large enough to seat at least twenty people. At the head of the table an easel held an aeronautical chart, on which my flight was plotted up to the North Pole. A sheet of paper was taped over the portion of the chart that would depict my flight after leaving the Pole. The Colonel told me to take a seat and General Power would be with us in a few minutes. When General Power did enter the room, eight other generals who looked as if they hadn't been out of their uniforms for days followed him. Their eyes were blood shot and some hadn't seen a razor the past 24 hours. I stood at attention while they were all seated. General Power was seated directly across the table from me. He looked extremely tired, but was clean-shaven and wore a clean uniform. I didn't recognize any of the other generals.

"As soon as everyone was seated, with their eyes riveted on me, General Power said, 'Captain Maultsby, how about briefing us on your flight yesterday.'

"I stood at the easel while describing the type mission, then took the pointer and indicated the route flown from Eielson to the North Pole. I mentioned the difficulty I had taking fixes, because of the Aurora Borealis.

"No one stopped me to ask questions, until I pointed to the North Pole. General Power then asked, 'Maultsby, do you know where you went after leaving the Pole?'

"I said, 'Yes sir.'

The other generals squirmed in their seats, as if they were sitting on tacks. General Power then asked, 'Show us please.'

"I took the pointer and lifted the paper that covered my flight path after leaving the Pole. The other generals really became excited now, but General Power only smiled.

He asked, 'How did you know?'

"I told him that I saw my flight path plotted in the radar site in Kotzebue. General Power turned and looked from one general to another and asked, 'Gentleman, do you have any more questions?' They all nodded negative. He then looked back at me and said, 'Too bad you weren't configured with a system to gather electromagnetic radiation. The Russians probably had every radar and ICBM site on maximum alert.'

"General Power thanked me for the briefing and told me not to discuss my over flight with anyone and left the room. The other generals followed in order of rank but the last to leave the room, a Brigadier General, stopped and said, 'You are a lucky little devil, I've seen General Power chew up and spit out people for doing a hellava lot less.'

"The Colonel who escorted me into the command post asked me if I'd like to wait in his office as there was a U-3A flying up from Laughlin Air Force Base, Texas, to pick me up. It wasn't due for another hour or so. I thought now would be a good time to find out why I wasn't given a steer when every Tom, Dick and Harry had my flight path plotted. The Colonel wouldn't tell me why I wasn't given a steer but he did say that my over flight came close to starting world war three. If it hadn't been for my 'May Day' calls, the Russians may have pulled the trigger. He also told me that when President Kennedy was informed about my over-flight, he simply said, 'There's always some son of a bitch that doesn't get the word.'

"Well, if I had gotten the word, I wouldn't be sitting here now. Just one steer would have prevented all this commotion.

"A phone call from Base Operations announced the arrival of a U-3A from Laughlin. I thanked the Colonel for his hospitality and left that underground command post, still wondering why I wasn't given a steer. It would bug me for years, before I found out why. Captain Ed Purdue was waiting for me in the flight planning room in base ops when I arrived and said everyone back at Laughlin had been sweating me out. He said he didn't think anyone had told Jeanne, for which I was thankful. He was anxious to hear all about my fiasco, but when I told him General Power told me not to discuss the flight with anyone, he didn't pursue the issue. Ed said he flew through some pretty nasty weather on his way up and hoped it had cleared for the flight back. The weather station forecast wasn't optimistic. Just north of Enid, Oklahoma, we ran into icing conditions and couldn't maintain altitude. We called Vance Air Force Base, which was located near Enid, and told them we were icing up and requested immediate landing instructions. To make matters worse, one engine was losing power, which increased our rate of descent. We requested a straight in GCA and declared an emergency. When GCA picked us up we were already below the glide path still descending.

"I thought...'What a way to go.' After all I had been through the past two days.

"For the next two hours I recited the same briefing I gave to General Power, et al, down to the last period. You could hear a pin drop throughout the entire briefing. Except for an occasional muttered, 'Oh shit' when I described the six MiGs after my fanny, no one asked a question until I finished. Everyone seemed more interested in the thoughts that went through my mind during the ordeal than the cause of the over flight. All agreed it was a flight that they were glad they weren't in my place. With that, my boss General Des Portes, thanked me and said, 'Now get back to Jeanne and the boys and take the next two days off.'

"Jeanne met me at the door with a cool one and said, 'After you change I'm dying to know what all the commotion is about. Just tell me one thing, with a quick yes or no, does it have anything to do with Rudy Anderson being shot down?' We had become good friends with the Andersons. 'I'll tell you all about the commotion, and no it doesn't have anything to do with Rudy's shoot down, but first let me change. By the way, if the boys come in, I'll have to wait until we are alone to fill you in on my latest escapade.'

"Jeanne sat as still as a mouse, her huge eyes looking even larger as I went through the events of the past three days. Well that's it, now you know what all the commotion was all about. She just shook her head and said, 'I let you out of my sight and you try to start world war three!'

"Before she could say another word, Chuckie and Shawn came bursting through the door shouting, 'What did you bring me?' I felt like saying, 'I brought your daddy's ass home!'"

Captain Chuck Maultsby's experience embodies several important features of the typical SAC aviator—his cool management and control of a critical situation; the cooperative efforts of the Air Defense Command F-102 pilots to get a fellow airman down safely; the professional and personal concern of CINCSAC, General Thomas Power and perhaps the most gratifying, the bravery and support of those behind the lines, his wife, Joanne, and two sons.

These were but a few of the unexpected events that occurred spontaneously during the critical days of Cuban Crisis. Similar, but unknown aberrations likely also transpired in the Soviet Union. Fortunately, neither side over-reacted! The conclusion of the Cuban Crisis resulted in the installation of the famous "Hot Line" between Moscow and Washington to avert potential future misunderstandings.

OPERATION ARC LIGHT

SAC was called early-on in the Vietnam Conflict. KC-135 tankers were initially located on Guam and Okinawa to support tactical fighter operations of both the Air Force and the Navy. As the intensity of the war increased such as Operation Arc Light, the rooting out of Viet Cong from their dense jungle hideouts, so did the requirement for aerial refueling with tankers being further deployed to Taiwan and Thailand. At its peak, SAC was operating 175 KC-135 tankers in Southeast Asia.

Skilled airmanship and heroism of SAC combat crews were demonstrated daily. One such example took place on May 31, 1967, on an Arc Light support mission when Major John Casteel and his tanker crew found themselves over the Gulf of Tonkin and instructed to contact the Navy task force about a possible emergency. When the call came, the tanker was in the process of off-loading fuel to two Air Force F-104's, so Casteel "took the two fighters along" refueling them along the way as he headed toward the designated location of the impending emergency. Arriving at the rendezvous point, the tanker crew discovered a pair of Navy A-3 aerial tankers low on fuel themselves and unable to make it back to their aircraft carrier, the USS Hancock. One of the A3's was down to 3 minutes of usable fuel, although he had plenty in his transfer tanks, unable to transfer fuel back into his own engine fuel tanks. The KC-135 quickly transferred 2,300 pounds of fuel to the first A-3 and then hooked up with the second one. As the refueling process was taking place, two desperate Navy F-8 fighters showed up, one of which was at dry tanks. The F-8 was instructed to hook-up to the A-3 that was still off-loading fuel from Casteel's KC-135. As it has been noted in several journals, this was probably the first and only "three-deep" refueling operation ever recorded. As this activity was taking place, the second A-3 began refueling the other F-8. Major Casteel's KC-135 had successfully refueled two F-104's, two A-3's and two F-8's, six different aircraft and then had to again refuel the F-104's who had stayed along side the tanker to fly "shotgun" in the event of possible enemy intercepts. But, the day wasn't over for Casteel and his SAC tanker crew. As they were about to head back to their home base at U Tapao, Thailand, two Navy F-4's based on the aircraft carrier, the USS Constellation, showed up with insufficient fuel to make it back to their carrier. The tanker crew gave them an emergency fill-up and then again to the F-104 escorts, which had only taken on short-loads during each previous refueling. By this time the KC-135 was beginning to run short of fuel itself, altered its mission and landed at Da Nang Air Base, Vietnam. During the extraordinary episode, the KC-135 crew had off-loaded 49,000 pounds of fuel to eight fighter aircraft in fourteen separate aerial refuelings! But another example of SAC combat crew discipline, airmanship and valor. Major Casteel's crew was awarded the coveted McKay Trophy for the most meritorious aerial accomplishment of the year.

OPERATION LINEBACKER

On the night of October 22, 1972, Captain N. J. Ostrozny and his B-52D crew were flying a mission over Vinh, North Vietnam. Within a few minutes after bombs away, the crew heard and felt a horrific explosion in the mid-section of the bomber. The bomb bay area of the aircraft had been hit by an anti-aircraft missile and fires quickly spread outward to both wings. The crew lost all communications within the bomber. There was no doubt among the crew that ejection was inevitable. Captain Ostrozny struggled to keep the flaming bomber under control as best he could while heading toward the border of friendly Thailand. Sergeant Ron Sellers was alone in his gunner's loft in the tail of the aircraft witnessing the fire spreading within each wing. One by one the engines flamed out until the fiery carcass became deadly quiet. Eventually, Sellers watched as the right wing tip dropped away and the aircraft swerved into a steep bank. Bailout was now imminent: Captain Bob Estes, the navigator, confirmed that they were over Thailand and Captain Ostrozny toggled the Bailout Switch. All six crew members safely escaped the doomed bomber and were promptly rescued near Nakhon Phanom, Thailand. The North Vietnamese had scored their first shoot-down of a B-52.

Linebacker II also known as the "Eleven-Day War," was conducted between December 18th and 29th 1972, and was the final assault on North Vietnam. Colonel (later Brigadier General) James R. McCarthy recalls: "The crew members were casually milling around the briefing room that afternoon, too casual, I thought. So I decided to try to get their attention...I began the first of three briefings with: Gentlemen, your target for tonight is Hanoi. That got their attention...thereafter you could hear a pin drop in the briefing room." McCarthy had directed the planning of this mission and also flew that day himself with a chest full of pneumonia. The Soviet trawler that had sat off the end of the runway at Guam during all the years of the B-52 operations in Vietnam, and had ostensibly radioed to the North Vietnamese information regarding expected strike missions throughout the war was also on duty that day. Shortly after 3:00 p.m. on the 18th, Major Bill Stocker and his crew began the take-off roll—the first of 120 B-52's that launched on their first mission to North Vietnam.

Lt. Colonel George Allison recalled as the mission aircraft began to launch: "We're finally going to do it! It's long overdue! It was difficult to describe the feeling which develops gradually around intuition, hunches, rumors, logic and so on. But we were really going to bomb the North."

The seemingly endless number of B-52's continued to start engines and taxi to the runway throughout the afternoon into the evening with the last bomber taking off around midnight. Suddenly, the island of Guam fell into a deadly quiet after thunderous hours of jet engines roaring into the dark sky. The first wave of bombers over the target area of Haiphong was led by Colonel (later Brig. General) Tom Rew. After dropping their 750 pound bombs, Rew reported that they witnessed at least 200 surface to air missiles (SAMs) fired at them. At least one B-52 had been shot down and two were unaccounted for. Surprisingly, there were no reports of MiG fighter attacks.

"The SAMs lighted up the sky like the Fourth of July. It was a beautiful sight if I hadn't known how lethal they were," Rew said later. "I was sitting on the jump seat behind the two pilots and as we began our turn away from the target area, a large KABOOM shook the aircraft. We had been hit! The pilot had the aircraft under control although we had been badly damaged. The left wing was on fire and the aircraft was losing airspeed. After we were safely out of missile range, we inventoried the damage…the left wing fuel tank was missing and number one and two engines were shut down. Fire was streaming out of the wing; we had lost most of the flight instruments and cabin pressurization. The pilot headed the aircraft toward Thailand and we were joined by two F-4s to escort us. I unfastened my seat belt and looked over the pilot to the left wing…it was totally engulfed in flames. There was little doubt that we would have to bailout. I unplugged my headset and climbed down stairs to the Bomb Nav station just as the red ABANDON light came on. The navigator promptly pulled his ejection handles and disappeared downward out of the bomber. The radar bombardier turned to me and pointed to the hole in the aircraft left by the navigator's ejection seat. I climbed over some debris and looked at the hole and dark night below. At that moment, the aircraft began to shudder. I rolled forward into the hole and was out of the aircraft…as soon as I felt I was clear, I pulled my rip cord. There was full moon and as I came closer to ground, I could see that I was going to land in a small village. I maneuvered as best I could to keep from hitting a roof top. I didn't want to land in someone's bedroom. I hit the ground and rolled over. It was good to be alive!" 113 B-52's made it over their targets that night and three were lost to surface to air missiles.

Colonel McCarthy led the second night's raid. With a chest full of what later turned out to be double pneumonia, he and his crew churned into the target area with his flight in tow. He recalls: "As we were turning from the IP into the target, the gunner reported two SAM's, low and heading in our direction. The electronics warfare officer (EWO) reported that he was tracking the two missiles. The co-pilot then reported four SAM's coming up in our direction. We had our bag of tricks...SHRIKE anti-radiation missiles. We fired them and it was nice to see something bright headed away from us! As we neared our target, Hanoi, more SAM's were fired at us. We could see the ground clearly and when they fired a missile, magnified by the clouds, it looked like a whole city block lighted up. As the missiles broke through the clouds they appeared to be the size of a basketball, illuminated by the exhaust of the rocket engine. As it approached the aircraft, it took on the appearance of a silver donut...our crews nicknamed them 'deadly donuts'. About two minutes from bomb release, the SAM's were replaced by conventional anti-aircraft AAA fire. Watching the multicolored flak below us was a welcome relief, that is until we arrived directly over Hanoi and the barrage of SAM's began all over again. Miraculously, there were no bombers lost on the second night. The B-52's had flown large strikes earlier but none that had the effect of this one. The turning point of the war had finally arrived. The U.S. kept up the pressure on succeeding days through December 29th flying sixty plane bombing missions to "clean-up" the previously bombed target areas. McCarthy was awarded the Air Force Cross for his brilliant leadership in planning and leading the mission.

ASSAULT ON HANOI

Captain John D. Mize and his B-52D crew were among the bombers making a massive attack on targets near Hanoi on the night of December 27, 1972. Looking out the cockpit window, Mize said he counted at least five or six surface to air missiles (SAM's) headed toward his aircraft. His tail gunner, TSgt Peter Whalen, sitting all alone in the isolated rear turret cone, counted the fiery glow of each of the SAM's and confirmed the incoming missiles aimed at their bomber.

"The clouds magnify exhaust and make the SAM look bigger than it really is," Mize said.

This was the ninth day of Linebacker II and the previous days' strikes had badly damaged the air defenses of the North Vietnamese Army. They were now making indiscriminate salvo launches in desperate attempts to knock down as many B-52's as they could. According to Captain Mize, he looked downward outside his cockpit again as they approached their target area and counted the flaring exhausts of 15 SAM's. And shortly after releasing their load of eighty four 500 pound bombs, the bomber was jolted by a missile impact on the left side of the aircraft. Captain Mize was wounded by shrapnel striking his left thigh, lower leg and right hand.

The Radar Navigator, Captain Bill North and Navigator, Lieutenant Bill Robinson, sitting directly below the pilots felt the jolt of missile strike. Robinson was hit in the leg by hot metal shards of shrapnel.

Captain Mize struggled to keep the bomber under control. Three engines on the left side had been shut down by the missile strike and the aircraft was in a steep dive. After losing several thousand feet, he was able to level the bomber and regulate the power on the remaining five engines. Bill Robinson, in severe pain from his wounds, gave Mize a heading toward Thailand, the nearest friendly territory and Nakhon Phanom (NKP) Air Base just across the border. If he couldn't reach NKP or another airfield on which to land the badly wounded bomber, the crew could at least bailout over a safe area.

Wounded, bleeding and in moderate pain, Mize struggled with a fourth engine on the left side that was in the process of failing. Afterward, he was quoted as saying, "I had not previously flown by the seat of my pants, but the B-52 can be flown that way."

All four engines on the left side were now silent with the wing in flames... The situation had become critical. Likewise, the navigation equipment had also shut down and the navigator, Bill Robinson, as best he could, used indicated airspeed and his watch to gauge the distance flown toward Thailand and friendly territory. Hearing their call for help, an HC-130 Hercules rendezvoused with the stricken bomber at the Thai/Laos border and flew along side the burning aircraft. They were now at 12,000 feet and a few miles inside Thailand when the bomber's operating systems began to react radically with the bomb bay doors dropping open and the landing gear cycling up and down on its own.

Captain Mize realized at this point that there was no possibility of making an emergency landing, he ordered the crew to eject. Four crewmen successfully ejected, Bill Robinson's ejection seat, apparently hit by the same shrapnel that had wounded him, failed to operate. He finally worked his way to the open hatch created by the radar-navigator's ejection and bailed out through the opening. Mize, not knowing if all of his crew had successfully departed the aircraft, held onto the crippled bomber until he lost complete control and it began to plummet toward the ground. He ejected at the last minute. The rescue and recovery effort of Mize and his crew was hailed as one of the lengthiest of the war, in that the crew members were strewn out over more than a hundred miles. Captain Mize's heroism and concern for saving his crew was rewarded with the Air Force Cross, the nation's second highest combat decoration pinned on by General John C. Meyer, Commander-in-Chief of SAC.

In the final analysis, the strategic air power employed in the Vietnam War was eventually used in the effective manner that it could have been eight years earlier. The SAC combat crews, which were redirected from Cold War mission responsibilities, were no less heroes in Vietnam than any of their counter-parts. They suffered casualties, became prisoners of war, and finally, were permitted to do the job they were trained to do. During the 11 days of LINEBACKER II, SAC aircrews flew combat missions with the same discipline and accuracy as they were trained to do in their Cold War nuclear role with the incredible capabilities of the aging B-52 which was averaging 17 years in age at the time. A total of 729 sorties were flown against Soviet-built air defenses dropping 15,000 tons of bombs with 15 bombers shot down, numerous crew members killed and captured. There had been an estimated 1,240 SAM's fired at the B-52's during the period.

Walter Boyne in his book, Boeing B-52, described the last days of the war best: "Eight years of the ARC LIGHT concentrated bombing missions had seen 126,615 B-52 sorties flown. The venerable bomber had grown from a desperation weapon, thrown-in when there was nothing else, to become the final instrument of the war."

ENDURANCE

Throughout the history of SAC, aircrew, bomber, aerial tanker and reconnaissance aircraft performance was mandated as being paramount to its strategic global capabilities and enemy deterrence. Following are but a few noteworthy examples of aircrew and aircraft achievements.

[Author's note: Early in my Air Force career I was a B-36 pilot assigned to the 95th Bomb Wing at Biggs Air Force Base near El Paso, Texas, during the 1950's. From our Texas base, our crews and bombers made frequent training deployments to Alaska, Japan, Okinawa, the Azores and the United Kingdom. The flights were always long—18 to 20 or more hours—filled with a multitude of activities; navigation legs, simulated bomb runs, practice gunnery and electromagnetic counter-measures. There was little or no casual time during these deployment flights. After a few days rest at the destination base, the return flights back home consisted of the same—one training event followed by the next. Our entire unit also rotated to Guam for periods of up to three months, where routine combat crew training continued. Our bomber crews also stood alert with the aircraft fully loaded with fuel and nuclear weapons in the event the Cold War suddenly turned hot. At the end of our deployments, our unit would be relieved by another B-36 unit back in the States.

One of my memorable flights in the B-36 was that of returning from a deployment to Guam back to our home base at El Paso, Texas. Our bomber performed unusually well with good fuel economy and no oil leaks, so much so that we were able to make the trip nonstop and of course, un-refueled. The flight was extremely monotonous; with the exception of the Navigator staying alert to keep us on course, there wasn't much for the rest of the crew to do except ride-out my longest airborne venture—34 hours and 40 minutes.]

In later years, there were other feats of SAC airborne endurance. One such was "Operation Powerflight," demonstrating the long-range capability of the B-52 with a round-the-world non-stop flight by three "C" models. Lt. General Archie Olds, Commander, 15th Air Force, led five bombers, including two spares, and their air crews which took off from Castle Air Force Base, near Merced, California, on January 16, 1957. Two of the B-52's dropped out of the mission along the way with the three remaining over-flew Newfoundland, Casablanca, Dhahran, Ceylon, Manila and Guam completing a record-breaking 24,235 mile, 45 hour and 19 minute flight, landing back at March Air Force Base near Bakersfield, California, on January 18th. The three bombers landed within an astonishing two minutes of the estimated time for the record-breaking flight with all eight engines on each aircraft operating normally. An interesting "crew comfort" initiative evolved from the long flight—bite sized pre-grilled frozen beef steak cubes packaged in foil wrap which were heated in the installed mini-ovens. These frozen beef cubes along with other creative food provisions became a staple when SAC began flying the 24-hour Chromedome airborne alert training missions. General LeMay awarded the Distinguished Flying Cross to each of the crew members on "Powerflight," commenting, "The flight was a demonstration of SAC's capability to strike any target on the face of the earth."

In a show of determination, global reach and presence during the Iranian crisis in 1979, a B-52H SAC combat crew took off from Grand Forks Air Force Base, North Dakota, to their planned destination of Diego Garcia in the Indian Ocean where other B-52's had been deployed in a show of force. As the bomber and crew approached the air base at Diego Garcia, General Richard Ellis, Commander-in-Chief, SAC, made a bold decision to demonstrate SAC's commitment and capability. He contacted the B-52 crew and asked how they felt about proceeding on their flight to Europe and if aircraft problems or fatigue set-in, to land in the United Kingdom. It would be up to the Aircraft Commander to decide when he should land. The crew continued to fly over the major cities in the Middle East and Europe and onward to the Atlantic Ocean. The bomber performed perfectly, the aircrew did not waiver and they had no desire to land any sooner than after they completed their "around the world" flight and back to their home base at Grand Forks.

THE HUSTLER

The B-58 Hustler for its size was a state-of-the-art incredibly high speed aircraft. It broke record after record over the course of its life. Only five months after SAC took delivery, a B-58 established six international speed and payload records, all in a single flight, on January 12, 1961. Pilot, Major Henry J. Deutschendorf and Navigator, Major William L. Polhemus along with Defensive Systems Operator, Captain Raymond R. Wagner, flying out of Edwards Air Force Base, California without a bomb payload, averaged 1,200 MPH in two laps over a 1,243-mile course. The same crew and aircraft proceeded to fly five additional speed patterns with varying load configurations averaging between 1,200 MPH and 1,061 MPH. Incidentally, Major Deutschendorf was the father of the late folk singer, John Denver.

A B-58, piloted by Major Elmer E. Murphy set a sustained speed record of 1,302 MPH on May 10, 1961. Less than a month later, however, tragedy struck Major Murphy and his crew when their bomber crashed later during a June 3rd demonstration flight at the Paris Air Show. All three crew members were killed.

On May 26, 1961, a B-58 piloted by Major William Payne flew nonstop from New York to Paris—4,612 miles—in 3 hours, 19 minutes, 41 seconds. On October 16, 1963, Major Henry Kubesch and his crew from the 305th Bomb Wing flew nonstop from Tokyo to London—8,028 miles—in 8 hours, 35 minutes, 20 seconds. Five aerial refuelings were required to complete the mission. In all, the B-58 set 15 world records for speed and altitude. Its achievements include winning the Bendix, Bleriot, Harmon, MacKay, and Thompson trophies. Meanwhile, the B-58 bomber and crew force remained combat-ready, performing training missions and remaining alert as a part of the 43d Bombardment Wing at Carswell Air Force Base, Texas and the 305th Bombardment Wing at Bunker Hill (later named Grissom) Air Force Base, Indiana. Later configured B-58s were modified to carry high-resolution cameras in the nose of the pod for performing a reconnaissance role.

Not to be outdone, the KC-135 aerial tanker also set its own endurance records. One such flight was piloted by General LeMay, himself, making a non-refueled 6323 mile flight during November 11-12, 1957.

THE BLACKBIRD

"I spent an entire military career fighting Communism, and was very proud to do so. We won that war, we beat one of the worst scourges to humankind the world has known. But it took a great effort, over many years of sustained vigilance and much sacrifice by so many whose names you will never know. And perhaps our nation, so weary from so long a cold war, relaxed too much

212

and felt the world was a safer place with the demise of the Soviet Union. We indulged ourselves in our own lives, and gave little thought to the threats to our national security." Brian Shul, United States Air Force.

As Brian Shul was flying his 212th combat mission in Vietnam, he was shot down near the Cambodian border in April 1974. He was so badly burned that he was given next to no chance to live. Following the agony of the aircraft crash, life-threatening burns, 15 major surgeries and related skin grafts, he did miraculously live and persevered to return to flying status to became qualified to fly SAC's and the world's fastest aircraft, the SR-71 Blackbird. The following is his own account of a critical mission he later flew in the SR-71 in support of the retaliation bombing attack against Omar Qaddafi's terrorist headquarters in Libya and his reflections about flying the supersonic Blackbird:

"In April 1986, following an attack on American soldiers in a Berlin disco; President Reagan ordered the bombing of Muammar Qaddafi's terrorist camps in Libya. My duty was to fly over Libya and take photos recording the damage our F-111's had inflicted. Qaddafi had established a 'line of death,' a territorial marking across the Gulf of Sidra, swearing to shoot down any intruder that crossed the boundary. On t he morning of April 15, I rocketed past the line at 2,125 mph.

"I was piloting the SR-71 spy plane, the world's fastest jet, accompanied by Major Walter Watson, the aircraft's reconnaissance systems officer (RSO). We had crossed into Libya and were approaching our final turn over the bleak desert landscape when Walter informed me that he was receiving missile launch signals. I quickly increased our speed, calculating the time it would take for the weapons-most likely SA-2 and SA-4 surface-to-air missiles capable of Mach 5 - to reach our altitude. I estimated that we could beat the rocket-powered missiles to the turn and stayed our course, betting our lives on the plane's performance.

"After several agonizingly long seconds, we made the turn and blasted toward the Mediterranean. 'You might want to pull it back,' Walter suggested. It was then that I noticed I still had the throttles full forward. The plane was flying a mile every 1.6 seconds, well above our Mach 3.2 limit. It was the fastest we would ever fly. I pulled the throttles to idle just south of Sicily, but we still overran the refueling tanker awaiting us over Gibraltar.

"Scores of significant aircraft have been produced in the 100 years of flight, following the achievements of the Wright brothers, which we celebrate in December. Aircraft such as the Boeing 707, the F-86 Sabre Jet, and the P-51 Mustang are among the important machines that have flown our skies. But the SR-71, also known as the Blackbird, stands alone as a significant contributor to Cold War victory and as the fastest plane ever-and only 93 Air Force pilots ever steered the 'sled,' as we called our aircraft.

"As inconceivable as it may sound, I once discarded the plane. Literally! My first encounter with the SR-71 came when I was 10 years old in the form of molded black plastic in a Revell kit. Cementing together the long fuselage parts proved tricky, and my finished product looked less than menacing. Glue, oozing from the seams, discolored the black plastic. It seemed ungainly alongside the fighter planes in my collection, and I threw it away.

"Twenty-nine years later, I stood awe-struck in a Beale Air Force Base hangar, staring at the very real SR-71 before me. I had applied to fly the world's fastest jet and was receiving my first walk-around of our nation's most prestigious aircraft. In my previous 13 years as an Air Force fighter pilot, I had never seen an aircraft with such presence. At 107 feet long, it appeared big, but far from ungainly.

"Ironically, the plane was dripping, much like the misshapen model had assembled in my youth. Fuel was seeping through the joints, raining down on the hangar floor. At Mach 3, the plane would expand several inches because of the severe temperature, which could heat the leading edge of the wing to 1,100 degrees. To prevent cracking, expansion joints had been built into the plane. Sealant resembling rubber glue covered the seams, but when the plane was subsonic, fuel would leak through the joints.

"The SR-71 was the brainchild of Kelly Johnson, the famed Lockheed designer who created the P-38, the F-104 Starfighter, and the U-2. After the Soviets shot down Gary Powers' U-2 in 1960, Johnson began to develop an aircraft that would fly three miles higher and five times faster than the spy plane-and still be capable of photographing your license plate. However, flying at 2,000 mph would create intense heat on the aircraft's skin. Lockheed engineers used a titanium alloy to construct more than 90 percent of the SR-71, creating special tools and manufacturing procedures to hand-build each of the 40 planes. Special heat-resistant fuel, oil, and hydraulic fluids that would function at 85,000 feet and higher also had to be developed.

"In 1962, the first Blackbird successfully flew, and in 1966, the same year I graduated from high school, the Air Force began flying operational SR-71 missions. I came to the program in 1983 with a sterling record and a recommendation from my commander, completing the weeklong interview and meeting Walter, my partner for the next four years He would ride four feet behind me, working all the cameras, radios, and electronic jamming equipment. I joked that if we were ever captured, he was the spy and I was just the driver. He told me to keep the pointy end forward.

"We trained for a year, flying out of Beale AFB in California, Kadena Airbase in Okinawa, and RAF Mildenhall in England. On a typical training mission, we would take off near Sacramento, refuel over Nevada, accelerate into Montana, obtain high Mach over Colorado, turn right over New Mexico, speed across the Los Angeles Basin, run up the West Coast, turn right at Seattle, then return to Beale. Total flight time: two hours and 40 minutes.

"One day, high above Arizona, we were monitoring the radio traffic of all the mortal airplanes below us. First, a Cessna pilot asked the air traffic controllers to check his ground speed. 'Ninety knots,' ATC replied. A twin Bonanza soon made the same request. 'One-twenty on the ground,' was the reply. To our surprise, a navy F-18 came over the radio with a ground speed check. I knew exactly what he was doing. Of course, he had a ground speed indicator in his cockpit, but he wanted to let all the bug-smashers in the valley know what real speed was 'Dusty 52, we show you at 620 on the ground,' ATC responded. The situation was too ripe. I heard the click of Walter's mike button in the rear seat. In his most innocent voice, Walter startled the controller by asking for a ground speed check from 81,000 feet, clearly above controlled airspace. In a cool, professional voice, the controller replied, 'Aspen 20, I show you at 1,982 knots on the ground.' We did not hear another transmission on that frequency all the way to the coast.

"The Blackbird always showed us something new, each aircraft possessing its own unique personality. In time, we realized we were flying a national treasure. When we taxied out of our revetments for takeoff, people took notice. Traffic congregated near the airfield fences; because everyone wanted to see and hear the mighty SR-71 you could not be a part of this program and not come to love the airplane. Slowly, she revealed her secrets to us as we earned her trust.

"One moonless night, while flying a routine training mission over the Pacific, I wondered what the sky would look like from 84,000 feet if the cockpit lighting were dark. While heading home on a straight course, I slowly turned down all of the lighting, reducing the glare and revealing the night sky. Within seconds, I turned the lights back up, fearful that the jet would know and somehow punish me. But my desire to see the sky overruled my caution, I dimmed the lighting again. To my amazement, I saw a bright light outside my window. As my eyes adjusted to the view, I realized that the brilliance was the broad expanse of the Milky Way, now a gleaming stripe across the sky. Where dark spaces in the sky had usually existed, there were now dense clusters of sparkling stars Shooting stars flashed across the canvas every few seconds. It was like a fireworks display with no sound. I knew I had to get my eyes back on the instruments, and reluctantly I brought my attention back inside. To my surprise, with the cockpit lighting still off, I could see every gauge, lit by starlight. In the plane's mirrors, I could see the eerie shine of my gold spacesuit incandescently illuminated in a celestial glow. I stole one last glance out the window. Despite our speed, we seemed still before the heavens, humbled in the radiance of a much greater power. For those few moments, I felt a part of something far more significant than anything we were doing in the plane. The sharp sound of Walt's voice on the radio brought me back to the tasks at hand as I prepared for our descent.

"The SR-71 was an expensive aircraft to operate. The most significant cost was tanker support, and in 1990, confronted with budget cutbacks, the Air Force retired the SR-71. The Blackbird had outrun nearly 4,000 missiles, not once taking a scratch from enemy fire.

"On her final flight, the Blackbird, destined for the Smithsonian National Air and Space Museum, sped from Los Angeles to Washington in 64 minutes, averaging 2,145 mph and setting four speed records.

The SR-71 served six presidents, protecting America for a quarter of a century. Unbeknownst to most of the country, the plane flew over North Vietnam, Red China, North Korea, the Middle East, South Africa, Cuba, Nicaragua, Iran, Libya, and the Falkland Islands. On a weekly basis, the SR-71 kept watch over every Soviet nuclear submarine and mobile missile site, and all of their troop movements. It was a key factor in winning the Cold War.

"I am proud to say I flew about 500 hours in this aircraft. I knew her well. She gave way to no plane, proudly dragging her sonic boom through enemy backyards with great impunity. She defeated every missile, outran every MiG, and always brought us home. In the first 100 years of manned flight, no aircraft was more remarkable.

"With the Libyan coast fast approaching now, Walt asks me for the third time, if I think the jet will get to the speed and altitude we want in time. I tell him yes. I know he is concerned. He is dealing with the data; that's what engineers do, and I am glad he is. But I have my hands on the stick and throttles and can feel the heart of a thoroughbred, running now with the power and perfection she was designed to possess. I also talk to her. Like the combat veteran she is, the jet senses the target area and seems to prepare herself.

"For the first time in two days, the inlet door closes flush and all vibration is gone. We've become so used to the constant buzzing that the jet sounds quiet now in comparison. The Mach correspondingly increases slightly and the jet is flying in that confidently smooth and steady style we have so often seen at these speeds. We reach our target altitude and speed, with five miles to spare. Entering the target area, in response to the jet's new-found vitality, Walt says, 'That's amazing' and with my left hand pushing two throttles farther forward, I think to myself that there is much they don't teach in engineering school.

"Out my left window, Libya looks like one huge sandbox. A featureless brown terrain stretches all the way to the horizon. There is no sign of any activity. Then Walt tells me that he is getting lots of electronic signals, and they are not the friendly kind. The jet is performing perfectly now, flying better than she has in weeks. She seems to know where she is. She likes the high Mach, as we penetrate deeper into Libyan airspace. Leaving the footprint of our sonic boom across Benghazi, I sit motionless, with stilled hands on throttles and the pitch control, my eyes glued to the gauges.

"Only the Mach indicator is moving, steadily increasing in hundredths, in a rhythmic consistency similar to the long distance runner who has caught his second wind and picked up the pace. The jet was made for this kind of performance and she wasn't about to let an errant inlet door make her miss the show. With the power of forty locomotives, we puncture the quiet African sky and continue farther south across a bleak landscape.

"Walt continues to update me with numerous reactions he sees on the DEF panel. He is receiving missile tracking signals. With each mile we traverse, every two seconds, I become more uncomfortable driving deeper into this barren and hostile land. I am glad the DEF panel is not in the front seat. It would be a big distraction now, seeing the lights flashing. In contrast, my cockpit is 'quiet' as the jet purrs and relishes her new-found strength, continuing to slowly accelerate.

"The spikes are full aft now, tucked twenty-six inches deep into the nacelles. With all inlet doors tightly shut, at 3.24 Mach, the J-58s are more like ramjets now, gulping 100,000 cubic feet of air per second. We are a roaring express now, and as we roll through the enemy's backyard, I hope our speed continues to defeat the missile radars below. We are approaching a turn, and this is good. It will only make it more difficult for any launched missile to solve the solution for hitting our aircraft.

"I push the speed up at Walt's request. The jet does not skip a beat, nothing fluctuates, and the cameras have a rock steady platform. Walt received missile launch signals. Before he can say anything else, my left hand instinctively moves the throttles yet farther forward. My eyes are glued to temperature gauges now, as I know the jet will willingly go to speeds that can harm her. The temps are relatively cool and from all the warm temps we've encountered thus far, this surprises me but then, it really doesn't surprise me. Mach 3.31 and Walt is quiet for the moment.

"I move my gloved finder across the small silver wheel on the autopilot panel which controls the aircraft's pitch. With the deft feel known to Swiss watchmakers, surgeons, and 'dinosaurs' (old- time pilots who not only fly an airplane but 'feel it'), I rotate the pitch wheel somewhere between one-sixteenth and one-eighth inch location, a position which yields the 500-foot-

217

per-minute climb I desire. The jet raises her nose one-sixth of a degree and knows, I'll push her higher as she goes faster. The Mach continues to rise, but during this segment of our route, I am in no mood to pull throttles back.

"Walt's voice pierces the quiet of my cockpit with the news of more missile launch signals. The gravity of Walter's voice tells me that he believes the signals to be a more valid threat than the others. Within seconds he tells me to 'push it up' and I firmly press both throttles against their stops. For the next few seconds, I will let the jet go as fast as she wants. A final turn is coming up and we both know that if we can hit that turn at this speed, we most likely will defeat any missiles. We are not there yet, though, and I'm wondering if Walt will call for a defensive turn off our course.

"With no words spoken, I sense Walter is thinking in concert with me about maintaining our programmed course. To keep from worrying, I glance outside, wondering if I'll be able to visually pick up a missile aimed at us. Odd are the thoughts that wander through one's mind in times like these. I found myself recalling the words of former SR-71 pilots who were fired upon while flying missions over North Vietnam they said the few errant missile detonations they were able to observe from the cockpit looked like implosions rather than explosions. This was due to the great speed at which the jet was hurling away from the exploding missile.

"I see nothing outside except the endless expanse of a steel blue sky and the broad patch of tan earth far below. I have only had my eyes out of the cockpit for seconds, but it seems like many minutes since I have last checked the gauges inside. Returning my attention inward, I glance first at the miles counter telling me how many more to go, until we can start our turn Then I note the Mach, and passing beyond 3.45, I realize that Walter and I have attained new personal records. The Mach continues to increase. The ride is incredibly smooth.

"There seems to be a confirmed trust now, between me and the jet; she will not hesitate to deliver whatever speed we need, and I can count on no problems with the inlets. Walt and I are ultimately depending on the jet now - more so than normal - and she seems to know it. The cooler outside temperatures have awakened the spirit born into her years ago, when men dedicated to excellence took the time and care to build her well. With spikes and doors as tight as they can get, we are racing against the time it could take a missile to reach our altitude.

"It is a race this jet will not let us lose. The Mach eases to 3.5 as we crest 80,000 feet. We are a bullet now - except faster. We hit the turn, and I feel some relief as our nose swings away from a country we have seen quite enough of. Screaming past Tripoli, our phenomenal speed continues to rise, and the screaming Sled pummels the enemy one more time, laying down a parting sonic boom. In seconds, we can see nothing but the expansive blue of the Mediterranean. I realize that I still have my left hand full-forward and we're continuing to rocket along in maximum afterburner.

"The TDI now shows us Mach numbers, not only new to our experience but flat out scary. Walt says the DEF panel is now quiet and I know it is time to reduce our incredible speed. I pull the throttles to the min 'burner range and the jet still doesn't want to slow down. Normally the Mach would be affected immediately, when making such a large throttle movement But for just a few moments old 960 just sat out there at the high Mach, she seemed to love and like the proud Sled she was, only began to slow when we were well out of danger. I loved that jet!"

ASSERTION

In 1988, as the Cold War began to wind down, Soviet Air Marshal Sergei Akhromeyev was invited to visit the United States in response to an orientation exchange program between the two governments. One of his visits took him to the SAC B-52 bomber and Minuteman missile units at Ellsworth AFB, South Dakota. The Air Marshal was impressed with the professionalism and outward dedication of the bomber and missile combat crews. During his visit, he asked a B-52 pilot his thoughts about dropping nuclear weapons on the Soviet Union. The young captain thought for a minute and said, "I understand your question, Sir, and the impact it would have on your country and the innocent women and children, but you should know that if the President of the United States directed me to bomb your country, I would do it!" The Air Marshal Akhromeyev remained stoic and only smiled at the young officer's response.

THE MISSILEERS

Intercontinental ballistic missiles (ICBMs) manned by a different breed of SAC warrior contributed greatly to deterrence during the Cold War period. The missile weapons systems discussed previously and first employed by SAC were the Snark, followed by the Thor, both ground-to-ground intermediate range missiles. The SM-65 Atlas became the first ICBMs deployed by SAC, followed in sequence with Titan I, Titan II, Minuteman and Peacekeeper.

By the fall of 1963, the Atlas systems were being retired, and the three Titan I wings were being augmented by an eventual 1050 Minuteman Missile silos dispersed across the Midwest and Western United States. Among the first Minuteman missiles deployed were the 150 assigned to the 44th Strategic Missile Wing at Ellsworth Air Force Base near Rapid City, South Dakota. The missile silos housing Minuteman were dispersed over broad expanses of farm and ranch land covering upwards to six thousand or more square miles. For every 10 missile silos a support structure known as the Launch Control Facility (LCF) was centrally located within the area. Within the LCF, a Facility Manager, cooks and several security police personnel were assigned to provide support for two Missile Combat Crew Members, "Missileers" as they became known, stationed in the Launch Control Center (LCC) capsule 30 or more feet below the surface. The assigned LCF personnel worked nominally three day shifts with three days off. The missileers in the underground LCC were on duty for 24-hour shifts at a time.

A typical LCF was "Delta One" located 80 miles east of Ellsworth Air Force Base on the plains of South Dakota. Delta One was typical of all the other Minuteman facilities which were eventually operational for nearly 30 years. This author remembers Delta One well as a member of the initial cadre of SAC Minuteman missileers and served as a missile combat crew commander (MCCC) assigned to the 44th SMW in the early 1960s. The SAC combat crews and support personnel on duty with the 44th SMW and at the five other Minuteman wings experienced some of the more tense moments during the Cold War. Just as the bomber and tanker combat crews on ground alert, missile crews were on the frontline of America's Cold War deterrence. The missileers might also have appropriately been called the "Silent Warriors"; they stood quietly on alert year after year within their underground 'cocoons' ready to launch the ten nuclear ICBMs under their control if directed. There were no engines running, no take-offs to be made, no missions to be flown, only the quiet whirring of the air exchanger and the periodic interruption by a practice alert exercise from the local unit command post or SAC Headquarters.

All of the duties performed by the men and women assigned to a SAC Minuteman LCF were dedicated to the missile combat crew standing alert in the LCC down below. The missile combat crew consisted of a commander and deputy commander; both were Air Force commissioned officers. The LCC served as their alert duty station for the 24-hour shift. Missile combat crew members underwent intensive training for several months before they were certified to go on alert. They were expected to become proficient beyond error in managing and operating the Minuteman missile system. A significant requirement for all missile combat crew members included being certified as psychologically stable to perform their tasks within the isolated and close confined environment of the underground capsule and importantly to not possess any reservations to take the necessary actions to launch their portion of the ICBM force if directed by the National Command Authority. Once the missile combat crew was trained, certified and on duty, they became an integrated part of the SIOP along with their bomber, tanker and SLBM counterparts.

A typical duty day for a Minuteman missile combat crew would begin early in the morning when they arrived at squadron operations; they would receive a local weather and security briefing covering the current international situation including any reasons that the U.S. might be placed on higher alert status. They would then depart for their LCF either in an Air Force vehicle or aboard a helicopter for their tour of duty. If they were required to drive, it would nominally take an hour or two—in the frequently brutal Midwest winter weather even longer. Arriving at the entrance gate and the security checkpoint for the LCF, the crew would identify themselves to the Flight Security Controller who in turn opened the gate to the complex. The crew commander would then phone downstairs to the combat crew on duty in the LCC and identify themselves and authenticate their identification codes.

From the Security Control Center the crew would take the elevator leading down to the capsule. Arriving at underground LCC, the deputy crew commander on duty inside would unlock and swing open the eight ton blast door to allow them in. The LCC was required to be a "No Lone Zone, Two Man Concept Mandatory," requiring that no one individual was authorized to be in the LCC alone. The off-going missile combat crew would give the oncoming crew an operational status briefing of the ten missiles under their direct control and hand over the keys to the safe that contained the classified "Launch Codes."

Missile crew duty was also perhaps the most boring duty with the most pending responsibility that any combat crew member endured. As the crews often lamented, "hours and hours of boredom punctuated with moments to stark terror."

Through most of the 24-hour duty tour, the crews generally refreshed their tech order system knowledge, read books and magazines or studied if they were enrolled in a professional military program or the masters degree program offered at all Minuteman units. In the early days television sets were prohibited to avoid distraction; that restriction was relaxed over the years. The "stark terror" referred to above, occurred when the ever anticipated, but always surprising "blurt" from the Primary Alert System (PAS) announcing a practice exercise from either the local wing command post or the SAC Command Center. The crew would immediately take their console positions, go to their checklists and proceed to coordinate a simulated "touch and tell" practice launch of their ten missiles. The most feared command a SAC missile or air crew could ever receive was an Emergency War Order (EWO). This would mean their missiles were to be actually launched according to the war plan and SAC alert bombers would launch toward their assigned targets.

Hot meals and quality food were a priority and the LCF cooks generally lived up to and took considerable pride in the preparation of meals for their missile crews, maintenance teams and security police. Following the evening meal, one missile crew member would usually go to bed in the enclosed bunk where he would attempt to rest for a few hours. After his rest period he would swap out for few more hours with the other crew member and the night would generally pass without interruption.

Though missileers never executed an actual launch there was always the distinct possibility that the time could come when they might be directed to carryout a launch directive. Although these silent warriors went relatively unnoticed by the general public and even their own fellow Air Force colleagues, they were an integral part of the brave shield that the deterrence protected America from an enemy thousands of miles away. This was the routine until the Cold War came to a quiet close in 1991.

When the Cold War ended and SAC was stood down, many of the Minuteman Missile facilities were also deactivated as their predecessor Atlas and Titan launch facilities had during the evolution of Cold War weapons systems. Each missile weapon system had acted as a silent deterrent guarding the United States for nearly four decades. Thousands of young Air Force men and women from all walks of life had their lives touched by the respective ICBM system; they served as combat crew members, maintenance support teams, cooks, administrators and security police. Likewise, the ICBM program touched the lives of the good farmer and rancher neighbors on whose land the thousands of silos and hundreds of launch control facilities resided.

THE WOMEN WARRIORS

Early on General LeMay initiated programs to recognize the contributions of women in SAC by placing them into more and more positions involved in the operations of the Command. In the beginning they became aircraft maintenance officers and technicians, but it wasn't long before women began training as Titan ICBM launch officers and enlisted crew members. The issue with the Minuteman missile program presented more difficult issues since the combat crews were "two-man" in composition and the social concern of pairing up male-female crews to spend 24-hour alert tours in the underground launch control capsules was obvious.

Colonel Larry Hasbrouck, a former Minuteman combat crew commander and later a wing director of operations during the period that SAC was incurring increasing pressure to allow female officers to serve on ICBM combat crews, laments: "I received a call from the wing commander. He said to go get Captain Rex Stone, (a Minuteman missile combat crew commander), "and get his wife, Becky, (who was also an Air Force captain stationed on the base), "and take the two out to a launch control center and have her go through as many weapon system checklist procedures as possible and report back how well she did. We did it. Becky followed the checklists and her husband answered her questions but did not assist her physically in any way. She encountered no problem with the eight-ton blast entry door or the elevator. No problem with the inspections and she did a great job with the 'touch and tell' launch procedures. When I called the wing commander back, I said, 'Sir, I know the people at SAC who called, want you to tell them that she failed miserably, but she didn't!' It wasn't very long thereafter that women were fully integrated into the ICBM force, both Minuteman and Titan."

Colonel Linda Aldrich was one of the first female officers to integrate into the Minuteman weapon system. At 30 years old, divorced, and with a young daughter, Colonel Aldrich decided she wanted to be an Air Force officer. Against long odds she succeeded in becoming one of few female space and missile officers in the Air Force. After three years at Little Rock Air Force Base, Arkansas, with the Titan II Intercontinental Ballistic Missile system, she transferred to Whitman Air Force Base, Missouri, to become one of the first female missileers on a combat crew with the Minuteman.

This was a significant career change; unlike the Titan II, the Minuteman II missile silos afforded little privacy for the newly mixed-gender crews. This created a stir in the Air Force community, especially among the wives of the male missileers. Overcoming gender-integration challenges in the Minuteman weapon system, Colonel Aldrich rose to become crew commander and instructor crew commander at Whitman before transferring to Vandenberg Air Force Base, California, where she became the first female Minuteman operations instructor in the Air Force and later a senior instructor at the Space and Missile Operations Course.

Thereafter, Colonel Aldrich served in a variety of assignments, including missile squadron commander at F.E. Warren Air Force Base, Wyoming, senior military advisor in the Office of National Drug Control Policy and a variety of senior staff positions.

"What the Air Force has given me is far greater than anything I have ever given the Air Force," she proudly lamented. "It is a gift to be in the military at all. This was absolutely not supposed to happen. My mom raised me to get a husband, have kids, and stay in Nebraska."

Throughout her years as an officer and single mother, her drive to succeed was fueled by devotion to her daughter, Ashley, the colonel said. Her experiences also made her very sensitive to the predicament of single parents in the service, she said, many of whom are forced to choose between work and family commitments.

"You must know yourself," she continued. "Figure out what you're willing to give up if you want to stay in the military and make it a career." Colonel

Aldrich's daughter, then Captain Ashley Shull, followed her mom's footsteps into the Air Force.

During the visit to Ellsworth Air Force Base, South Dakota, Soviet Air Marshal Akhromeyev mentioned above, was introduced to a young female Minuteman missile officer, 1st Lt Jill E. Nagel; who accompanied him and his delegation into the Minuteman training simulator. Throughout the orientation, she answered all of the Air Marshal's questions with confident professionalism. The Marshal finally asked her how she felt about launching a nuclear missile toward the Soviet Union.

Without hesitation, Lt. Nagel replied: "My job is to maintain the missiles and make sure they will fire on demand; and Marshall, I want to assure you the missiles at Ellsworth Air Force Base will do it."

Once the barrier was lifted, more and more young women became missileers, pilots and navigators. SAC brought women into the KC-135 flight operations in the early 1980's, as co-pilots, navigators, boom operators and crew chiefs. The co-pilots eventually became fully qualified aircraft commanders. The first "all-female" KC-135 crew flew an operational mission on June 10, 1982. The crew included Captain Kelly S. C. Hamilton, SAC's first female KC-135 aircraft commander with co-pilot, Lieutenant Linda Martin, Captain Cathy Bacon, instructor navigator, Lieutenant Diane Oswald, navigator and Sergeant Jackie Hale boom operator, performed a five-hour air refueling training mission off-loading fuel to a B-52. SAC noted that the flight was 'token' in nature and would not become the norm, because to develop a program of all-female crews would in fact defeat the whole concept of integrating women into all phases of combat crew operations.

These were but a select few of the exploits of the SAC warriors along with some of the more routine ventures and experiences encountered along the way——most taken in stride and many not ever to be forgotten.

SEVEN

THE SHADOW WARRIORS

"Brave men who work while others sleep; who dare while others fly—they build a nation's pillars deep and lift them up to the sky."

Ralph Waldo Emerson

Joe Sewell was a wise beyond his young tech sergeant years whom this author served with during Vietnam. One day we were kicking around our situation over there and the broader specter of the Soviet threat that encompassed the situation in Southeast Asia and beyond; he looked at me and commented thoughtfully, "Sir, did you know we are just a nation of sheep. Sheep are mostly productive, harmless and passive," he continued. "They don't want to hurt each other. But the wolf, you know, is an enemy of the sheep and they viciously kill at random, sometimes for food and sometimes just for fun. I am just a sheepdog, but it's my job to protect the sheep by killing the wolf and any other predator. So, I guess we are all sheepdogs over here in Vietnam protecting all those sheep back home."

Later, as we moved on respectively with our careers, Joe and I joined up again, by then a Chief Master Sergeant; he became my Air Division Senior Enlisted Advisor. Chief Joe Sewell left us several years ago; may God rest his soul and bless his equally courageous family. Joe was right, the heroics of those "sheepdogs"—Cold Warriors all—served with distinction during a critical period of our history. Neither was Joe an ordinary "sheepdog", but he was typical of the truly great enlisted and noncommissioned officer (NCO) warriors that served so valiantly and bravely during the protracted Cold War conflict.

Aviator and missileer Cold Warriors took considerable pride and confidence in the fact that the weapon systems placed under their control had been made ready by a skilled operations and maintenance team of NCOs and airmen. Pilots started the engines of their aircraft with the assurance that it had been properly prepared for flight and refueled by technicians, maintenance personnel and a ground crew of competent NCO's and airmen. They commenced to taxi only after a young airman removed the chocks and gave the thumbs-up signal to proceed and—"Have safe flight, Sir!" Flight crew members turned on and tuned-up their respective operating systems with full reliance that those responsible for installation and calibration had properly completed their tasks. Missile combat crews entered launch control facilities and assumed nuclear alert with the same full confidence that their systems had been made operational ready by skilled and competent NCOs and airmen.

Those responsible for these duties requiring extraordinary skilled performance were the men and women—the "Shadow Warriors"—this author's chosen term for the often unheralded enlisted men and women, NCOs and airmen, and the untold number of civil servants who worked diligently, often behind the major scenes of action, throughout the Cold War era.

The performance of these Shadow Warriors was not limited to the direct support of weapons system operations; they also participated in equally important roles as flight and missile crew members, security police, within supply, logistics, food service, finance and accounting, human resources, administration and multiple other critically essential areas. Neither were these warriors drafted into Cold War military service; they stepped forward voluntarily to serve the nation in a time of need. Many of them found a comfortable home in serving; they performed extraordinarily and were rewarded with increasing responsibilities, rank and leadership roles in their professional careers.

In the mid-1960s, the Air Force recognized the need for a Senior NCO at unit levels of command, major air commands (MAJCOMS) and at USAF Headquarters to work closely with commanders as a liaison with the enlisted force. The result was the creation of the positions of Senior Enlisted Advisor and Chief Master Sergeant of the Air Force (CMSAF) respectively. The Chief Master Sergeant of the Air Force and Senior Enlisted Advisors added considerable prestige to the noncommissioned officer corps. The CMSAF acts as a personal advisor to the Air Force Chief of Staff and Secretary of the Air

Force on matters concerning the welfare, effective management and progress of the enlisted force.

PAUL W. AIREY
CHIEF MASTER SERGEANT OF THE AIR FORCE
1967 - 1969

Chief Paul Airey was appointed as the first Chief Master Sergeant of the Air Force on April 3, 1967. Chief Airey had spent much of his career as a unit First Sergeant. During World War II, he became a hero in his own right, serving as a B-24 aerial gunner and credited with 28 combat missions in Europe before being forced to bail out of his flak-damaged aircraft. He was captured and became a Nazi prisoner of war from July 1944 to May 1945. During the Korean conflict, he was awarded the Legion of Merit while assigned at Naha Air Base, Okinawa. The award, an uncommon decoration for an enlisted man, was earned for his creation of a system for constructing equipment from salvaged parts that improved corrosion control of sensitive radio and radar components. Fourteen CMSAFs have succeeded Chief Master Sergeant Paul Airey, eight of whom served at various times and positions during their extraordinary careers in Strategic Air Command. Two served as Senior Enlisted Advisor, Strategic Air Command, before being selected Chief Master Sergeant, United States Air Force.

The eight Shadow Warriors who served in Strategic Air Command before moving on to reach the highest pinnacle, included:

DONALD L. HARLOW
CHIEF MASTER SERGEANT OF THE AIR FORCE
1969 - 1971

Chief Master Sergeant Harlow, as did his predecessor, Chief Airey, joined the Army Air Corps during World War II in 1942 following graduation from Lawrence Academy in Groton, Massachusetts. He served with SAC as a Personnel Chief Clerk at Travis Air Force Base, California. A 'fast burner', he was promoted to Chief Master Sergeant after only 16 years of active duty. CMSAF Harlow succeeded CMSAF Airey, becoming the second Chief Master Sergeant, U.S. Air Force, on August 1, 1969.

Chris Adams

THOMAS N. BARNES
CHIEF MASTER SERGEANT OF THE AIR FORCE
1973 - 1977

CMSAF Thomas Barnes became the fourth Chief Master Sergeant of the Air Force in October 1973. He was key in bringing many African-American related issues to the attention of senior military leaders. Chief Barnes enlisted in the Air Force in 1949 and received his basic training at Lackland Air Force Base, Texas; afterwhich he attended Aircraft and Engine School and Hydraulic Specialist School at Chanute Technical Training Center, Illinois. In November 1950, he transferred with the 4th Troop Carrier Squadron to Ashiya, Japan, in support of the Korean War. Shortly after arrival in Japan, he completed on-the-job training as a flight engineer.

Chief Barnes transferred in June 1952 to the 30th Air Transport Squadron, Westover Air Force Base, Massachusetts, where he attended C-118 school and continued flight engineer duties. In September 1952, he volunteered for temporary duty with the 1708th Ferry Group at Kelly Air Force Base, Texas, and participated in ferrying aircraft from various depots to Air Force organizations in Hawaii, Japan and Northeast Air Command. Upon completion of temporary duty, he returned to Westover. In December 1952, he transferred to Andrews Air Force Base, Maryland, and served as crew chief and flight engineer on B-25, T-11, C-45 and C-47 aircraft in support of various requirements of Headquarters U.S. Air Force, Headquarters Military Air Transport Service, and the Air Research and Development Command. It was during this time that Barnes applied for commissioning and was accepted but had to turn down the opportunity due to the fact that the pay cut which officer candidates experience while undergoing training would not allow him to continue to support his wife and children.

In June 1958, Chief Barnes joined Strategic Air Command with the 42nd Bombardment Wing at Loring Air Force Base, Maine, as a B-52 crew chief, flight chief and senior controller. In September 1965 he went to Fairchild Air Force Base, Washington, and continued duties as senior controller. He was transferred to the 8th Tactical Fighter Wing in Southeast Asia in December 1966 to serve as noncommissioned officer in charge of the reparable processing center, senior controller and noncommissioned officer in charge of maintenance control. Promoted to the grade of chief master sergeant on December 1, 1969, and moved on to Headquarters, Air Training Command in October 1971, to assume duties as command senior enlisted adviser. Chief Barnes, as was Chief McCoy and Chief Parish, selected to attend the first class of the Senior NCO Academy. He was appointed Chief Master Sergeant of the Air Force on October 1, 1973. At the expiration of the initial two-

228

year tenure, he was extended for an additional year by the Chief of Staff. In February 1976, he was again selected to serve an unprecedented second year extension.

Chief Barnes retired on July 31, 1977, following 28 years of active duty including nine years as a flight engineer on a variety of aircraft and service in Korea, the Cuban missile crisis and Vietnam. Following retirement from the Air Force, he worked for the First National Bank of Fort Worth as Employee Relations Officer for seven years. From there he moved to The Associates Corporation of North America as Vice President/Director of Employee Relations. CMSAF Barnes died on March 17, 2003, after a long battle with cancer.

ROBERT D. GAYLOR
CHIEF MASTER SERGEANT OF THE AIR FORCE
1977 – 1979

Chief Bob Gaylor became the fifth CMSAF. He entered the Air Force in September 1948 and was assigned to the security police career field where he served until 1957. From there he served as a military training instructor at Lackland Air Force Base, Texas, until February 1962 before returning to security police. During his security police years, he served successively at James Connally Air Force Base, Texas; Laredo Air Force Base, Texas; Kunsan Air Base, Korea; Tachikawa Air Base, Japan; Columbus Air Force Base, Mississippi; Barksdale Air Force Base, Louisiana and Korat Air Base, Thailand. He served as Senior Enlisted Adviser to the Commander, Second Air Force (SAC) and accompanied the Commander, U.S. Air Forces, Europe (USAFE) to establish the USAFE Command Management and Leadership Center which eventually became the USAF NCO Academy. In June 1972, he established the USAFE Command Management and Leadership Center, an in-residence program of instruction for NCOs. In September 1974, Chief Gaylor was assigned to the Air Force Military Personnel Center where he traveled extensively as a management and leadership instructor. He became Chief Master Sergeant of the Air Force in 1977 and retired July 31, 1979. Chief Gaylor and his wife live in San Antonio where he remains active as a renowned public speaker.

JAMES M. MCCOY
CHIEF MASTER SERGEANT OF THE AIR FORCE
1979 - 1981

Chief Master Sergeant Jim McCoy, born in Creston, Iowa, in 1930, became the sixth CMSAF on August 1, 1979. He graduated from Maur Hill High

Chris Adams

School in Atchison, Kansas, in 1948. He entered the U.S. Air Force in January 1951 after attending St. Benedict's College in Atchison and St. Ambrose College in Davenport, Iowa. In 1966 he received a Bachelor of Science degree in business administration from Centenary College of Louisiana. An honor graduate of the Second Air Force Noncommissioned Officer Academy, he graduated with the first class of the U.S. Air Force Senior Noncommissioned Officer Academy at Gunter Air Force Station, Alabama, in 1973. Chief McCoy's illustrious career included service with the Air Defense Command as a radar operator and instructor, Air Force Basic Military Training instructor and assistant commandant of cadets, Air Force Reserve Officer Training Corps at the University of Notre Dame. In 1960, he became Commandant, Strategic Air Command Noncommissioned Officer Preparatory School and later as an instructor and Sergeant Major of the Second Air Force NCO Academy at Barksdale Air Force Base, Louisiana. In 1966, he was appointed Chief, Training Branch, DCS, Personnel, Second Air Force and moved on to Headquarters, Strategic Air Command in June 1967 as NCO, Professional Military Education deputy chief of staff, personnel. While there, he established and monitored the SAC Noncommissioned Officer Academy and Noncommissioned Officer Leadership School programs. Chief McCoy transferred to the 41st Aerospace Rescue and Recovery Wing, Hickam Air Force Base, Hawaii, in 1970 as NCO in charge of operations training. There, he supervised and monitored all training programs for the H-3, H-43, H-53 and HC-130 aircraft crews assigned to units throughout the Pacific and Southeast Asia. In April 1973, he moved to Chief, Military Training Branch, DCS, Personnel, Headquarters, PACAF, where he revitalized the on-the-job training programs. During this assignment, he was selected as one of the 12 Outstanding Airmen of the Air Force. Returning to Strategic Air Command in March 1975, Chief McCoy became Command's first Senior Enlisted Adviser where he served as the personal representative of CINCSAC to the enlisted men and women of the command, traveling extensively throughout the command helping to identify issues affecting quality of Air Force life.

In 1979, he became the sixth chief master sergeant appointed to the ultimate position of Chief Master Sergeant of the Air Force. Chief McCoy retired November 1, 1981, and has remained active over the years with many business and civic organizations, councils and board of directors within Omaha and at the national level. He has also served two terms as National President, two terms as Chairman of the Board of the Air Force Association and Chairman of the Air Force Retiree Council—the first retired enlisted member to hold either of the positions.

SAM E. PARISH
CHIEF MASTER SERGEANT OF THE AIR FORCE
1983 - 1986

Chief Master Sergeant Parish became the third Strategic Air Command Senior Enlisted Advisor and the eighth chief master sergeant appointed to the ultimate noncommissioned officer position as CMSAF. Chief Parish was born in Marianna, Florida. He joined the U.S. Air Force in December 1954 and graduated along with Chiefs Barnes and McCoy with the first class from the Senior Noncommissioned Officer Academy at Gunter Air Force Station, Alabama, in 1973. Following basic military training at Lackland Air Force Base, Texas, he was assigned to Chanute Air Force Base, Illinois, for training as a ground weather equipment operator. After completing the course as an honor graduate in August 1955, Chief Parish was assigned to the 18th Weather Squadron, Wiesbaden Air Base, West Germany, as noncommissioned officer in charge of weather communications. In January 1960, he returned to Chanute Air Force Base for the weather observer technician course and again was an honor graduate. From August 1960 to May 1966, the chief was assigned to the Air Force Systems Command, Electronics Systems Division, Hanscom Air Force Base, Massachusetts, as NCO in charge of operational procedures for the 433L Systems Program Office. While assigned at Hanscom, he attended the Air Force Systems Command Noncommissioned Officer Academy and was honor graduate of his class. He returned to West Germany as chief observer for the 7th Weather Squadron at Heidelberg from June 1966 until June 1969. He then transferred to Headquarters Air Weather Service, Scott Air Force Base, Illinois, as the command's chief observer and later as chief, observing services and procedures division, Office of the Deputy Chief of Staff, Operations. Chief Parish attended the Senior Noncommissioned Officer Academy in January 1973, and in July 1973, was chosen senior enlisted adviser for Air Weather Service. In October 1975, he was assigned as the weather assignments adviser for Military Airlift Command's deputy chief of staff, personnel. In August 1976, Chief Parish began his third tour of duty in West Germany as sergeant major for the 36th Combat Support Group consolidated base personnel office at Bitburg Air Base. From November 1977 to August 1980, he served as U.S. Air Forces in Europe senior enlisted adviser at Ramstein Air Base, West Germany. He then became 40th Air Division senior enlisted adviser at Wurtsmith Air Force Base, Michigan. In November 1981, the chief was selected as the Strategic Air Command senior enlisted advisor at Offutt Air Force Base, Nebraska. In 1983, he became Chief Master Sergeant of the Air Force. He retired from the Air Force June 30, 1986.

JAMES C. BINNICKER
CHIEF MASTER SERGEANT OF THE AIR FORCE.
1986 - 1990

Chief Binnicker was born in Orangeburg, South Carolina, in 1939, graduated from Aiken High School in 1956 and entered the Air Force in August 1957. His first assignment was with the 96th Air Refueling Squadron, SAC, at Altus Air Force Base, Oklahoma, as a life support specialist. His early years included assignments in base and wing operations in Hawaii, North Dakota, Georgia, North Carolina, Vietnam, and Taiwan. He served as the Senior Enlisted Advisor for 12th Air Force, Headquarters Pacific Air Forces (PACAF), and Headquarters Tactical Air Command (TAC). He also represented the Air Force as Senior Enlisted Advisor on the President's Commission on Military Compensation. In February 1985, Chief Binnicker was selected for the 33-year extended tenure program. Chosen as the ninth Chief Master Sergeant of the Air Force, he served from July 1, 1986 to July 1990.

Following his retirement from active duty in 1990, Chief Binnicker became president and CEO of the Air Force Enlisted Village (AFEV), a non-profit charity located in Fort Walton Beach, Florida, that provides a home for the surviving spouses of enlisted military personnel. He has been a member of the AFEV Board of Directors since 1992.

CMSAF Binnicker's major awards and decorations include the Air Force Distinguished Service Medal, the Legion of Merit, the Bronze Star, the Meritorious Service Medal with three oak leaf clusters, the Joint Service Commendation Medal, Air Force Commendation Medal with oak leaf cluster, the Vietnam Service Medal with three service stars, the Republic of Vietnam Gallantry Cross with Palm, and the Republic of Vietnam Campaign Medal.

GARY R. PFINGSTON
CHIEF MASTER SERGEANT OF THE AIR FORCE
1990 - 1994

Chief Gary Pfingston became the tenth CMSAF and the seventh who served in Strategic Air Command during the Cold War. Chief Pfingston was born in Evansville, Indiana, on January 2, 1940. In 1958, he graduated from Torrance High School California, and attended El Camino College. He entered the Air Force in February, 1962. Chief Pfingston spent his early years in Strategic Air Command as a B-52 crew chief at Castle AFB, California, from 1962 to 1968 and continued working with B-52s and KC-135s at Plattsburgh AFB, New York, from 1968 to 1972. Following a tour of duty at U-Tapao Royal Thai Air Base, Thailand, he became a military training instructor at Lackland AFB in 1973. In 1979 he was appointed Commandant of the Military Training

Instructor School.   On August 1, 1990, Chief
Pfingston was selected to become Chief Master Sergeant of the Air Force. Chief
Pfingston's focus during his tenure was tackling the Air Force's post-Cold War
personnel drawdown and budget reductions. His most difficult challenge was
Air Force downsizing. With a goal of avoiding involuntary separations during
the on-going force drawdown, he worked to get the Voluntary Separation
Incentive and Special Separation Bonus programs established.
Chief Pfingston retired October 25, 1994, and succumbed to an untimely
death from cancer June 23, 2007.

DAVID J. CAMPANALE
CHIEF MASTER SERGEANT OF THE AIR FORCE
1994 - 1996

Chief Campanale, born in Worcester, Massachusetts, became the eleventh
appointed to the highest noncommissioned officer position in the United
States Air Force and the eighth who had served in Strategic Air Command.
He graduated from North High School and entered the Air Force in October
1970. He completed technical training as an aircraft maintenance specialist
at Sheppard Air Force Base, Texas. In February 1971, he was assigned as
a B-52 Stratofortress crew chief in the 2nd Organization Maintenance
Squadron, Barksdale Air Force Base, Louisiana. While there, he completed
three successive tours at Andersen Air Force Base, Guam, in support of B-52
Operation Arc Light missions in Southeast Asia. His career includes tours at
bases in Indiana, Hawaii, New Hampshire, and Nebraska. He served as Senior
Enlisted Advisor to the 93rd Bomb Wing, Castle Air Force Base, California,
and Air Mobility Command, Scott Air Force Base, Illinois.

CMSAF Campanale served as the Chief Master Sergeant of the Air Force
from October 1994 to November 1996. He retired from active duty effective
January 1, 1997. He now resides in southern Arizona, and frequently speaks
at USAF gatherings.

His most notable contributions during his time on active duty in the
CMSAF slot include a major push for single dorm occupancy (which led to
the current dorm single occupancy policy,) and a reduction of DUI incidents
at Castle AFB in one year from over 190, to less than five.

Chief Campanale also disagreed with the proposed Air Force uniform
change which removed name tapes and rank insignia from the battle dress
uniform. The Air Force leadership persisted and swapped the sleeve "stripes"
insignia for a short time to a single black label worn over the left breast pocket
which contained text including the rank, name, and position of the invidiual.
In total disagreement with the uniform insignia change, Chief Campanale

said, "To prove my point, I had the secretary of a 3-star General remove the stars (rank insignia) from the Generals' BDU (utility uniform) collar, then affixed the black label over his nametape as would be worn by everyone else. I then challenged that if he were to walk with me around the base, nobody would salute or render courtesies, since they couldn't read it. He accepted my challenge, and after about an hour of walking, someone finally recognized the General and said, 'Hey.. aren't you General so and so?'" Within a few weeks, the black patch was being phased out, and the rank insignia/name tapes were on the way back in.

These men cited above are but a few of the extraordinary hundreds of thousands of noncommissioned officers that served in the Air Force and Strategic Air Command during the 45-year Cold War era. The challenge to recruit and retain quality young enlisted men and women during the period was ever-present. Retention became challenging, increasingly difficult and persistent as industry clamored for the exceptionally well-trained, skilled, disciplined and motivated young SAC airmen who had attained all of the afore-mentioned attributes and who became highly vulnerable to the better paying jobs on the 'outside'. It was here that senior NCOs from the Chiefs on down worked diligently to assist in retaining these bright and well-trained young minds. Patriotism played a major role in keeping many young airmen motivated to serve beyond their initial enlistment and to look toward to rewarding careers in the service of their country. In spite of compensation wages well below their civilian counterparts, frequent moves and hours and days away from home and family, they remained on active duty and served with distinction. The Chief Master Sergeants of the Air Force highlighted in this chapter exemplified the Leadership of all those who served in those critically important positions during the Cold War.

In summarizing the story of the Shadow Warriors, CMSAF Jim McCoy reminded me of a story attributed to former CINCSAC, General Russell Dougherty relating an episode when he was a young B-47 aircraft commander. It seems the aircrews were lounging around the alert facility one quiet evening when an argument ensued about which of the three combat crew members on the B-47 was the most important. The pilot in the group asserted that "he" was the most important because of his flying ability and that he was in charge of the aircraft and crew. The radar-navigator stated that "he" was the most important crew member because, "If I don't get you to the correct place and the right time, and drop the bombs on the target, then the mission would be a failure."

The young co-pilot remained out of the discussion, knowing full-well that he couldn't compete with the other two members of the crew. Finally, the crew chief, an experienced NCO, who had been quietly listening to the back and forth argument, quietly walked over to the group and said, "I have been listening to you officers arguing about who is the most important member on your crew. I just want to remind you that you are not ever going anywhere until I pull the chocks so that you can taxi out." End of story.

EIGHT

THE CIVIL WARRIORS

Herein, we have singled-out the Cold War leaders, the nine Presidents of the United States during the period; the Commanders-in-Chief of Strategic Air Command; the Cold Warriors and the Shadow Warriors, and in closing I take pride in acknowledging another bloc of special people who also worked and performed behind the scenes, often deep within the shade of the Cold War—the "Civil Warriors"...more correctly, the Civil Servants. These mostly unheralded Civil Service employee professionals worked quietly in varied, important and frequently critical positions too numerous to name.

Civil service based on meritocracy was the Imperial bureaucracy of China, traced as far back as the Qin Dynasty (221–207 BC). During the Han Dynasty (202 BC–220 AD) the Xiaolian System of recommendation by superiors for appointments to office was established. In the areas of administration, especially in the military, appointments would be based solely on merit. This system was reversed during the shortlived Sui Dynasty (581–618), which initiated a civil service bureaucracy recruited by written examinations and recommendation. The following Tang Dynasty (618–907) would adopt the same measures of drafting officials, and would decreasingly rely upon aristocratic recommendations and more and more upon promotion based on the written examinations and job performance.

The Chinese civil service became known in Europe in the mid-18th century, and influenced the development of the American systems. Ironically, and in part due to the Chinese, the first European civil service, distinguished its civil servants from its military servants. In order to prevent corruption and favortism, promotions within the system were based on examinations. The system spread to the United Kingdom in 1854, and to the United States in 1883, with the Pendleton Civil Service Reform Act.

The Pendleton Civil Service Reform Act became federal law in 1883, establishing the United States Civil Service Commission, which placed most federal employees on the merit system and marked the end of a so-called "spoils system." Each of the Military Services rely heavily on the steady and stable civil service system for specialists, scientists, technicians all the way down to the interim clerk typist. Strategic Air Command was no exception.

I could have chosen from any one of thousands of notable Cold War civil servants who typified that special cadre of professionals and did so in making a personal choice of one who sums up not only the pride in serving, but one whose special performance and patriotism reflects on all the others from that clerk typist to the highest level civil service executive.

Dorene Sherman began her civil service career with Strategic Air Command in 1960. She applied for a job as an administrative clerk and was hired. Finding her 'niche' in serving, first as a file clerk, she steadily worked herself up to staff secretary, secretary to the Commander-in-Chief, SAC and finally to her last position as Deputy Director of Protocol, where she served until her retirement in 1999. Earning her "stripes" as a competent professional, she was well-grounded, self-confident and exuded animated energy and enthusiasm in every position she was assigned. She was also the first to retreat into the background when the situation dictated. Within the SAC Headquarters staff of 8,000 or so officers, NCO's, airmen and civilians, she was known to all for her personal enthusiasm, "can do" spirit, exceptional competence and trust.

The Omaha World Herald newspaper featured Dorene Sherman in a 2006 personal profile as, "One who stood near commanders and celebrities, politicians and many generals; a prince and a queen."

She traveled the world. On an Air Force trip to Belgium and Germany, she recalls thinking, 'How can this little farm girl from Nebraska even be here? Although lots of kids from Nebraska have gone on to do great things; President Gerald Ford and Johnny Carson among others.'"

Still, this shy farm girl who grew up near Wausa, Nebraska, can't forget milking cows and slopping hogs before school, nor does she wish to. "Those were the experiences that developed my character and work ethic," she was quoted as saying. The term Warrior fits her perfectly—always working behind the scenes with the same shyness, grace, dignity and astute awareness of everything going on around her. At formal receptions for national political, senior military and local civic leaders, she was ever-quietly present; more often than not, standing near the Commander-in-Chief, she discreetly whispered names of the guests to him. When the famous visited SAC Headquarters, she arranged and organized their itineraries. Within her numerous career positions, she was also entrusted with the most sensitive of national security information in order to understand the requirements necessary to coordinate visits of special dignitaries. Like her civil service colleagues, she didn't wear an Air Force uniform, but she was just as committed and loyal to the Cold War mission as those in command, sat at the controls of nuclear bombers or the ICBM's.

Her scrapbook is a personal treasure trove within which she appears in many of the pictures. The Omaha World Herald article characterized her photo album as a walk through history: Queen Elizabeth, Saudi Prince Bandar, Prime Minister Margaret Thatcher, President George H.W. Bush and numerous other dignitaries and personalities, including Senators and generals galore; several Chairmen of the Joint Chiefs of Staff; even World War II hero General Jimmy Doolittle, Bob Hope, Rita Moreno, Bob Newhart, the Osmond brothers and Tom Clancy. She escorted many of the notables through the highly classified and sensitive SAC underground command post.

During her many years of service, she traveled extensively with SAC commanders and staff virtually all over the world; she even once attended a White House luncheon.

Dorene Sherman claims that the Omaha area has benefited greatly not only from Offutt Air Force Base, Strategic Air Command and later, U.S. Strategic Command, but especially from the many Air Force officers and enlisted personnel who were assigned there; "and civilians, too;" she says proudly, "even me!"

Like many who retire from military service, this civilian warrior hasn't slowed down either. She plays the piano and organ at her church. She continues to utilize and share her talents, serving on the boards of numerous organizations, including the Salvation Army, Eppley Cancer Center, Omaha Symphony and Opera, Omaha Community Playhouse, Boys and Girls Clubs and Lauritzen Gardens.

This extraordinary "Civil Warrior" smiles as she recalls serving on the staff of every Commander-in-Chief of Strategic Air Command with the exception of Generals Kenny and LeMay; both of whom preceded her joining the civil service. From General Thomas Power onward, each she says was a great Commander-in-Chief for the time they served, yet each was uniquely different. "Of course I loved hearing all the stories and lore of the great General LeMay era," she says. "He was most certainly the single brilliant architect of SAC. Most of the CINCs who followed him remained in awe of his great ability and accomplishments as the true architect of Strategic Air Command, for as most of them reflected, "Unless you have been CINCSAC, you cannot possibly realize the miracle of this great organization.

"I was so delighted and blessed," she continued, "to have had the opportunities to be in the company, so close and to escort, the many SAC commanders over the years."

NINE

THEY ALSO SERVED

"The bravest are the tenderest; the loving are the daring."

Henry Wadsworth Longfellow

In developing this reflection on the Cold War and its many heroes, I attempted to derive a measure of thought and reflection about the wives and families of the valiant men who served. Of each of them, it can truly be said, they also served! It was common knowledge throughout Strategic Air Command and the United States Navy that the greatest burdens of the Cold War often fell on the wives and families of those in uniform. The combat crews and the support personnel seemed to always be away when they were needed most.

Having personally known literally thousands of the Cold Warrior's wives over the years and being familiar with the challenges of keeping their homes and families intact while their husbands were frequently either far away on a deployment, on ground alert, in a missile capsule or at sea, I marveled at their resilience and steadfast loyalty to their husband's jobs and responsibilities. Most took the long duty days, alert and prolonged separations in stride, seldom complaining. They became mother and father to the kids, took care of the upkeep of house and home, paid the bills and nurtured the family automobile when it needed repair. In spite of all the pressures and anxiety, the divorce rate among SAC and the Navy submariner families was exceptionally low.

Looking back at troubling and stressful times, many wives pointed to the Cuban Crisis as the most frightening period of their military service lives.

SAC combat crews and support personnel were called on alert with their respective bomber, tanker, reconnaissance or missile weapons systems. Many aircrews were moved out immediately to forward bases and overseas locations. The men were forbidden to tell their families where they were going or when they would return. Their only related source of information came from the radio, TV and newspapers, and neither of those media had an inkling of what was really happening with the military forces. Some wives did not hear from husbands for weeks after their departure. The "war of nerves" that pervaded the country through the media only added to their fear and concern.

[Author's note: As a B-52 pilot and Wing Command Post Controller at Ramey AFB, Puerto Rico, when the Cuban Crisis began to unravel, I participated in two airborne alert sorties during the anxious period. The President had directed airborne alert missions to commence immediately after the Crisis began and the combat crews were either in the air or on ground-alert with our bombers fully generated and ready to launch. The consequences of the situation, unquestioned among the combat crew force, did not fully impact the families until the Air Force casualty assistance people began collecting personal affairs information and requesting each family to pack for immediate evacuation if necessary. At that point, the true specter and fear of war became a reality.

I was amazed, as were others who have told me since, that there was virtually no panic among the wives and children—they simply went about their necessary preparations—just in case.]

Rumors, of course, were always a part of military life and the lives of their families, especially during such tense periods when their husbands were deployed across the world for several months at a time or potential crises such as that with Cuba. Wives frequently responded to stressful situations by participating in support groups, led by other wives, many with special education and training to deal with unpredictable circumstances. Those who stepped forward were exceptionally beneficial in providing counsel and comfort to the younger wives when husbands were away, rumors flying about, or when a tragic accident happened. They all bonded a family of one—relying upon and supporting one another.

Someone once said to me early in my career, "Air Force always gets two for the price of one." And, the same held true for the Navy. Only one, the military spouse gets paid for serving, but both clearly serve. SAC and the Navy were not unique in this tribute to wives and families; it was equally true for the other military services as well. The families of the submarine SSBN crews endured great frustration and maintained tempered patience as their husbands and fathers departed on their underwater patrols literally for months without receiving word of any kind until they returned.

I would have been remiss if I had not acknowledged the true bravery and spirit of the wives and families of the Cold War warriors. And while this has been but a brief acknowledgment of that special group of silent and unsung heroes—the wives and families—who carried out perhaps the most difficult duties of all, it is a heartfelt tribute to each. They also served!

TEN

THE LAST FULL MEASURE

"It is rather for us to be here dedicated to the great task remaining before us—that from these honored dead we take increased devotion to that cause for which they gave the last full measure of devotion."

Abraham Lincoln

A RB-47 reconnaissance aircraft flying out of Eielson Air Force Base, Alaska on April 17, 1955, was skirting along the Kamchatka Peninsula in international airspace when it was intercepted by Soviet MiG-15 fighters. The RB-47 abruptly disappeared. Most speculated that the crew was lost at sea after being shot down; others held that the crew may have been rescued by a Soviet vessel, imprisoned, tortured for what information they might gain and then executed.

When SAC stood down the Command in 1992, and its hundreds of thousands of assigned people over the years had served their country and the Free World very well—global peace had been sustained. SAC's nuclear delivery systems and combat crews were distributed to other operational and reoriented commands within the Air Force. During the 46 years, 2 months, and 10 days of SAC's life, 2,637 combat crew fatalities were recorded. The record, however, does not include fatalities that could not be officially attributed to SAC operations due to the sensitivity of the missions at the time. These losses resulted principally from classified reconnaissance missions that, in time, will likely be declassified. Only then will proper recognition be given to those individual Cold War heroes and their families for their ultimate sacrifice. To recognize each individual whose heroism so deserves would fill several volumes. Accordingly, I attempted to highlight and acknowledge the brave feats of a few SAC warriors in Chapter Six. In recognizing those special mission accomplishments, I also join my former Cold Warrior colleagues in offering the highest praise to all those on the SAC Honor Roll. May God bless their courageous families, gallant bravery and ultimate sacrifice.

The following quote from an old SAC comrade and former Cold Warrior colleague sums up our story:

"My overriding memory of my Cold War years in SAC is the great cadre of professionals who made the system work. It was truly a privilege to be associated with them. In retrospect, I find it almost incredible that such a group could have been put together and maintained without the need of the coercion of conscription. And, truly I think, they served out of love for their country and the conviction they were essential to its survival. God knows they didn't do it for the money (of which there was often very little) or for the easy life (which they didn't have). The work was hard, the life demanding, the rewards other than personal satisfaction, few and far between. Separation from family by alerts, TDYs, short duty tours, and so forth, went with the territory, but that didn't make them easy to take. But I loved it, I'm proud I did it, and I'd do it again if the good Lord would give me the chance. I really believe that what we did was crucial for the nation; and that we did it with an élan that would have made Jeb Stuart proud. Our country is better, and perhaps even exists, because we passed this way. I love my country without reservation and consider it the highest of all honors that I had the opportunity to serve her in a time of need. I think all true Cold Warriors feel exactly the same way!"

Bill Brooksher
Brigadier General, USAF (Ret)
Cold Warrior

CLOSING PERSPECTIVE

"Victory at all cost; Victory in spite of all terror;   Victory no matter how long and how hard the road may be; for without victory there is no survival"

Winston Churchill
May 13, 1940

In 1991, less then two years after the Berlin Wall fell, the Soviet Union began to crumble within. The Soviet economy had been faltering for years. The cost of keeping up with advanced American military weapons technologies, systems and strategies had led the Soviet economy to the brink of bankruptcy. Their entire infrastructure began to fall apart. For decades, the Soviets had barely been able to take care of its military needs which came largely at the expense of the sacrifices of their citizens. By the beginning of the 1990s, the Soviet people began to grow increasingly restless as they saw democracy and free enterprise economics take hold in the nations of Eastern Europe that had once professed their loyalty to communism. In a remarkable series of events which included street protests, rallies and the attempted overthrow of leader Mikhail Gorbachev, the Soviet Union finally dissolved in December of 1991.

At the heart of the long period of success of the United States in maintaining deterrence against Soviet aggression was a compelling national will, great leadership, innovative technologies, a superior industrial base and most importantly, young American men and women. The United States clearly enjoyed the unsurpassed patriotism and loyalty of its Cold War military forces. They served, they trained hard and they performed incredible tasks and missions without fanfare and mostly without recognition by the rest of the world passing them by. They worked long hours with compensation considerably less than that of their contemporaries on the "outside." Their families sacrificed with them, weekdays blended with weekends, long absences from home were the norm rather than the exception and yet morale remained amazingly high. The discipline was exacting and their commitments were unsurpassed, and the young warriors of the late forties and fifties grew into older Cold Warriors and commanders of the seventies and eighties. With the passage of time, the strategic nuclear deterrent warriors of SAC and the Navy became a disciplined, committed and elite professional deterrent force—— second to none other in the world before them.

The imprint of these airmen and sailors was indelible as a reminder that they fought in a virtual silent war of nerves through four and a half decades with several generations of men and women who continuing to step forward to serve. They transitioned through a dramatic evolution of weapon systems technologies over the period more so than ever in history. The awesome responsibilities of the "care and feeding" of nuclear weapons alone was tremendous. From the young airmen technicians to the NCO's to the bomber, ICBM combat crew members and the nuclear Navy, all of whom bore individual and collective responsibility for attention to the minutest detail in handling and managing special weapons entrusted to them. Errors of omission or mistakes could not and were not tolerated at any level.

While the revolutionary growth in the sophistication of weapons and operational hardware was extraordinary, along with the attendant personal responsibilities, they did not compare with dedication of those who chose to walk a different path than their childhood, high school or college contemporaries. 'Chose' is important in this context, because the entire U.S. strategic nuclear deterrent force was sustained during the Cold War and continues to be today, by men and women who chose patriotism and service with a belief in the nation's ideals over other available pursuits. During the Cold War era not a single draftee or conscript served aboard a SAC aircraft, in an ICBM launch control center or aboard a Navy nuclear submarine.

The national leaders, military commanders and warriors, young and old, rode through tides of soaring technologies, numerous changes in perceptions of military prestige, critical periods of national roller coaster politics, inconsistent diplomacy and radical social changes. Yet, each continued to come forward and excelled in their chosen profession and moved on as others with the same ideals followed. The term "professionalism" seems not quite enough to fully embody or characterize the Cold War servants, but I cannot think of another term that better describes those who willingly served, sacrificed, performed, excelled and above all preserved the peace during the greatest period of threat that our country had ever known at that time. The young heroes became the 'friendly' envy of many of those served in other military units and capacities. But none could sell SAC or the Navy short on its mission responsibilities, the commitment of its people or the consistent sharp edge of readiness and performance.

Finally, what of the future? The decade following the end of the Cold War was telling for America's future security in many ways. One major mighty force that provided deterrence during the tenuous period—Strategic Air Command—was stood down and promptly dismantled; its Cold War deterrent and fighting capabilities along with the seasoned leaders, strategic thinkers and planners were distributed out among other Air Force commands. The Navy's strategic nuclear submarine missions were all but ended. The political mantra of the early '90s became "The Peace Dividend", an overly optimistic benefit of the end of the Cold War and, "It's the economy, stupid," a contradictory, but a politically convenient statement for election year rhetoric. A result of that rhetoric was drastic down-sizing of U.S. military forces across the board. A zealous post-Cold War 'peace-seeking' Congress created policies which critically disrupted the U.S. Intelligence Community by imposing radical constraints on funding and hiring practices. The result of the latter Congressional acts resulted in cutting the various Intelligence Agencies' budgets by almost half. An additional act placed restrictions on the CIA———curbing the recruiting of foreign nationals as undercover agents.

As the years of the nineties moved on, a subtle, but highly volatile new enemy of American peace and freedom was on the move. The indicators, although increasingly evident, were by and large ignored by leaders in Washington. One needed only to assess the provocative intrusions of this new enemy of militant terrorists to recognize that the United States was the prime target. From the first attempt to destroy the World Trade Center in 1993, the random bombings of U.S. interests overseas, the bombing of two U.S. Embassies in Africa, and the bombing of the USS Cole, the pattern should have been obvious as it led finally to the attack and catastrophic destruction of the World Trade Center on September 11, 2001, by zealous Islamic terrorists.

In conclusion and in reference to earlier comments in my Author's Note, the 21st Century President of the United States in remarks to students during his 2009 visit to Moscow concluded the Cold War as such: "The American and Soviet armies were still massed in Europe, trained and ready to fight. The ideological trenches of the last century were roughly in place. Competition in everything from astrophysics to athletics was treated as a zero-sum game. If one person won, then the other person had to lose. And then within a few short years, the world as it was ceased to be. Make no mistake: This change did not come from any one nation. The Cold War reached a conclusion because of the actions of many nations over many years, and because the people of Russia and Eastern Europe stood up and decided that its end would be peaceful."

As we have observed in this latter day review of the Cold War, the conflict was by no means a "competition in astrophysics and athletics." It was a global battle between tyranny and freedom. The Soviet "sphere of influence" was delineated by walls and barbed wire and tanks and secret police to prevent people from escaping. American deterrence was an unmatched force for winning in the Cold War. The Cold War did not end because the Soviets decided it should, but clearly because they were no match for the 'capability' of forces of the United States and the 'will' of the people and the leadership to defend our liberty and defeat Communism.

If American leaders and others among us persist in pushing the 'reset button' to politically correct history to meet their own social, political and personal goals of appeasement and claiming moral equivalence with known adversaries, thence this great nation will soon collapse under the weight of false historical narratives created for that very purpose. Notably, the assertion of equivalence between acts of the United States, the Islamic terrorists of 9/11 and the preceding years of provocative violence can only further demean American strength and resolve. The 21st Century leadership of America need only to heed the words of President Harry Truman as he explained the requirement to reorganize the U.S. Military establishment in 1950 to address the Cold War threat from the Soviet Union: "No people in history have preserved their freedom who thought that by not being strong enough to protect themselves they might prove inoffensive to their enemies."

This new enemy, although with different motives and tactics than that of the Cold War, is not unlike any other that has sought to bring America down. And the nation has responded in defense with another generation of war fighters; these, too, will not be unlike those that preceded them—youthful, bright, determined and voluntarily serving their country in a time of need.

DETERRENCE

The enduring and undeniable strategy for peace and security

God Bless America!

SOURCES

While literally hundreds of books, reference documents, periodicals and cyber searches were consulted and researched, the following are those that were most valuable in this work.

PUBLISHED BOOKS:

Adams, Chris, Inside The Cold War: A Cold Warrior's Reflections. Maxwell Air Force Base, Alabama, The Air University Press, 1999.

Adams, Chris, Ideologies in Conflict: A Cold War Docu-story, New York, Writers Showcase, 2001.

Aiken, Jonathan, Nixon, A Life. New York, Regency Publishing, Inc., 1993.

America's Shield: The Story of Strategic Air Command and Its People. Paducah, Kentucky, Turner Publishing Company, 1992.

Anderson, David A. Strategic Air Command: Two Thirds of the Triad. New York, Scribner's: 1976.

Aspin Report, The Strategic Defense Initiative And American Security. Boston, University Press of America: 1987.

Baar, James and Howard, William E., Spacecraft and Missiles Of The World. New York, Harcourt, Brace and World: 1966.

Baldwin, Hanson W., The Great Arms Race: A Comparison of United States and Soviet Power. New York, Frederick A. Praeger, Publisher: 1958.

Ball, Desmond, Politics And Force Levels: Strategic Missile Program of the Kennedy Administration. Berkley, California, University of California Press: 1980

Barnet, Richard J., The Giants. New York, Simon and Shuster: 1977.

Bender, David L., The Cold War, Opposing Viewpoints. San Diego, Greenhaven Press, Inc.: 1992.

Beschloss, Michael R. and Talbott, Strobe, At The Highest Levels. Boston, Little, Brown and Company: 1993.

Beschloss, Michael R., May Day -- Eisenhower, Khrushchev and the U-2 Affair. New York, Harper & Row: 1986.

Betts, Richard K., Soldiers, Statesmen and the Cold War Crisis.

Cambridge, Massachussets, Harvard University Press: 1977.

Bohn, John, Development of Strategic Air Command. Offutt Air Force Base, Nebraska, Office of the Historian, Headquarters, Strategic Air Command: 1976.

Borklund, C.W., Men Of The Pentagon: From Forrestal To McNamara. New York, Praeger Press: 1966.

Bottome, Edgar M., The Missile Gap: A Study Of The Formulation Of Military And Political Policy. Rutherford, New York, Farleigh Dickinson University Press: 1971.

Bottome, Edgar M., The Balance Of Terror: A Guide To The Arms Race. Boston, Beacon Press: 1971.

Boyne, Walter, Boeing B-52, A Documentary History. New York, Jane's Publishing Company: 1982.

Britten, Stewart, The Invisible Event. London, Menard Press: 1983.

Burgess, Eric, Long Range Ballistic Missiles. New York, The MacMillan Company: 1962.

Burton, James G., The Pentagon Wars. Annapolis, Maryland, Naval Institute Press: 1993.

Calder, Nigel, Nuclear Nightmares. London, British Broadcasting Corporation: 1979.

Chapman, John L., Atlas, The Story Of A Missile. New York, Harper: 1960.

Coffee, Thomas M., Iron Eagle. New York, Crown Publishers: 1986.

Current, Richard N., Williams, T. Harry and Freidel, Frank, American History -- A Survey. New York, Alfred A. Knopf: 1965.

Divine, Robert, Eisenhower And The Cold War. New York, Oxford University Press: 1981.

Dolgikh and Kuraniov, Communist Ideals And The Atheistic Indoctrination Of The Troops. Moscow, Military Publishing House: 1976.

Donald, David, Spyplane. Osceola, Wisconsin, Motorbooks International: 1987.

Donovan, Robert J., Nemesis – Trumam and Johnson: The Coils Of The War In Asia. New York, St. Martin's - Marek: 1984.

Duignan, Peter and Rabushka, The United States In The 1980'S. Hoover Institution, Stanford University Press: 1980.

Eisenhower, Dwight D., Mandate For Change: 1953-1956. Garden City, New York, Doubleday: 1963.

Gaddis, John Lewis, Strategies of Containment. New York, Oxford University Press: 1982.

Gates, Robert M., From The Shadows. New York, Simon & Schuster: 1996.

Ginsberg, Colonel Robert N., USAF, U.S. Military Strategy In The Sixties. New York, W.W. Norton: 1965.

Goldman, Eric F., The Tragedy Of Lyndon Johnson. New York, Dell Books: 1969

Goldman, Marshall, Gorbachev's Challenge: Economic Reform in the Age Of High Technology, New York, W.W. Norton: 1987.

Gorbachev, Mikhail, Perestroika. New York, Harper & Row: 1987.

Gray, Colin S., The Soviet-American Arms Race. Farnsborough, UK, Saxon Books: 1976.

Griffith, Thomas E., MacArthur's Airman: General George C. Kenney and the War in the Southwest Pacific (Modern War Studies), Lawrence, Kansas, University Press of Kansas, 1998.

Griffin, William E., The Superpowers And Regional Tensions. Lexington, Massachusetts, Lexington Books: 1982.

Gunston, Bill, Modern Bombers. New York, Salamander Books Ltd.: 1988.

Halberstadt, Hans, FB-111 Aardvark. Stillwater, Minnesota, Specialty Press: 1992.

Harris, Edgar S., Jr., Lt. General, USAF (Ret), U.S. Air Force Oral History Interview, by Lt. Col. David L. Young, USAF, Edited by Pauline Tibbs. Washington D.C., Office of Air Force History: 1985.

Horelick, Arnold L. and Rush, Myron, Strategic Power And Soviet Foreign Policy. Chicago, University of Chicago Press: 1966.

Hosking, Geoffrey, The Awakening Of The Soviet Union. Cambridge, Massachusetts, Harvard University Press: 1991.

Hubler, Richard G., SAC – The Strategic Air Command. New York, Duell, Sloan and Pearce: 1958.

Hyland, William G., The Reagan Foreign Policy. New York, New American Library: 1987.

Jane's All The World's Greatest Aircraft. London, Jane's Publishing, Ltd.: 1979-80, 185-86.

Jacobsen, Meyers K. and Wagner, Ray, B-36 in Action. Carrollton, Texas, Signal Publications: 1980.

Jordon, Amos A. and Taylor, William J., American National Security - Policy And Process. Baltimore, The Johns Hopkins Press: 1981.

Kahn, Herman, Thinking About The Unthinkable In The 1980's. New York, Simon & Schuster: 1984.

Kahan, Jerome H., Security In The Nuclear Age: Developing U.S. Strategic Arms Policy. Washington, Brookings Institution: 1975.

Kanter, MacKinley, Mission With LeMay; My Story. Garden City, New York, Doubleday: 1965.

Katz, Nick, Wild Blue Yonder: Politics and the B-1 Bomber. New York, Pantheon Books: 1988.

Kaufman, William W., The McNamara Strategy. New York, Harper & Row: 1964.

Kearns, Doris, Lyndon Johnson And The American Dream. New York, Harper & Row: 1976.

Kennedy, Robert F., Thirteen Days. New York, W.W. Norton & Company: 1969.

Kennen, George F., The Nuclear Delusion. New York, Pantheon Books: 1982.

Kennen, George F., The Cloud of Danger: Current Realities Of American Foreign Policy. Boston, Little, Brown: 1977.

Kissinger, Henry, Necessity For Choice. New York, Harper & Row: 1961.

Kissinger, Henry, Diplomacy. New York, Simon & Schuster: 1994.

Knorr, Klaus, Historical Dimensions Of National Security Problems. Lawrence, Kansas, University Press of Kansas: 1976.

Kohn, Richard and Harahan, Joseph P., Strategic Warfare. Washington DC, Office of Air Force History: 1988.

Kuniholm, Bruce R., The Origins Of The Cold War In The Near East. Princeton, New Jersey, Princeton University Press: 1980.

Ladislav, Bittman, The New Image Makers. Washington DC, Pergamon-Brassey's International Defense Publishers: 1988.

Laird, Melvin R., A House Divided: America's Strategy Gap. Chicago, Henry Regnery: 1962.

Leckie, Robert, The Wars of America -- Volume II, San Juan Hill To Tonkin. New York, Harper & Row: 1968.

Lewin, Moshe, The Gorbachev Phenomenon. Berkeley, California, University of California Press: 1991.

Lippman, Walter, The Cold War: A Study in U.S. Foreign Policy. New York, Harper: 1947.

Love, Jay and Kimmel, Neal, Peacemaker, The History of the B-36 At Carswell Air Force Base, Ft. Worth, Texas, 1948 -1958. Ft. Worth, Taylor Publishing Company: 1995.

Mastny, Vojtech, Russia's Road to the Cold War: Diplomacy, Warfare and the Politics Of Communism. New York, Columbia University Press: 1979.

Douglas, The Balance of Military Power. New York, Salamander Books: 1981.

Miller, Jay, CONVAIR B-58. Arlington, Texas, Aerofax Inc: 1985.

Morris, Charles R., Iron Destinies, Lost Opportunities. New York, Harper & Row: 1988.

Mueller, John, Retreat From Doomsday. New York, Basic Books, Inc.: 1989.

Newhouse, John, Cold Dawn - The Story of SALT. Washington, Pergamon-Brassey's: 1989.

Newman, John N., JFK and Vietnam. New York, Warner Books: 1992.

Noonan, Peggy, What I Saw At The Revolution. New York, Random House: 1990.

Parmet, Herbert S., Nixon And His America. Boston, Little, Brown and Company: 1990.

Patterson, Bradley H., Jr., The Ring of Power. New York, Basic Books, Inc.: 1988.

Polmar, Norman and Laur, Timothy M., Strategic Air Command. Baltimore, The Nautical and Aviation Publishing Company of America: 1990.

Pipes, Richard, U.S. - Soviet Relations in the Era of Détente. Boulder Colorado, Westview Press: 1981.

Power, General Thomas S., USAF, Design For Survival. New York, Pocket Books: 1965.

Powers, Francis Gary with Curt Gentry, Operation Overflight. New York, Holt, Rinehart and Winston: 1970.

Prados, JohN, Presidents' Secret Wars. New York, William Morrow and Company, Inc.: 1986.

Pringle, Peter and Arkin, William, SIOP. New York, W.W. Norton & Co.: 1984.

Rhodes, Richard, The Making of the Atomic Bomb. New York, Simon and Schuster: 1986.

Sagan, Scott D., The Limits of Safety. Princeton, N.J., Princeton University Press: 1993.

Schick, Jack, The Berlin Crisis, 1958-1962. Philadelphia, University of Pennsylvania Press. 1971.

Schlesinger, Arthur M., The Imperial Presidency. Boston, Houghton Mifflin: 1973.

Schlesinger, Arthur M., The Cycles of American History. Boston, Houghton Mifflin: 1986.

Schuman, Frederick L., The Cold War Retrospect And Prospect. Baton Rouge, Louisiana State University Press: 1988.

Shul, Brian and Watson, Walter L., The Untouchables: Mission Accomplished. Chico, California, Mach One, Incorporated: 1993.

Singer, J. David, Deterrence, Arms Control and Disarmament. Columbus, Ohio, Ohio State University Press: 1962.

Slessor, Sir John, Strategy for the West. New York, William Morrow and Company: 1954.

Smith, Joseph B., Portrait of a Cold Warrior. New York, Putnam's: 1976.

Snyder, Glenn H., Deterrence and Defense: Toward a Theory of National Security. Princeton, New Jersey, Princeton University Press: 1961.

Snyder, William P. and Brown, James, Defense Policy in the Reagan Administration. Washington DC, National Defense University Report: 1988.

Sorenson, Theodore C., Kennedy. New York, Harper and Row, Publishers: 1965.

Stockman, David A., The Triumph of Politics. New York, Avon: 1987.

Sulzberger, C.L., A Long Row of Candles. Toronto, The MacMillan Company: 1969.

Taylor, General Maxwell D. USA (Ret), Responsibility And Response. New York, Harper & Row: 1967.

Taylor, General Maxwell D., USA (Ret), The Uncertain Trumpet, New York, Harper & Brothers: 1959.

Taylor, William J. and Maaranen, Steven A., The Future of Conflict in the 1980's. Lexington, Massachusetts, Lexington Books: 1982.

Toffler, Alvin and Heidi, War and Anti-War. New York, Little, Brown and Company: 1993.

Weisberger, Bernard A., Cold War Cold Peace. New York, Houghton Mifflin Company: 1985.

Wise, David and Ross, Thomas B., The U-2 Affair. New York, Random House: 1962.

Wettig, Gerhard, High Road, Low Road - Diplomacy & Public Action in Soviet Foreign Policy. Washington DC, Pergamon - Brassey's International Defense Publishers: 1989.

Wolfe, Alan, The Rise and Fall of the Soviet Threat. Washington DC, Institute of Policy Studies: 1979.

Yenne, Bill, S A C, A Primer of Modern Strategic Airpower. Novato, California, Presidio Press: 1985.

Yergin, Daniel, Shattered Peace: The Origins of the Cold War and the National Security. Boston, Houghton Mifflin: 1978.

PUBLISHED REPORTS, INTERVIEWS AND NEWSPAPER ARTICLES:

Alert Operations and the Strategic Air Command, 1957-1991. Office of the Historian, Headquarters, Strategic Air Command, Offutt Air Force Base, Nebraska, 7 December 1991

Bohn, John T., A Conversation With LeMay. Office of the Historian, Strategic Air Command, Offutt Air Force Base, Nebraska, November 1972.

Cheney, Liz, New York Times, Copyright 2009 Dow Jones & Company, Inc. All Rights Reserved.

Conversino, Mark J., PhD., Major, USAF, Back to the Stone Age: The Attack on Curtis E. LeMay. A Paper presented at America's Shield Symposium, Offutt A.F.B., 15 - 17 May 1996.

Hopkins, Charles K., Unclassified History of the Joint Strategic Target Planning Staff (JSTPS). Offutt Air Force Base, Nebraska: 26 June 1990.

Michael Kelly, Omaha World Herald: "Offutt Takes 'Farm Girl' On World Tour:" February 12, 2006.

Peck, Earl G., B-47 Stratojet, Aerospace Historian, Volume 22, No. 2. Manhattan, Kansas, Department of History, Kansas State University: June 1975.

The National Security Archive, The George Washington University. A repository of open source material, government records, declassified documents and interviews of prominent political and military leaders on a wide range of topics pertaining to the national security, foreign, intelligence, and economic policies of the United States.

U.S. Air Force Almanac Series, 1997, 1978, 1981. Air Force Magazine. Washington DC.

PERIODICALS:

Alexander, George, "Life With The Minuteman, Newsweek, April 7, 1969.

Alsop, Joseph, "The New Balance of Power", Encounter Magazine, v. 10, no. 5, May 1958.

Alsop, Stewart, "How Can We Catch Up?" Saturday Evening Post, v. 230, no. 24, December 14, 1957.

Austin, Harold (Hal), "A Cold War Overflight of the USSR", Daedalus Flyer, Spring, 1995.

Edmundson, James V., Lt. General, USAF (Ret), "Six Churning and Four Burning" - Three Part Series. Omaha, Nebraska, Klaxon Magazine, Volume 3, Issues 3 and 4, Volume 4, Issue 1: 1995-1996.

Garthoff, Raymond, "Russia – Leading the World In ICBM and Satellite Development?", Missiles and Rockets, v.2, no.12, October 1957.

Murray, Stanley H., "Treasure Of The Czar", The Retired Officer Magazine, October 1994.

"Soviet Pilot Says He Downed U-2 'Unarmed'", Plane Talk, Employee Publication of Lockheed Martin Tactical Aircraft Systems, Vol. 4, No. 18, October 22, 1996.

Rhodes, Richard, The General and World War III, The New Yorker, New York: June 19, 1995.

Sagan, Scott, Nuclear Alerts and Crisis Management, "In International Security," Volume 9.

Pratt, Colonel Henry J., "The Buck Stops Here," The Retired Officer Magazine, v. LI, no. 4, April 1995.

Roberts, Steven, Stanglin, Douglas, Pasternak, Doug and Walsh, Kenneth T., "Why There Are Still Spies," U.S. News & World Report, v.116, no.9, March 7, 1994.

Sowell, Thomas, "An Unnecessary War," Forbes Magazine, v. 158,   no. 10, August 1995.

ABOUT THE AUTHOR

Chris Adams is a graduate of Tarleton State University; Texas A&M University-Commerce and the Industrial College of the Armed Forces. Following 31 years of active duty in the Air Force, he retired in the grade of Major General after an extraordinary career leading up to his final assignment as Chief of Staff, Strategic Air Command (SAC). A veteran of the Cold War and Vietnam he logged 8,000 hours in a variety of aircraft including the B-36, B-52, EC-135 and numerous others, including 1100 hours in the venerable C-47 *Gooneybird* in Southeast Asia. He enjoyed a diverse career serving a tour of duty as a Minuteman ICBM combat crew commander. With increasing rank and responsibilities, he moved on to become a SAC wing commander, air division commander, Assistant Deputy Chief of Staff, Operations (SAC) and Deputy Director, Strategic Target Planning (JSTPS) as well as six years on the senior staff of the Defense Nuclear Agency.

He retired from the Air Force to accept an appointment as Associate Director, Los Alamos National Laboratory. Thereafter he became Vice President, Government Systems, ANDREW Corporation, which included managing business enterprises in China, throughout the Far East, Saudi Arabia, the Soviet Union and the former Soviet States; in the latter, directing the recovery of the post-Cold War badly degraded telecommunications systems in that region. He currently remains active serving on numerous government and public service boards and foundations.

A published author, he has drawn from his extraordinary knowledge and experience in strategic air operations, nuclear weapons and the culture of the former Soviet Union in publishing six books; two nonfiction Cold War research studies and four spy novels.

His military awards include The Distinguished Service Medal, the Department of Defense Meritorious Service Medal, two Legions of Merit, two Air Medals for service in Vietnam and numerous other decorations. He is a Distinguished Alumnus of Tarleton State University and Texas A&M University-Commerce, and is listed in Who's Who in America.

INDEX

A

Airey, Paul 227
Akhromeyev, Air Marshall 219, 224
ALCM (air launched cruise missile) 42, 47, 56, 57, 160, 164
Aldrich, Linda 223, 224
Allen, Lew 52, 133, 157
Anderson, Rudolph 193, 201
Anderson, William R. 58
Arnold, Henry H. "Hap" 29, 118
ATLAS missile 54, 74
Austin, Harold "Hal" 181, 182, 187, 258

B

B-1 39, 48, 56, 92, 95, 96, 98, 112, 113, 125, 149, 160, 164, 254
B-2 39, 98, 160
B-29 8, 16, 18, 26, 27, 36, 39, 49, 66, 68, 121, 123, 134, 148, 159
B-36 17, 18, 28, 29, 30, 32, 33, 34, 35, 36, 39, 42, 43, 45, 47, 106, 122, 123, 124, 129, 137, 172, 174, 175, 176, 177, 210, 254, 255, 261
B-47 29, 35, 36, 37, 38, 39, 40, 41, 42, 45, 49, 78, 122, 123, 125, 135, 139, 159, 179, 183, 192, 194, 234, 258
B-50A 27, 123

B-52 22, 33, 38, 39, 40, 41, 42, 43, 44, 45, 47, 49, 56, 78, 80, 85, 86, 87, 92, 98, 112, 122, 124, 125, 136, 137, 139, 142, 144, 149, 157, 159, 164, 167, 172, 192, 193, 194, 206, 207, 208, 209, 210, 211, 219, 224, 228, 232, 233, 242, 252, 261
Bacon, Cathy 158, 224
Bahia de Cochinas (Bay of Pigs) 77, 79
Barents Sea 187, 191
Barry, Harold 174
Benn, William 118
Berlin Blockade 12, 32
Biggs Air Force Base 35, 138, 210
Bissell, Richard 52
Bogan, Gerald 18
Bohn, John 252, 257
Brooksher, Bill 246
Burke, Arleigh 21
Bush, George H.W. 63, 64, 100, 109, 110, 111, 112, 167, 239
Butler, George 166, 167
Byrnes, James F. 10

C

C-47 49, 200, 201, 228, 261

Carter, James (Jimmy) E. 21, 48, 56, 57, 63, 91, 92, 93, 94, 95, 96, 97, 98, 110, 111, 112, 126, 132, 149, 160

Castro, Fidel 77, 80, 87, 90, 95, 193, 194

Chain, John T. 163, 164

Chernenko, Konstantin 101, 103

Chromedome 22, 43, 193, 211

Churchill, Winston xvii, 3, 4, 5, 6, 8, 9, 65, 66, 67, 247

Clancy, Tom 239

Clark, Orion 159, 180

Cold War vii, ix, x, xi, xvii, xviii, 3, 4, 7, 11, 12, 13, 17, 19, 20, 22, 24, 25, 26, 38, 50, 51, 59, 63, 64, 65, 67, 68, 69, 70, 71, 74, 80, 82, 83, 84, 88, 89, 90, 93, 95, 98, 101, 106, 107, 109, 110, 111, 112, 113, 115, 116, 124, 125, 127, 128, 129, 133, 139, 150, 158, 160, 167, 168, 171, 172, 173, 180, 181, 188, 189, 192, 193, 210, 214, 216, 219, 220, 222, 226, 232, 233, 234, 237, 238, 239, 241, 243, 245, 246, 247, 248, 249, 250, 251, 252, 254, 255, 256, 257, 258, 261

Containment Strategy 7, 10

Crommelin, John 17, 18

Cuban Crisis xvii, 12, 22, 86, 135, 136, 137, 173, 194, 195, 196, 204, 241, 242

D

Davis, Bennie L. 149, 159, 160, 163, 176

Defense Nuclear Agency 261

Denfeld, Louis 18

Denver, John 44, 212

Department of Energy 96

Deutschendorf, Henry 212

Dobrynin, Anatoli 111

Doolittle, Jimmy 239

Dougherty, Russell ix, 148, 149, 150, 151, 152, 153, 154, 168, 234

Draper, Charles 59

Dulles, Allen 52

E

Edmundson, James W. 15, 174, 175, 176, 258

Eisenhower, Dwight D. 5, 20, 21, 52, 54, 63, 69, 70, 71, 72, 73, 74, 75, 76, 77, 78, 79, 84, 111, 150, 151, 174, 186, 190, 252, 253

Ellis, Richard 125, 126, 156, 157, 158, 168, 211

Ellsworth, Richard 179, 180, 181, 219, 220, 224

Ermath, Fritz 100

Estes, Bob 206

F

Ford, Gerald 63, 76, 89, 90, 91, 100, 110, 111, 132, 238

Franklin, Benjamin 25, 59

G

Gaylor, Robert D. 229

Goforth, Oscar L. 187

Gorbachev, Mikhail 13, 102, 103, 104, 105, 106, 107, 108, 109, 110, 111, 167, 247, 253, 255

Göring, Hermann 117

Gray, Colin 100, 101, 253

Great Patriotic War 4

Groves, Leslie 7

Gunter, Lester E. 145, 179, 230, 231

H

Hale, Jackie 224

Halloran, Pat xi, 196

Hamilton, Kelly 224

Harris, Edgar S. xi, 127, 253

Hasbrouck, Larry 222
Heavlin, Vance 182
Hillman, Donald 178, 179
Holloway, Bruce K. 132, 143, 144, 145
Holt, Carl 181, 182, 183, 256
Hope, Bob 239

I

Ikle', Fred 100, 101

J

JSTPS 17, 21, 157, 258, 261

K

Kampelman, Max 103
KC-10 50
KC-97 36, 38, 49, 148, 179, 182, 191
KC-135 22, 36, 43, 45, 49, 78, 142, 144, 149, 191, 194, 201, 202, 205, 212, 224
Kennedy, John F. 20, 63, 73, 76, 77, 78, 79, 80, 81, 82, 83, 92, 95, 100, 110, 111, 124, 136, 150, 153, 188, 192, 193, 203, 251, 254, 256
Kennen, George 9, 10, 11, 72, 91, 92, 100, 254
Kenney, George 17, 28, 29, 67, 117, 118, 119, 120, 122, 253
KGB 13, 101, 188, 192
Khrushchev, Nikita 12, 22, 52, 73, 74, 76, 79, 80, 86, 101, 136, 152, 186, 188, 190, 192, 252
Kiev, Ukraine 102
Kissinger, Henry 73, 84, 85, 88, 90, 91, 94, 110, 111, 254
Korean War 18, 28, 33, 35, 71, 123, 148, 190, 228
Kremlin 74, 80, 86, 91, 97, 99, 101, 105, 187, 194
Kubesch, Henry 212
Kvitsinsky, Yuli 97

L

LeMay, Curtis E. 8, 17, 19, 21, 29, 31, 40, 46, 47, 66, 68, 78, 79, 115, 119, 120, 121, 122, 123, 124, 125, 126, 127, 128, 133, 134, 135, 139, 147, 153, 156, 164, 168, 171, 173, 174, 176, 177, 182, 183, 211, 212, 222, 239, 254, 257
Lodge, Henry Cabot 188
Looking Glass 22, 23, 24, 161
Los Alamos 7, 8, 9, 65, 66, 97, 261
Lovell, Bernard 195
Luttwak, Edward 100

M

MacArthur, Douglas 69, 118, 253
Manhattan Project 7, 129, 258
Marshall, George 7, 66, 68, 69, 107, 128, 224, 253
Martin, Linda 26, 36, 51, 54, 123, 224, 253, 258
Matthews, Francis 18
Maultsby, Charles (Chuck) 196, 202, 204
Maultsby, Jeanne 196
Maxwell, Joseph 183, 184, 185
McCarthy, James R. 206, 207, 208
McCoy, James M. xi, 193, 228, 229, 230, 231, 234
McKone, John 187, 188, 189, 190, 192
Mentyukov, Igor 186
Meyer, John C. xiv, 145, 146, 147, 209
MiG-15 51, 179, 180, 182, 245
Minuteman missile (ICBM) 98, 219, 220, 221, 222, 224
MIRV 55, 58, 59
Mize, John D. 208, 209
MK-17 nuclear weapon 32, 177
Moreno, Rita 239

Moscow 6, 9, 10, 19, 52, 74, 79, 84, 85, 86, 97, 99, 105, 186, 188, 204, 249, 252
Murphy, Elmer E. 212

N

Nagasaki 8, 9, 17, 121, 134
Nagel, Jill E. 224
Nazzaro, Joseph J. 141, 142
Newhart, Bob 239
New York Times 40, 78, 121, 257
Nixon, Richard M. 21, 47, 63, 70, 76, 78, 84, 85, 86, 87, 88, 89, 90, 91, 93, 100, 110, 111, 112, 132, 251, 255
Nuclear submarine (SSBN) ix, xviii, 21, 57, 58, 115, 116, 171, 216, 248, 249

O

Obenauf, James E. 183, 185
Okimoto, Fred 196
Olmstead, Bruce 187, 188, 192
Ostrozny, N.J. 206
Oswald, Diane 224

P

Palm, Wilford G. 137, 139, 140, 165, 187, 188, 232
Parish, Sam 228, 231
Pavlichenko, Vladimir 97
Payne, William 212
Peck, Earl 37, 258
Phillips, Dean 187
Polaris 20, 21, 57, 58, 59, 78, 79, 131, 151, 153
Polhemus, William L. 212
Posa, Eugene 187, 188
Poseidon 57, 58, 59
Powers, Gary xvii, 12, 51, 52, 74, 149, 156, 164, 185, 186, 188, 198, 214, 256

Power, Thomas 21, 73, 120, 134, 135, 136, 137, 139, 147, 149, 168, 192, 201, 202, 203, 204, 239, 251, 253, 255, 256, 258
Pruett, Jacob 180
Purdue, Ed 148, 203

R

Radford, Arthur 18
Reagan, Ronald 12, 13, 48, 63, 64, 90, 94, 95, 96, 97, 98, 99, 100, 101, 102, 103, 104, 105, 106, 107, 108, 109, 110, 111, 112, 113, 157, 158, 160, 164, 213, 254, 256
Rew, Tom 207
Rickover, Hyman 57, 58, 59, 115, 116, 128, 129, 130, 131, 132, 133
Roosevelt, Franklin 3, 5, 6, 7, 9, 10, 25, 65, 66, 128
Russia x, 4, 5, 6, 7, 16, 52, 65, 70, 107, 200, 201, 250, 255, 258
Ryan, John D. 138, 139, 140, 168

S

Schairer, George 125
Schriever, Bernard 54
Sellers, Ron 206
Sewell, Joe 225
Shelepin, Alexandr 188
Sherman, Dorene xi, 18, 238, 239
Shul, Brian 213, 256
Shull, Ashley 224
Soviet Union xviii, 3, 4, 7, 10, 11, 12, 13, 18, 20, 22, 40, 51, 63, 64, 66, 68, 73, 76, 78, 79, 80, 82, 86, 87, 89, 90, 91, 92, 93, 99, 101, 102, 103, 104, 105, 107, 109, 110, 111, 112, 113, 122, 125, 129, 136, 167, 171, 176, 178, 183, 187, 189, 190, 192, 193, 194, 204, 213, 219, 224, 247, 250, 253, 261

Sputnik xvii, 12, 72, 73, 135
Stalin, Josef 3, 4, 5, 6, 7, 9, 10, 11,
        12, 16, 18, 19, 65, 66, 67, 68,
        70, 72, 86, 87, 101, 107
Stone, Rex 222, 257
Strategic Air Command (SAC) ix,
        xviii, 15, 16, 17, 19, 21, 23, 24,
        44, 57, 59, 60, 67, 73, 80, 85,
        106, 115, 116, 117, 119, 120,
        122, 128, 129, 134, 138, 141,
        143, 145, 146, 147, 148, 149,
        156, 160, 161, 164, 167, 168,
        171, 173, 189, 193, 227, 228,
        230, 231, 232, 233, 234, 237,
        238, 239, 241, 249, 251, 252,
        253, 255, 257, 261

T

Timmins, Edward 179
Titan missile 54, 55, 78, 135, 160,
        195, 219, 222, 223
Tolsma, Charles (Chuck) 137
Triad 151, 251
Truman, Harry 3, 4, 7, 8, 9, 10, 11,
        17, 18, 63, 64, 65, 66, 67, 68,
        69, 71, 72, 95, 107, 111, 112,
        178, 250

U

U-2 (spy plane) xvii, 12, 51, 52, 53,
        73, 74, 79, 80, 185, 186, 187,
        193, 196, 198, 199, 200, 201,
        214, 252, 257, 258

United States iv, ix, x, xvii, xviii, 3, 4,
        5, 7, 9, 10, 11, 12, 13, 17, 19,
        23, 24, 26, 31, 33, 40, 51, 52,
        55, 63, 65, 66, 69, 70, 73, 74,
        77, 78, 80, 81, 82, 84, 85, 86,
        88, 92, 93, 94, 95, 96, 99, 100,
        101, 102, 103, 104, 105, 106,
        107, 109, 110, 111, 112, 113,
        116, 121, 127, 128, 131, 138,
        139, 140, 141, 143, 145, 146,
        148, 149, 150, 151, 154, 158,
        159, 161, 162, 166, 167, 171,
        176, 180, 183, 188, 189, 193,
        194, 213, 219, 222, 227, 233,
        237, 238, 241, 247, 249, 250,
        251, 253, 258
Ustinov, Demitri 101

V

Vietnam xvii, 12, 42, 46, 47, 77, 82,
        83, 84, 85, 86, 87, 89, 95, 112,
        139, 141, 144, 149, 159, 161,
        163, 165, 166, 194, 205, 206,
        209, 210, 213, 216, 218, 225,
        229, 232, 255, 261

W

Wagner, Raymond 212, 254
Wallace, Henry 10
Watson, Walter L. 213, 256
Welch, Larry D. 161, 162
Wilkie, Wendell 10
World War I x, 50, 111, 117
World War II x, xvii, 3, 4, 7, 16, 17,
        18, 26, 35, 49, 50, 51, 55, 67,
        68, 71, 80, 91, 100, 107, 111,
        112, 113, 115, 117, 118, 119,
        120, 121, 127, 129, 134, 143,
        145, 148, 149, 156, 227, 239
Wright, Frank 27, 35, 117, 125, 148,
        175, 180, 213

Y

Yates, Bob 196

Printed in the United States
by Baker & Taylor Publisher Services